Unity in Islam
Reflections and Insights

by
Tallal Alie Turfe
Professor
University of Michigan

Published by
Tahrike Tarsile Qur'an, Inc.
Publishers and Distributors of Holy Qur'an
80-08 51st Avenue
Elmhurst, New York 11373-4141
www.koranusa.org
E-mail: orders@koranusa.org

Published by

Tahrike Tarsile Qur'an, Inc.

Publishers and Distributors of Holy Qur'an
80-08 51st Avenue
Elmhurst, New York 11373-4141

First U.S. Edition 2004

Library of Congress Catalog Number: 2004112175
Copyright © 2004 Tallal Alie Turfe

British Library Cataloguing in Publication Data
ISBN: 0-940368-61-7

Distributors in U.K. and Europe
Murtaza Bandali/ALIF International
37 Princes Avenue
Watford, Herts WD1 7RR
England, U.K.

Cover Courtesy: Space Images.com

UNITY IN ISLAM:
REFLECTIONS AND INSIGHTS

Unity is magnificent and attractive, but it has circumstances that cannot be forced. Traditionally, Muslim leaders have worked to develop unity. Yet it has become more and more evident that one of the greatest threats to unity is not only the divergence created by differences between denominations but also the divergence found within denominations. How we come together and bridge the divergence is the theme of this book. It is our intent to find the balance in the hope that all Muslims will lay aside their fears and desires for the betterment of the Muslim community. The challenge is to regain this unity in light of the complexity of issues causing problems in the Muslim world.

If we can recapture the Islamic dream of unity that motivated Prophet Mohammad (peace be upon him), then we can recapture our Islamic heritage. While we need to deal with the unavoidable conflict between our desire for unity and our commitment to truth, Muslims need to reflect on those things that drive home the unity. As Allah has already given us the passion for unity, we must move forward to fulfill His Command. We can no longer preach unity and practice division. Our pledge to unity must begin within ourselves, within our families, within our communities, and with each other. As we engage in dialogue, let us seek to understand before we seek to be understood.

The author has written another book, _Patience in Islam: Sabr_, which has received worldwide acclaim. That book has been published in several languages: Arabic, English, French and Indonesian.

Table of Contents

PREFACE

"And hold fast, all together, by the Rope which Allah stretches out for you, and be not divided among yourselves…." (Qur'an 3:103)

This book is written in the hope that all peaceful loving Muslim believers will make every effort towards unity in Islam. Holding fast to the *Rope of Allah* protects us from misguidance and destruction. Holding fast also protects us from deviation. Holding fast is to attain the Shelter and Protection of Allah.

This book is dedicated to the Twelfth Imam, Imam Mohammad al-Mahdi, and may he forgive me for any errors I may have made. In addition, I would like to dedicate this book to my parents, Haj Alie Turfe and Hajjah Hassaney Turfe, who were constant and steadfast in their faith and good deeds as they secured a unified family.

Each of us goes through life wanting to understand more clearly our metaphysical relationship with Allah. In search of knowledge and wisdom, we broaden our horizons and equip ourselves with the tools to help fulfill this mission. As we strive towards self-actualization, we find ourselves thirsty and eager to learn even more about Islam. This book will enlighten those who wish to reflect on Islam, with particular focus on the bedrock of Islam - unity!

I would like to thank the dedicated Muslim scholars who provided counsel with their comments and guidance. May Allah shower them with His Blessings?

Tallal Alie Turfe

ABOUT THE AUTHOR

Haj Tallal Alie Turfe was born in Detroit, Michigan. He is the son of Haj Alie Turfe and Hajjah Hassaney Turfe. He has four brothers (Bennett, Haj Fouad, Feisal, and Atallah) and one sister, Hajjah Wanda Fayz. His wife is Hajjah Neemat Turfe, and they have four sons (Alie, Haj Norman, Robert, and Hassan) and one daughter (Summer). Two of his sons graduated from the United States Military Academy at West Point. This achievement is a first for a Muslim to have entered and graduated from that Academy. That institution has produced the greatest American generals, and it also was the school from where some of America's presidents graduated. filling the gap in international law and to restore peace, security, understanding and prosperity among the peoples of different faiths and cultures around the world. It was stated that *"Tallal's participation as a speaker was crucial to the success of the conference and its ultimate goal in achieving lasting peace and security in the world."*

In August 2003, Tallal became a member of the International Council of the Millennium World Peace Summit Global Ethics Initiative. The Global Ethics Initiative has been created to facilitate the implementation of the goals envisaged in the Millennium World Peace Summit of Religious and Spiritual Leaders *Commitment to Global Peace.* The Global Ethics Initiative will advance and promote the achievement of peace, the protection of children and the environment, and the promotion of ethics in all walks of life. The Council is comprised of a small number of global humanitarian leaders some of whom are Nobel Peace Prize winners, former Presidents of countries, educators, entertainers, religious clerics and business entrepreneurs.

Tallal has also been instrumental in securing gainful employment for thousands of Muslim and non-Muslim immigrants primarily from the Middle East. For this achievement, his community gave a testimonial dinner in his honor in February of 1974.

Another testimonial dinner was given in his honor in October of 1995 as he was presented with the *Knight of Charity Award* by the Pontifical Institute for Foreign Missions, an international community of Christian priests and lay missionaries who *maintain a preferential and evangelical option for the poor and marginalized of society.* Frequently, Tallal gives lectures on Islam in various mosques and churches located in the Detroit Metropolitan area. He has published several articles on Islam.

Since 1998, Tallal has been a Management Consultant engaged in e-commerce strategies for Fortune 500 companies on a global basis. His focus has been on strategic use of technology to gain new market opportunities, competitive advantages, operational efficiencies and cost reduction. Previously, Tallal spent over 40 years in the automotive industry (Ford Motor Company and General Motors Corporation). During that period, he held various positions in industrial relations, purchasing, production control, export-import, marketing, trade relations, business planning, product planning and development, competitive intelligence, decision-making and risk analysis, geodemographic information systems, and corporate strategy. Tallal has interacted with heads of states in the Middle East and Africa while employed with General Motors Corporation, resulting in assembly operations in Egypt and Tunisia. He has also generated hard currency for General Motors Corporation by countertrading products and services for third-world developing countries.

Additionally, he is a Professor at several universities such as the University of Michigan, Wayne State University, Eastern Michigan University, Central Michigan University, and the University of Windsor (Canada). On a part-time basis since 1969, he has taught graduate and undergraduate courses in business administration with concentration primarily in the disciplines of marketing, management, and business policy. A prolific writer, he has published several marketing and finance articles in leading business journals as well as a book, entitled *Patience in Islam: Sabr*, written in Arabic, English, French and Indonesian.

Tallal is the former President and Chairman of the Greater Detroit Interfaith Round Table, National Conference for Community and Justice, an organization that helps build bridges between various religious faiths and ethnic groups. He is also the former Chairman of the Arab-American and Chaldean Council, a social services agency that assists immigrants in the areas of job training, mental health, substance abuse, teen counseling, school counseling, and immigration. He is a member of the American Task Force for Lebanon, a Washington, D.C.-based group engaged in facilitating the peace process and reconstruction in Lebanon. He has served on the board of directors of the Citizens Council for Michigan Public Universities and the Oakwood Healthcare System

Foundation Strategic Board. Currently, he serves on the board of directors of the American Red Cross, the Detroit Medical Center, and the Henry Ford Health System's Multicultural Dermatology Center. Tallal was also a member of former U.S. President Bill Clinton's *Call to Action: One America* race relations group. Tallal was also chosen by Dubai Television as one of the most prominent and influential Arab Americans and as such was interviewed by them.

In August 2000, Tallal was one of 200 spiritual and religious leaders of the world to be chosen by the United Nations to participate in the Millennium World Peace Summit of Religious and Spiritual Leaders. This Summit was held at the United Nations, and it focused on four objectives: (a) conflict transformation; (b) forgiveness and reconciliation; (c) elimination of poverty; and (d) environmental preservation and restoration. Tallal gave a presentation and was interviewed by several television networks. All the participants signed a Declaration of Peace. That Summit preceded the political summit of the world's kings, presidents, and prime ministers.

In May 2003, Tallal was a keynote speaker at a global conference held by the World Council of Religious Leaders at the United Nations headquarters in New York. The topic presented was *Islam's Perspective on Violence and Terrorism*. The purpose of the conference was to review and analyze the use of religion to incite for violence within the context of contemporary human rights and humanitarian laws. The conference was attended by United Nations diplomats and staff as well as distinguished international jurists and public figures. The conference took a major and essential step in filling the gap in international law and to restore peace, security, understanding and prosperity among the peoples of different faiths and cultures around the world. It was stated that *"Tallal's participation as a speaker was crucial to the success of the conference and its ultimate goal in achieving lasting peace and security in the world."*

In August 2003, Tallal became a member of the International Council of the Millennium World Peace Summit Global Ethics Initiative. The Global Ethics Initiative has been created to facilitate the implementation of the goals envisaged in the Millennium World Peace Summit of Religious and Spiritual Leaders *Commitment to Global Peace*. The Global Ethics Initiative will advance and promote the achievement of peace, the protection of children and the environment, and the promotion of ethics in all walks of life. The Council is comprised of a small number of global humanitarian leaders some of whom are Nobel Peace Prize winners, former Presidents of countries, educators, entertainers, religious clerics and business entrepreneurs.

Tallal has also been instrumental in securing gainful employment for thousands of Muslim and non-Muslim immigrants primarily from the Middle East. For this achievement, his community gave a testimonial dinner in his honor in February of 1974.

Another testimonial dinner was given in his honor in October of 1995 as he was presented with the *Knight of Charity Award* by the Pontifical Institute for Foreign Missions, an international community of Christian priests and lay missionaries who *maintain a preferential and evangelical option for the poor and marginalized of society.*

Frequently, Tallal gives lectures on Islam in various mosques and churches located in the Detroit Metropolitan area. He has published several articles on Islam.

In the Name of Allah,
the Beneficent, the Merciful

The Rope of Allah
By Tallal Alie Turfe

Come pray with me let there be no divide,
Cemented all together side by side.
Declaring our faith as we kneel and stand,
Reciting verses that secure each strand.
As we raise our hands to affirm our hope,
Reaching on high to Hold Fast to the Rope.

Interlocked as we continue to pray,
Seeking His Guidance to show us the way.
Connecting our thoughts with a common plea,
Fulfilling our promise in harmony.
As we cling to the power of the strand,
Uniting our minds with the Rope in hand.

Our hearts are cleansed as we come to the end,
Renewing our vow to join with a friend.
Paying our respects with a word of peace,
Embracing our love with a sense of ease.
Tied to a Rope that manifests our souls,
Unifying in trust as truth unfolds.

INTRODUCTION

Unity is magnificent and attractive, but it has circumstances that cannot be forced. Muslims would celebrate to accept the reinstatement of unity if it were offered on the basis of truth, but they have been unable to accept it on the basis of a form of agreement that would cover up and compromise the real issues. Let there be no misunderstanding. There can be no union without unity. Over the centuries, disagreement has been portrayed by politics, theology, and provincialism. Traditionally, Muslim leaders have worked to develop unity, but it has become more and more evident that one of the greatest threats to unity is not the divergence created by differences between denominations but the divergence found within the denominations.

Purpose of the Book

It is the intent of the author to delve into the problems of disunity among Muslims and to seek ways of bringing together the religious leaders and scholars to pursue productive opportunities toward driving home the unity. How we come together and how we bridge the differences is the purpose of this book.

We come together by enjoying our unity as we live our faith. Islam works best and enjoys its greatest strength and permanence when all Muslims are working together in unity towards the noble goal of adhering to Allah's Commands. Therefore, the primary and genuine requirement of Muslims is the need for unity, a proactive unity of mind and heart. What is Islamic unity and why did the Muslims lose that unity is the thesis of this book? The challenge is to find the means to regain this unity in light of the complexity of issues causing problems in the Muslim world.

Central Issue in Achieving Unity

While the issue of unity is on every Muslim's mind, then why is it not a reality? As we explore this issue throughout the book, we come to realize that the answer is deep and complex. There are many reasons for disunity, and some of these are the result of hatred, suspicion, intolerance, and deficiencies in control and collaboration.

This disunity is the direct result of ignorance (*jahil*), which thrives on the absence of education. Those who are **ignorant** evidently have been devoid of the teachings of proper Islamic principles and beliefs. One example of **ignorance** is not being tolerant and understanding as to the differences between various Islamic philosophies. This example unfolds into a major aspect of **ignorance**, which is the reluctance to engage in diversity. Although **ignorance** continues to spread throughout the Muslim world, there are scholars who will emerge to rectify the misunderstandings in the minds of others. In addition, these scholars will educate others as to what Prophet Mohammad (peace be upon him) had preached, and will caution against those who breach the laws of Islam. The challenge is to remove **ignorance** from all of the different sects within Islam.

However, in bringing these Islamic sects to the table for effective dialogue, we must recognize that **ignorance** by either party can be an impediment to success. We must understand that **ignorance** exists primarily at two levels: **simple ignorance (*jahil basit*)** and **compound ignorance (*jahil murakkab*)**. [1] A person who is candid and admits that he simply does not know the answer to a question falls under the category of *jahil basit*. This is a fundamental unawareness that is simply resolved and replaced with **knowledge (*'ilm*)**. A far more complex and real problem is that of *jahil murakkab*. Here the person will say that he knows the answer to a question when he really does not know the answer. He is **ignorant** that he is **ignorant**! In other words, the person is not only **ignorant** but is **ignorant** of his **ignorance**. In other words, **compound ignorance** is a state at which point the afflicted are **ignorant** of the fact that they are **ignorant**. People who fall in this category frequently possess insufficient **knowledge**. Such **ignorance** is considered an affliction on the human soul, as it impedes learning and understanding. The danger with *jahil murakkab* is that those afflicted with this disease will render Islamic views and analyses even though they lack the **knowledge** to do so. The tragedy is that they think they have the **knowledge** when, in reality, it is only their invention of what they think they know. In addition, they think that they can reform others without first reforming themselves.

Yet, in the divergence of opinions and multiplicity of obstacles and impediments, there is one central axis to the issue of whether or not unity is achieved. The axis at which a myriad of obstacles converges is that of **ignorance** (**Figure 1**). Conversely, the axis at which a myriad of solutions converges is that of **knowledge** (**Figure 2**). Through **knowledge** we gain wisdom. And it is education that is the vehicle for increasing our **knowledge** and nurturing our wisdom as we overcome **ignorance**:

Figure 1
Obstacles to Unity

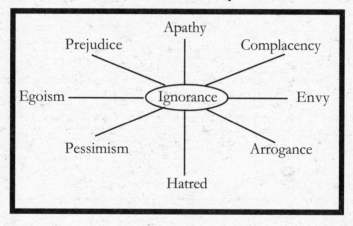

Figure 2
Solutions to Unity

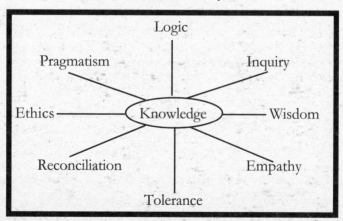

Discord runs rampant in the Muslim society, because Muslims are **ignorant** about their obligation to achieve and maintain unity. Some of the obstacles relative to **ignorance** are: apathy, complacency, envy, arrogance, hatred, pessimism, egoism and prejudice. Some of the solutions relative to **knowledge** are: logic, inquiry, wisdom, empathy, tolerance, reconciliation, ethics and pragmatism. **Compound ignorance** naturally dampens any sense or desire to broaden a viewpoint or opinion. Still another form of **ignorance** is termed **dangerous ignorance**, particularly for those who think they know for sure but is based on superstition. How we overcome **ignorance** with knowledge will determine what kind of Judgment awaits us:

"Do they then seek after a judgment of (the Days of) Ignorance? But who, for a people whose faith is assured, can give better judgment than Allah?" (Qur'an 5:50)

"When those come to you who believe in Our Signs, say 'Peace be on you: your Lord has inscribed for Himself (the rule of) Mercy: verily, if any of you did evil in ignorance, and thereafter repented, and amended (his conduct), lo! He is Oft-Forgiving, Most Merciful.'" (Qur'an 6:54)

"But verily your Lord, - to those who do wrong in ignorance, but who thereafter repent and make amends, - your Lord, after all this, is Oft-Forgiving, Most Merciful." (Qur'an 16:119)

"Judgment is of two kinds — the Judgment of Allah — the Great and Almighty — and the judgment of the people of ignorance (jahiliyah). So whoever misses Allah's Judgment surely will judge according to the judgment of the people of jahiliyah." (Imam Ja'far as-Sadiq)

In order to understand the consequences of **ignorance**, it is vital to separate **simple ignorance** from **compound ignorance**, the latter that is also labeled close-mindedness. Everyone is **ignorant** about something. **Ignorance**, by itself, is no reason for embarrassment. While one is **ignorant** about something, he is willing to listen and learn. A closed mind, however, is one that is not willing to listen and learn. The fundamental difference is that a mind that is simply **ignorant** does not defend its **ignorance**. As it is open-minded, it will accept guidance and new knowledge. By contrast, a mind in the clutch of **compound ignorance** employs a range of strategies to prevent new knowledge. It has obtained a particular set of beliefs and obstinately refuses to change them. What we should remember about **compound ignorance**, or close-mindedness, is that it is a defensive position. We must be cognizant of the fact that **compound ignorance** is not only a spiritual disease but is also detrimental to one's life. As **compound ignorance** is an illness, it is dangerous to one's well being. It is also the cause of discord and fragmentation within the Islamic society.

Knowledge (*'ilm*) is the panacea for overcoming **ignorance**. By seeking **knowledge** we are enlightened. **Knowledge** is not only a cure for **ignorance**, but it also guides us. Unity in Islam cannot come about if **knowledge** is absent. The **Book of Knowledge** is the Qur'an, which enlightens us and provides the guidance in our daily lives:

"...Are those equal, those who know and those who do not know? It is those who are endued with understanding that receive admonition." (Qur'an 39:9)

"It is He Who brought you forth from the wombs of your mothers when you knew nothing; and He gave you hearing and sight and intelligence and affections: that you may give thanks (to Allah)." (Qur'an: 16:78)

Undoubtedly, those who have **knowledge** of Allah are not equal to those who do not. Those who have **knowledge** are conscious of the truth and have a favorable influence on those with whom they come in contact. In contrast, those who are **ignorant** muddle through their lives, unsuccessfully trying to gratify their desires. In short, the **ignorant** fail to gain consciousness of their purpose and duty in this life. For Muslims, **knowledge** is a means to an end. When Allah created us from the wombs of our mothers, we were **ignorant**. Allah gave us the senses of hearing and sight and of touch and smell as well as of taste. Through these senses we are able to acquire **knowledge**. Whether we acquire **knowledge** from reading or hearing the Qur'an or whether we witness the marvels of creation, it is through these senses that we are able to function. Allah has provided us with the sources of **knowledge**, two of which are His Creation and His Revelation.

While **knowledge** has many branches, for our purposes we are focusing on **Islamic knowledge**, which provides us with a clear understanding of Allah. Even worship is manifested through **Islamic knowledge**. We increase our faith (*iman*) via **Islamic knowledge**. Believers constantly seek **knowledge** in order to increase their faith and direct their course to the straight path. Each time a believer searches for **knowledge**, he will have driven further on the path to Paradise. Seeking **knowledge** is part of our faith, as it helps us get a clear perception about our origin, our purpose, and our way of life. **Knowledge** becomes the lamp that illuminates the soul and brings about happiness. There is a great difference between those who seek **knowledge** and those who wish to remain **ignorant**. Those who seek **knowledge** learn the truth and obtain insight, while the **ignorant** remain blind trekking the path of Satan.

Islamic knowledge is acquired in many ways. For example, we are encouraged to explore and study the Qur'an and the *Hadiths* (Traditions), which provide the bases for **Islamic knowledge**. Listening to a *khutbah* (sermon) and reading a scholarly Islamic article or book are other means of acquiring **knowledge**. When seeking **Islamic knowledge**, we should always make our intention (*niyyah*) to spend time to understand it and to plan our daily lives around it. Seeking **knowledge** provides us with the necessity to teach others about Islam. Allah looks favorably upon those who acquire and spread **knowledge**.

Knowledge is vital in understanding from whence we came and to where we are going. How we conduct our daily lives is based on **knowledge** of Islam and what Islam asks of us. Therefore, it is apparent that to self-actualize as Muslims in our daily lives, we need to increase our **knowledge** and understanding of Islam. In addition, as we increase our **knowledge** we must also put it to practice. Faith and **knowledge** without practice is insignificant. Always **knowledge** should be sought for the purpose of obtaining Allah's Pleasure. The capacity of **knowledge** is Allah's Gift, which, when exercised, will lead the individual to a deeper **knowledge** of himself and the wonders of creation. One of the primary causes of fragmentation in Islam is the lack of **knowledge** of even the simple and basic laws of Islam. Even those who have read books and studied the Qur'an extensively can be **ignorant** of many basic canons of Islam. What is important is that as **knowledge** leads to serving the Islamic society, it also gives life and strength to that society. We must find the means whereby **knowledge** can be the vehicle for driving home the unity in Islam.

There is a great deal of truth in the adage that **knowledge** is freedom and **ignorance** is slavery. Human freedom cannot and does not rely on **ignorance** and randomness. Human freedom is the capacity to make choices based on reasons, and this expands with **knowledge**, not shrinks. The best way to combat **ignorance** is to heighten our struggle (*jihad*) against our ego, the major barrier to clear thinking. The struggle against **ignorance** requires that we continue to escalate our understanding of Islam, which provides the prescription for dealing with social issues including ethnic conflicts, religious and cultural differences, poverty, and ethics and moral values. The struggle against **ignorance** is the most important struggle we will ever fight and a struggle that we ultimately must win, if Islam as we know it is to survive. Winning the struggle against **ignorance** will require leaders with great knowledge and wisdom who understand the dilemma we face. Winning the struggle against **ignorance** represents a major challenge. The issues facing us today are far more difficult and complex than they ever have been before, and the stakes are getting progressively higher. For Muslims, our survival is dependent on our abilities to participate in the quest for unity. Yet, to participate requires that we understand the issues before us. **Knowledge** is indeed power. The less we know, the less we can contribute. We have a major job ahead of us to ensure that education becomes our number one priority and that we ultimately are victorious in the struggle against **ignorance**.

Relevant Issues

Division among Muslims is a horrid evil. How can Muslims work for unity without compromising the truth? How can Muslims insist on maintaining their own views without sacrificing their desire for unity? Some Muslims may say that their insistence on truth is a prerequisite for unity, and that they cannot and will not compromise the truth.

If we can recapture the Islamic dream of unity that motivated Prophet Mohammad, then we can recapture our Islamic heritage. To become united will necessitate the humility to rethink some things that have been very important to us. While we need to deal with the unavoidable conflict between our desire for unity and our commitment to truth, Muslims need to reflect on those things that bring about the unity.

We are going to have to revive a passion for the principle of the unity of all believers. Having the commitment to abide by Allah's Commands is the avenue towards brotherhood and solidarity. We must be cognizant of the fact that our passion to reject each other over issues of politics, theology, and provinciality are not virtues. They are indications that we are too often controlled by our ego and not by Allah's Commandments. We need a passion for unity. Unity is not something we invent; it is Allah's Gift. Let us make every concerted effort to be unified. Let us exhaust every possibility and leave no stone unturned in the quest for unity. Let our efforts be the result of an earnest desire and willingness to succeed as we celebrate our differences as windows of opportunities. As Allah has already given us that passion for unity, we must move forward to fulfill His Command.

In order to unify, we need to allow for diversity among Muslims. Without diversity of opinion, our hope for unity is severely weakened. Unity must prevail over uniformity, because the latter allows no room for personal opinion because the slightest deviation destroys it. Furthermore, the Qur'an discourages uniformity. The Qur'an is replete with verses calling on the Muslim brotherhood to be united in a common identity and a common trust. We can no longer preach unity and practice division. This requires Muslims to find the means by which to have a sound and workable dialogue. Our pledge to unity must begin within ourselves, within our families, within our communities, and with each other. With an open mind and open heart, we can have effective dialogue with each other. As we engage in dialogue, let us seek to understand before we seek to be understood.

Steps in Resolving Issues

Within the framework of this book, the author discusses the important steps toward achieving the unity. These steps are respect, communication and support. Relative to respect, there needs to be a concerted effort by everyone not to disparage any group or individual that shares in the common interest of unity. Relative to communication, information must be shared and conflict must be avoided. Relative to support, there must be autonomy and the freedom for groups or individuals to advocate their beliefs and practices. It is of little consequence to speak of unity on a theological level if there is no experience of unity in the day-to-day encounters between Muslims. On the other hand, theological conviction forms experience. Yet, it must always be remembered that theological positions are forged as a result of, and interpretation of, experience. On a practical level, we must work to forge an experience of solidarity, mutual respect, and reciprocal familiarity.

Then the unity for which we have labored so strenuously will become a living reality among us – a reality in which our common grip to the *Rope of Allah* is strengthened.

In resolving these issues we need to first understand the common elements that comprise a nation in general and the common elements that comprise a nation in Islam.

Common Elements of A Nation
Concept of Nation in General

Historically, there have been contrived interpretations or creations as to what constitutes a nation, for example, Indochina was a creation by the French. The concept of nation is more comprehensive and profound than just a country, state or republic. It is evolutionary in the sense that it has diverse characteristics and languages. In short, a nation is a natural creation that continues to evolve over time. Institutions, such as political, education, cultural, demographic, legal, technology, social and economic, derive from the notion of nation.

Any nation is an intricate social order with analogous differences in culture and customs. In structure it is comprised of different ethnic and race groups, class distinctions, geographical regions and civilizations. Nonetheless, overlaying these differences are universal elements of formal language, institutions, and traditions that interweave together to form a nation. If we were to identify the essential components that constitute a nation in general, we would come up with three basic elements: geography, community and governance. The geographical element is most discernible, but the absence of community with shared beliefs or principles collapses unless there is governance to tie it together. Irrespective of how a nation is defined, a common thread is one of homogeneity with common traits that rise above internal divisions of class, status and region.

Still another way of looking at the composition of a nation is from the perspective of the people who live there. Here a nation is distinguished by the self-consciousness of its people. Characteristics such as ethics, morals, perceptions and values form the self-consciousness of the nation's inhabitants. How this self-consciousness unfolds is when people are able to differentiate themselves from people of other nations. Let us explore some of the differences between nations of the East and nations of the West.

In the East, the concept of nation essentially advanced to convey cultural and ethnic sentiments of connecting with a community. Here the people that comprised the nation did so on the basis of tribal characteristics, class or caste systems, cultural identification or religion. The word nation was used to express a feeling of friendship and solidarity. Conversely, the concept of a nation in the West predominantly came into existence after the emergence of capitalism, which feeds on dominance and exploitation. The West used the word nation in a more narrow and distinct sense, as it wanted to delineate its boundaries so as to have absolute supremacy for exploitation of markets. As a result of capitalism, philosophical ideologies arose to counter it, such as Marxism. Marx preached the notion of revolutionary nationalism that meant struggle for national liberation. Even Stalin defined the word nation as one with a shared territory, a shared history, a shared economy and a common culture based on a common language.

Depending on which part of the world we connect with, there is a different perspective as to exactly what a nation is. It does not matter which perspective is right or wrong but, rather, how the people in each nation truly believe and stand by their perspective. However, there is a consensus and agreement that a nation is more than just a geographical boundary. It is a kind of implicit agreement among a body of people who are bound together within its influence. When people cooperate and work together, a nation thrives, but when that cooperation disappears so too does the nation. Since a nation is a package in which the various elements of social cooperation are contained, it is clear that a nation exists for the purpose of uniting the efforts of people and improving the quality of their lives. If it does not, then it fails in its central task. A nation and its essential components, such as government, social customs and economics, exist solely to serve its people.

As a result of our natural differences, we can never have a perfect nation. There are no shared body of laws and customs in a nation that meet the needs of its entire people. For example, no economic system provides for the comfort of everyone under its authority. Therefore, a nation must be imperfect because its components and elements as practiced are imperfect. A nation evolves and manifests itself through change, which is in direct proportion to how people within a nation change. Some of the instruments of change are diversity, dialogue, compromise, tolerance and patience. Without them there is only continual unsteadiness and ultimate obliteration of the nation.

Concept of Nation in Islam

The concept of nation in Islam is manifested in the word *Ummah*, which comes from the root *umm* or *mother*. A mother who cares and nurtures her children knows that each has different needs. Likewise, the ideal *Ummah* cares and nurtures its members in much the same way. In Islam, the word *Ummah* means the nation or community of believers that the Muslims know no second to, as they not only belong to it but are proud of it as well. The *Ummah* not only refers to individual communities but to the global community of believers as well. The Muslim *Ummah* is distinctive with the qualities and principles of mercy, flexibility, ease and brotherhood. The Qur'an states that some of the responsibilities of the *Ummah* are to maintain an impartial balance between extremes and to pursue the path of moderation. Muslims should avoid extremism and extravagances by seeking the middle way in their daily affairs (*Ummah Wasat*):

"Thus have We made of you an Ummah justly balanced, that you might be witnesses over the nations, and the Messenger a witness over yourselves...." (Qur'an 2:143)

Therefore, Islam encourages us to seek the middle way, which is the path of mercy and justice. For example, Islam does not teach us to be conceited or **ignorant**, which are both extremes. Rather, Islam teaches us to pursue the middle course in order to attain the Pleasure of Allah.

The *Ummah* is united by elements such as the belief in the principles of Islam, emotions, common goals, prayers done in the Arabic language, and the holy shrines of Mecca, Medina and Jerusalem. Although the basic elements of a nation in general are akin to those of the *Ummah*, the latter incorporates faith-based elements. With these additional elements, the *Ummah* comes full circle, as it now integrates the foundation whereby Muslims can experience a complete way of life (*deen*).

The primary principle of governance is to provide Muslims with the full extent of self-development, whether it is nourishment of the body or development of the Islamic personality. With governance in Islam, Muslims not only develop their persona but also enjoy the fruits of freedom as they conduct themselves in their daily activities. Relative to geography, the *Ummah* is not demarcated by national boundaries and territorial autonomy. The *Ummah* transcends geography. It is an open-ended community that transcends the boundaries of race and ethnicity. The *Ummah* permeates through all cultures and races throughout the world. The only condition for membership in the *Ummah* is one's devotion to Islam. The *Ummah* is acknowledged to be an essential part of a global community. It asserts the concept of a community based on mutual involvement of Muslims towards a more sanctified life. In Islam, the *Ummah* community is one of moderation that is positioned between the extremes of excess and deficiency.

Over the course of history, the term *Ummah* has taken on several meanings, such as caliphate and sultanate. At the inception of Prophet Mohammad's mission, the *Ummah* represented a somewhat small contingent of believers who adhered to his teachings. Subsequently, the *Ummah* extended to people of other regions and nationalities. This extension continued for centuries until it reached the entire global community, which was comprised of many nations built upon many civilizations. Today, the term *Ummah* implies a more constricted meaning. We find Muslims living in the East and West as part of an ethnic or racial group, and are often classified as the *Ummah* of Arabs or the *Ummah* of Pakistanis, for example. Many Islamic movements have now emerged, and the term *Ummah* signifies association and attachment within each of these movements, for example, the African American movement called the Nation of Islam.

The *Ummah* is a body of believers in Islam. It transcends all nationalities and ethnicities and is the concept that makes brothers and sisters of Muslims:

"To every people (was sent) a Messenger: when their Messenger comes (before them), the matter will be judged between them with justice, and they will not be wronged." (Qur'an 10:47)

"Mankind was but one nation, but differed (later). Had it not been for a Word that went forth before from your Lord, their differences would have been settled between them." (Qur'an 10:19)

Believers in Islam seek **knowledge** in compliance with the Words of Allah. Here **knowledge** leads us to at least two obligations: (a) individual obligation (*fardh 'ain*), which is the **knowl-**

edge that is required by any individual in his particular situation; and (b) general obligation (*fardh al-kifaya*), which is all forms of **knowledge** that are required for the needs of the *Ummah*, such as science, mathematics and medicine. [2] If the *Ummah* is without **knowledge** in these areas, it will suffer adversities.

Over the centuries, the *Ummah* has suffered hardships. It has been severely impacted by a lack of morals and ethics, which has resulted in the negligence of fulfilling the requisite obligations. Why? The answer is apparent. Muslims have become habitual in regarding Islam as a mere religion and not as a way of life (*deen*). For these Muslims, the word religion is generally used in a rather narrow sense. Its extent is restricted to a set of principles and social customs that commemorate important events in the society in which they live. The concept of *deen*, however, is a complete way of life in which Muslims submit their will to the Will of Allah. Therefore, it means a way of life where Allah is worshipped and obeyed in a manner that includes all facets of human life. *Deen* is a collective system, and Muslims need to practice it. This collective system defines the nation, which is the *Ummah*. Over time, the *deen* became a state of mind and a form of social consciousness that united the Muslims in order to lead a righteous life and to preserve and to expand the boundaries of the *Ummah*.

Topics Covered

It is the intent of this book to find the means towards unity in the hope that all Muslims will overcome ignorance as they lay aside their fears and desires for the betterment of the Muslim *Ummah*. The book covers two sections. Section I deals with reflections relative to the concept of unity, the concept of Oneness, the continuity of unity, the unity in the Qur'an, and the unity of community, family and self. Section II deals with insights relative to societal weaknesses, requisites for unity, convergence and promoting the unity.

Methodology

The methodology of this book is one that focuses on unity by way of the *Rope of Allah*, which are the Qur'an and the *Sunnah* of

Prophet Mohammad and his *Ahl al-Bayt*. It is the *Rope of Allah* that inculcates every aspect and every fiber of unity. It is the *Rope of* permeates throughout the entire book, and it is the means by which to overcome ignorance and achieve the unity of the *Ummah*. The methodology is simple, as it takes the notion of unity from its foundation, Allah, and proceeds to infuse the Blessings of Allah as the means that can achieve unity. This is a book for a broad spectrum of readers, from the curious to the committed. The curious are those who talk about unity but do little to achieve it. The committed are those who see the light but aren't sure whether it's the other side of the tunnel or the train – and want some help. In addition, this book can be helpful to those already building the unity, with reflections and insights on how to interact with other Muslims to achieve that unity.

SECTION I: REFLECTIONS

CHAPTER 1: CONCEPT OF ONENESS

"We dwell in ignorance only to be rescued by knowledge."
(Tallal Turfe)

In the most primitive stage of ignorance, man thinks that the great objects of nature whose grandeur and glory are visible, and which appear to be injurious or beneficial to him, hold in themselves the real power and authority and, therefore, are divine. Thus, he worships trees, animals, rivers, mountains, fire, rain, air, heavenly bodies and numerous other objects. This is the worst form of ignorance. When his ignorance dissipates to some extent and some glimmers of light and knowledge appear on his intellectual horizon, he comes to know that these great and powerful objects are in themselves helpless and dependent.

As man progresses still further in knowledge, and as he reflects more and more deeply on the fundamental problems of existence, he finds an all-powerful law and all-encompassing control in the Universe. He calls this greatest deity by different names, such as Allah or God. But as the darkness of ignorance still persists, he continues worshipping minor deities along with the Supreme One. The more a man increases his knowledge, the greater becomes his dissatisfaction with the multiplicity of deities. More enlightened men bring each one of them under the searchlight of scrutiny and ultimately find that none of these man-made deities has any divine character, they themselves are creatures like man, though rather more helpless. They are thus eliminated one by one until only one God remains. But the concept of one God still contains some remnants of the elements of ignorance. Some people imagine that He has a body as men have, and is in a particular place. Some believe that God came down to Earth in human form; others think that God, after settling the affairs of the Universe, retired and is now resting. Some believe that it is necessary to approach God through the media of saints and spirits, and that nothing can be achieved without their intercession. Some imagine God to have a certain form or image, and they believe it necessary to keep that image before them for the purposes of worship. [3]

Historical Beliefs in God

Throughout history, man has created a plethora of gods. Some are ancient in origin, while others were developed relatively recently. Most of the gods have evolved from a core group of deities, particularly, in pagan society. Man has created gods in his own image with human characteristics. Mankind has often used the existence of a supernatural being to explain occurrences that were beyond comprehension. Mysticism surrounded phenomena such as comets, eclipses, earthquakes and volcanic eruptions.

Animistic beliefs maintain that everything is part of God, and God is within all that exists. Pantheism maintains that God and the Universe are the same, that God has no existence independent of the Universe, and that God cannot be the creator of the Universe. Further, since there is neither beginning nor end, everything is cause and effect. Hinduism is associated with polytheism, as its concept of Avatara clearly reflects that idea. Avatara means an incarnation on earth of the Divine being and holds to the notion of a Trinity: that God is called Brahma when viewed as creator; Vishnu as the preserver; and Shiva as the destroyer.[4] Monotheistic faiths such as Judaism, Christianity, and Islam maintain that there is a common Creator, and that Messengers descended through Prophet Abraham.

Basically, Judaism is broken down into three main groups: Orthodox, Conservative, and Reformed. The Orthodox view God as spirit rather than form. That He is a personal God: omnipotent, omnipresent, omniscient, eternal and compassionate.

The Conservative's concept of God is non-dogmatic and flexible. There is less atheism in Conservative Judaism than in Reformed Judaism, but most often God is considered impersonal and indescribable.

Reformed Judaism allows a varied interpretation of the concept of God, with wide room to naturalists, mystics, super naturalists, or religious humanists. It holds that the truth is that we do not know the truth.

In Judaism, the concept of God is that He is One:
"Hear, O Israel: the Lord our God, the Lord is One." (Deuteronomy 6:4)
"I am the Lord thy God, which have brought thee out of the land of Egypt,

out of the house of bondage. *Thou shall have no other gods before me.*"
(Exodus 20:2-3)

Any attempt to divide God into parts and claim to understand God's structure, essence, and compassion runs counter to what Jewish tradition teaches. Many Jews comprehend God to be the one supernatural being whose presence is acknowledged through Divine revelation and is avowed through prayer. Other Jews understand the nature of God to be revealed within human life as the power that makes for salvation. There are spiritual values that actually sustain life and can be seen, as signs of the Divine, for example, values like justice, love and freedom. These values are celebrated during the Jewish religious year. Progressive Judaism identifies with both science and philosophy as helping to mold beliefs and religious perceptions. God is understood as infinite, while human beings are understood as finite. Judaism speaks of God of history and a covenant between the Jewish people and God. Jews find religious inspiration in the concept of the moral and ethical imperative.[5]

In Christianity, there are five main groups: Roman Catholic, Orthodox, Protestant, Anglican, and Pentecostal. Roman Catholics see themselves as directly inheriting an apostolic line of succession from the earliest Christian leaders. The Pope leads them.

The Orthodox see themselves as being in continuity with the undivided Church before its separation into Eastern and Western traditions. Orthodox Churches are independently governed, each with their own leaders who are bound together by their recognition of the Patriarch of Constantinople.

Protestants vary considerably, and especially concerning forms of Church organization and government. They emphasize the supremacy of scriptural authority and faith in Jesus. There are various denominations in the Protestant Churches, such as Baptist, Brethren, Congregationalist, Lutheran, Methodist, Moravian, Presbyterian or Reformed, and Salvationist.

Churches of the Anglican traditions see themselves as both Reformed and Catholic. They are autonomous Churches that look for international leadership to the Archbishop of Canterbury.

The Pentecostal tradition emerged within the broader Protestant tradition and additionally emphasizes the possibility of contemporary sharing the spiritual gifts and experience of the earliest

Christians. Restorationist and House Church Movements have more recently emerged seeking what they believe to be more biblical forms of Church life.

All Christians strongly believe that there is but one God, and He alone must be the object of their worship and service. Christians adhere to the pluralistic concept of God, that He is Three in One, i.e., the Holy Trinity. To correspond with Biblical revelation, Christians equally emphasize that God is One and Three. Today, the church has adapted the word to mean Three in Unity. According to Christian theology, the Trinity is God the Father who loves and saves the world by God the Son through God the Holy Spirit:[6]

"Therefore go and make disciples of all nations, baptizing them in the name of the Father and of the Son and of the Holy Spirit." (Matthew 28:19)

Though the word Trinity does not occur in the Bible, Christians believe that this concept is throughout the very fabric of both the Old Testament and New Testament. They believe that it is not something invented, but a truth revealed by God. The Trinity does not say there is more than one God. It is an attempt to explain what the Bible reveals about the One God, that within this One, there are three persons sharing the one essence in perfect unity.

Islamic View of Allah's Unity

The unity of consciousness within man helps him to know that Allah exists. Man explores his surroundings and perceives the flawless creation as part of a perfect Cosmos. Our conscience acknowledges that the perfection of the Cosmos is the work of Allah. By referring to our conscience we have awareness. Awareness is achieved through wisdom, and wisdom comes about by following one's conscience. Even the cellular structure of the human body is proof of the Creator, and wisdom and conscience helps us arrive at that conclusion.

In Islam, the first Article of Faith is the absolute belief in the Oneness (*Tawhid*) of Allah. Islam revolves around the principle of Oneness. With this belief, there can be no partners to Allah and there can be no association with Allah. How one professes his or her belief in Islam is by reciting the words *"La Ilaha Illallah"* signifying that *"there is no God but Allah."* In addition, the concept of Oneness or Unity also implies that Allah has no wife nor any children nor any kinfolk. A Muslim submits his will to the Will of Allah, and the foundation for this submission is faith (*iman*).

To become a true Muslim one must have faith as the basis for fulfillment in the way of Allah. What a Muslim takes with him in the hereafter are his earthly actions (*a'mal*) and deeds. Punishment or reward in the hereafter is predicated on how one performed during his life on earth. The individual acts as one and is judged on his earthly actions alone. The individual does not, for example, plead his case on the basis of having been wealthy. However, how that wealth was spent is a basis for rendering a decision. If wealth were used for good deeds, then the individual will be rewarded as such in the hereafter. If wealth were used for such acts as corruption, gambling or other abominable actions, then the person will be punished in the hereafter.

The word *"Allah"* means "God." And there is no God but God. Saying that *"there is no God but God and Mohammad is the Messenger of God"* extends the first Article of Faith. This creed is the bedrock of Islam. The belief in one Supreme God is essential. In Islam, the concepts of polytheism and atheism are forbidden. All people are dependent on God, while God is dependent on no one. This concept of unity transcended to all of God's Messengers, and each of them conveyed to their people the Oneness of God.

"Say: He is Allah, the One and Only; Allah, the Eternal, Absolute; He begets not, nor is He begotten; and there is none like unto Him." (Qur'an 112:1-4) The Unity of Allah means that Allah is Self-Dependent. He is not dependent on anything, and that everything depends on Him. He is the Creator and the ultimate source of all existence. Since Allah is the Cause of creation, this Universe has only one source, one end and one truth. The Universe and everything in it are the reflections of absolute unity, coherence and discipline. All of the components in the Universe have a common origin, a common purpose and a common end, as they are the creation of Allah. Allah has many Attributes, and each of His Attributes is linked together as One. There can be no pluralism in Allah's Essence. Therefore, the Unity of Allah's Divine Attributes means to accept the Oneness of Allah's Essence and His Attributes.

As everything is dependent on Allah, there is no self-existence in this world. Allah has no partners and no associates in his Divine Essence. Like man, everything in existence is the result of Allah's Divine Power and Will. None of Allah's creation has authority or input in that creation. While the Unity of Allah's Essence, His Attributes, and His Work are a matter of doctrine, the Unity of Worship is one of practicality. Here man must perform as he seeks Allah's Benevolence and Mercy. Here man worships Allah alone, as he prostrates in prayer.

Although Allah reveals Himself manifestly, He is invisible and hidden. Knowledge of Allah's existence is given in the Qur'an, which has given us clear and convincing arguments appealing to human reason in support of the existence of Allah:

"...Our Lord is He Who gave to each created thing its form and nature, and further, gave it guidance." (Qur'an 20:50)

This was Prophet Moses responding to Pharaoh who asked him as to who is the Lord. Prophet Moses is explaining that there is only one Lord, the Cherisher and Sustainer of creation. That Allah has given man the free will, and in order for this free will to be utilized righteously, Allah sent Messengers to guide mankind. Pharaoh is no exception, as he too needed guidance in the exercise of his own free will; yet, Pharaoh did not pay heed and continued to choose the wrong path. Allah is the cause of causes.

"That to thy Lord is the final goal." (Qur'an 53:42)

All things return to Allah, and that all our hope should be in Him. Here we have the natural order of cause and effect that pervades the Universe. And Allah is the First Cause and the Final Cause, and He alone gives life and death and life again.

The greatest obstacle to knowing the truth is ignorance. People who think they already know the truth do not have a humble, teachable spirit and are reluctant to change their beliefs. Unbelievers remain spiritually blind, unless they turn to Allah. Until then, they are darkened in their understanding because of the hardening of their hearts and the ignorance that is in them. As soon as ignorance is annihilated, darkness vanishes and the heart and mind come together to know that only by reliance on Allah can ultimate bliss be achieved. Those who are ignorant of Allah's Power do not fear Him and do not seek His Mercy. The fear of Allah is the beginning of knowledge, and consciousness is the spark that ignites the will to learn.

Divine Unity of Allah in Islam

The doctrine of the Unity of Allah is based on the belief that

Allah is One, Sovereign, Supreme, Absolute and Indivisible. Allah has established a structure and orderly Cosmos in the Universe that is essential for humans to relate to. Prophet Mohammad fulfilled the revelations previously given to Prophets Abraham, Moses and Jesus, that is, he laid the foundation for a pure monotheistic way of life. The Qur'an is replete with verses on the Unity of Allah (*Tawhid*). By believing in One Allah, the notion of mercy and justice unfold by clearly underscoring the idea of brotherhood and equality.

Even the nation of Islam is seen as one with no preferential treatment given to any country, race, ethnicity, color or creed. Here Islam is seen as universal serving all humanity. Even the unity of man is postulated in Islam, and Prophet Mohammad emphasized this. The Prophet was not a divine being, rather, human like the rest of mankind. The central concept around which all Quran'ic teaching revolves is that of *Tawhid*, the Unity or Oneness of Allah. Such a concept emphasizes a rigorous monotheism, stating Allah to be a unique absolute reality.

In the Qur'an, we read that Allah has Ninety-Names or Attributes. For example, He is Compassionate, Merciful, Kind, Loving and Wise. He is the Creator, the Sustainer and the Healer. He is the One Who Guides, the One Who Protects and the One Who Forgives. Muslims are strictly monotheistic, and reject any attempt to make Allah visible or human. Islam rejects any form of idol worship, and rejects the Trinity. In denying plurality, the Qur'an rejects all forms of idolatry, disallows any association of other divinities with Allah, and specifically denies all other definitions of Allah that might compromise Unity.

Muslims pray directly to Allah, with no intermediary, and seek guidance from Him alone. Quran'ic revelation requires Muslims to look around them for the Signs of Allah in the natural world. The Universe is in perfect order, and this order is neither chaotic nor random. The Omniscient, Omnipresent and Omnipotent One created the world, and everything in it, with a perfect plan.

Allah makes known His Will through angels. For example, Gabriel is known as the Angel of Revelation. Allah's Attribute of Mercy has full manifestation in His Attribute of Justice. Those who oppress people do not get the same treatment from Allah as those who suffer from starvation and hunger or those who prostrate in piety in worship of Allah. Islam rejects characterizing Allah in any human form or depicting Him as favoring certain individuals on the basis of wealth, power or race. He created humans as equals. The concept that Allah rested on the seventh day of creation is considered blasphemy from the Islamic point of view, as slumber never overtakes Allah. As the foundation of Islam is the belief in the Unity of Allah, this means that there is only One Creator and Sustainer of everything in the Universe, and that nothing is divine or worthy of being worshipped except for Him.

Religions other than Islam also claim the belief in the One Allah, believing that there is only One Creator and Sustainer of the Universe. However, Islam not only insists on this, but also rejects using such words as Lord and Savior for anyone besides Allah. Islam also rejects the use of all intermediaries between Allah and man, and insists that people approach Allah directly and reserve all worship for Him alone. Muslims believe that even though Allah is Unique and beyond comprehension, He has no partners or associates. Undoubtedly, the basic pillar of the Islamic faith is believing in Allah as the One and only God, asserting His freedom of human or other creatures characteristics, and recognizing His absolute perfection and possession of *Asma al-Husna* (Beautiful Names).

Based on the doctrine of Divine Unity, Muslims believe that Allah is Just in the obligations He imposes on His worshippers and in His recompense of them. Allah does not impose duties on mankind in excess of their capabilities. There is only One Allah for the entire Cosmos. He deals with it as He pleases without having anyone to share His Authority or to help Him. For Muslims, Allah is the only One Who legislates every rule of their lives. Such a Code of Legislation, the *Shari'a*, regulates everyone's relationship with each other as well as with their Lord. The Qur'an clearly indicates that no man-made law or constitution is acceptable, that the only law is the Qur'an. Only obedience of Allah's Commandments displays one's submission to Him.

A Muslim is required to do only what pleases Allah and what He has ordered as allowable. Allah is the Judge of Judges and His Authority is above that of anyone else. His Word is the Law as His Injunctions are compulsory on everyone. Vision does not comprehend Him, while He comprehends all vision. Allah is not a physical form and does not occupy a space, nor does He move from one place to another, nor can He be seen by anyone. Allah does not descend, nor does He need to descend.

Devotion to Allah

Through self-refinement of our souls we secure our faith by way of devotion to Allah. Our reliance on Allah guides us to the straight path and manifests itself in seeking Allah's Contentment, Gratitude, Generosity and Patience. We seek reliance by complete obedience to Him. This obedience takes the shape of piety, love and loyalty to Allah. For us, we begin with our steadfastness in belief, to resist temptations and inferior desires, and to be firm in hardship and difficulties. Allah tests our faith. How we score on these tests determines the extent of our devotion to Allah. Assurance of the highest score on these tests can be achieved through one's faith, righteous deeds, truth and patience. With man's self-refinement of his soul, heart and mind, Allah will reward him in the Hereafter.

Seek Allah's Contentment, Gratitude, Generosity and Patience by persevering in our own constancy. And the command is to be obedient to Allah. How we reach the level of obedience is through adherence to Islam by way of the example of Prophet Mohammad:

"And obey Allah and His Apostle; and fall into no disputes, lest ye lose heart and your power depart; and be patient and persevering; for Allah is with those who patiently persevere." (Qur'an 8:46)

Justice - An Attribute of Allah

Islam's most important principle is monotheism, which is the cornerstone of all Islamic teachings. Allah has no associate or partner. Allah has infinite existence as He pervades everything. As Allah is the only source of existence, we cannot associate any creature with Him in adoration. He alone is to be worshipped. As there is the belief in Islam of the One Allah, Muslims also acknowledge the Just and Righteous Allah. Justice imbues perfection, and Allah possesses all aspects of perfection. The Qur'an is replete with verses relative to justice and injustice. Allah enjoins people to perform justice and forbids them from engaging in acts of injustice.

To emphasize this concept of the Justice of Allah we observe the existence of this world, which is the most intelligent and well thought-out system. This world, in its creation, is the best possible and most perfect system. This is, of course, the result of Allah's Justice. While there are what man would consider defects and ugliness in this world, this does not apply to Allah. Allah's Justice is one whereby He enables existing things to reach the goal of their existence, which leads them to their inherent perfection. In other words, the purpose of every creation is inherent in its own nature, to which Allah leads and perfects it. The principle of Allah's Justice is an Article of Faith in Islam.

As man has the free will and volition, he alone engages in good deeds or bad deeds. Therefore, humans have the freedom and right to choose as they wish. This then logically follows with the concept of reward and punishment in the hereafter, which is based on justice for all. A Just Allah is One Who judges us on our own freedom to do right or wrong, and not on the basis of Allah controlling our destiny to do right or wrong. Therefore, Allah is Just and never deprives anyone of his rights. Allah never discriminates between His creatures or mankind relative to their obligations.

The dominion of justice is declared in the Qur'an:

"Say: My Lord hath commanded justice...." (Qur'an 7:29)

"We have sent down to thee the Book in truth, that thou might judge between men, as guided by Allah: so be not used as an advocate by those who betray their trust." (Qur'an 4:105)

"Allah commands justice, the doing of good, and liberality to kith and kin, and He forbids all shameful deeds, and injustice and rebellion: He instructs you that ye may receive admonition." (Qur'an 16:90)

Therefore, these Quran'ic verses unequivocally underscore that the Islamic way of life is based on justice, and that justice should be exercised and promoted at all times. The virtuous man must be vigilant and cautious, and ask for Allah's Protection against dishonesty. He must seek Allah's Help to be steadfast in dealing the most stringent justice without apprehension or partiality. Justice is an inclusive term with many meanings and applications. However, justice is heightened and brought to a greater meaning when the righteous person performs good deeds such as treating an enemy with kindness or helping someone whom did him harm. Attempts will be made to defeat the system of justice. Here, believers are reminded by the Quran'ic verses to be on guard against the unjust, and urges the believers to always seek the help of Allah for protection and justice. It is the Qur'an that provides the most inclusive *Code of Justice.*

Islam commands Muslims to sustain the cause of justice. As justice is the linkage between peace and prosperity, it becomes the basis of structure within the Islamic society. In addition, Muslims are commanded to resolve disputes on the basis of fairness, justice and truth. Justice in Islam has no preference for color, creed, race, ethnicity, tribalism, nationalism or biases. All people are created equally in this regard. Humanity must enjoy the fruits of justice albeit differences and disputes.

Ideally, justice is realized when a Muslim is truly free and optimistic as he pursues the fulfillment of his obligations as enjoined by Allah. Muslims need to engross themselves in the realm of ideas, exploring and evaluating competing and conflicting points of view in order to explore the deeper logic, the tacit suppositions, and that which is concealed. Muslims need to seek moral significance, ethical consequences and implications of ideas, which broaden and expand the concept of justice in the society. Muslims need to self-actualize in their personality by practicing and living the concept of leadership. And they do this by being serious thinkers, by having an open mind, and by evaluating each and every idea from the standpoint of justice.

The Justice of Allah means that there is always a reason why something happens, even though we may not know it or understand it. Whatever occurs is by the Will of Allah. And Allah always brings about what is good, right and just. If we do not see or understand the Justice of Allah in this world we will most definitely understand His Justice in the next world, the Hereafter. In this life, Allah grants everyone what is due to him. Allah puts everything in its right place; nothing ensues from Him except Justice. Even the Cosmos and nature have a sense of balance and justice imbued within them. The Qur'an promulgates what one may call a cosmology of justice. This cosmology of justice takes into its fold the realm of the human within the cosmic.

CHAPTER 2: CONCEPT OF UNITY

"Unity derives from knowledge; division from ignorance."
(Tallal Turfe)

When ignorance prevailed prior to Prophet Mohammad, the people were disunited, as hostility and hatred were widespread between them. Prophet Mohammad brought the knowledge of Islam to his companions who accepted it and became united. Today, we are facing major challenges in how to bring about the unity in Islam. As our knowledge of unity increases, the awareness of the extent of our ignorance increases in parallel. Ignorance wants to conquer the world by warfare and hostility. Knowledge wants to illuminate the world by becoming one with the world. Ignorance is hunger for constant separation. Knowledge is hunger for constant unity. Knowledge about people leads to peace and unity. Ignorance leads to prejudice and misunderstanding towards fellow human beings. The starting point of knowledge is the knowledge of ignorance.

Meaning of Unity

Just saying the word unity can cause turmoil for some people. There are many meanings to the term unity. For example, the philosophy of unity deals primarily with questions having to do with synthetic ideas, theories, viewpoints and value systems. It emphasizes synthesis and unification as the key to understanding rather than the opposite divisive movement of thought. The principle of unity mediates understanding through finding the common ground in or behind several viewpoints. These viewpoints may lie anywhere along a continuum between the individual and the universal viewpoints on any issue.

Understanding grasps the unity in any series of interconnected acts. All understanding aims likewise at some higher unity of purpose. We understand each thing and action in terms of what it is all for. Education may, for example, be seen as good serving national unity, or also for world peace unity, or unity at yet more universal levels.

The basic faith that lies behind the ideal of unity is that the existence of life and humanity has meaning, and that it is not a blind

41

accident of some unknown cause. One may well believe that there is unity in the essential nature or ultimate purpose of humanity; yet, the cultures of the world still exhibit amazing diversity. There is not only a divergence between different world cultures; it increases in volume and quality, if not in essence, the more closely one examines doctrines and beliefs within any given culture.

Unity of Consciousness

Consciousness consists of inner, qualitative, subjective states and processes or awareness. Oversimplifying, it includes everything from feelings of love or hate, joy or sadness, comfort or anxiety, to perceiving objects visually, to making mortgage payments, to discussion on politics or economics, or to just wishing we were somewhere else. Every conscious state has a certain qualitative feel to it. For example, the experience of tasting a soft drink is very different from hearing the sound of thunder, and both of these have a different qualitative character than the fragrance of a flower or the sighting of a rainbow. While these examples illustrate the different qualitative features of conscious experiences, they also imply subjectivity. In order to have a qualitative feel to some extent, there must be a subject that experiences the event, because if there is no subjectivity there is no experience. While a qualitative state of conscious implies subjectivity, subjectivity implies unity. For example, if one is driving his car, he does not only see the road ahead of him but also the scenic view as well. At the same he does not just feel the pressure of his back in the driver's chair and the thoughts that run through his mind. Rather, he experiences all of these as part of a single unified conscious field.

The unity of consciousness means to be aware of a number of things at the same time. It is a group of representations being related to one another such that to be conscious of any of them is to be conscious of others as a single group. The concept of intention in Islam is a form of consciousness. For example, it is our intention to face the *qiblah* (direction of prayer) when praying. Here our conscious state has both a qualitative and a subjective effect. As we face the *qiblah* in prayer and supplication, we feel and experience a sense of unification within ourselves. This unified feeling is heightened as we perform our group prayers together.

As there is only one *qiblah*, it is the pivotal point that unites the entire Muslim *Ummah* (community) and brings into harmony the feelings of Muslims. It is the point at which the emotions of Muslims converge. It is the axis at which the feelings of mercy and unity are interconnected.

There is a unity of consciousness of objects that one has of the world around him. Suppose one is aware of the furniture in his office as well as of the furniture in the office adjacent to him. If awareness of these two items is not unified, he will lack the subjective ability to compare the two. If he cannot bring the furniture in his office, as he is aware of it, to the state in which he is aware of the furniture in the other office, he could not know whether the furniture is the same color as his. We can compare represented items only if we are aware of both items together, as parts of the same field or state of consciousness.

Muslims need to restore the unity by eradicating the seeds of ignorance, which have paralyzed the human consciousness. This paralysis has afflicted both their steadfastness and their vital intellectual behavior. How we overcome this paralysis is by understanding the causes of this intellectual dilemma and remedying the logic by sound reflection and contemplation. The connection between logic and education must be restored. While reasoning is encouraged, it must be within the aegis of Islamic principles. These principles are manifested in the Qur'an, which guides the Muslim *Ummah* as to the proper course in achieving harmony within the conscious mind. Conscious Muslims are responsible for developing a firm and secure foundation for the restoration of the unity of the *Ummah*, and ultimately rebuilding the nation of Islam.

Problems in Achieving Unity

When there is no harmony in unity of consciousness, we have chaos. Our perceptions become distorted and discord sets in. For example, the apparent disparities in religions are due to erroneous beliefs or false impressions of the principles they were originally founded on. These differences may result from prejudice and bigotry. There are other problems that are barriers to achieving the unity. Some of these problems are political and economical while others are social, cultural, or institutional. Still other problems impeding unity could be due to complacency. Egoism is the biggest obstacle to a life of harmony and peace.

Often, man forgets about the principles of his religion on account of ignorance. Or man substitutes the truth of his religion for power and greed. In effect, he has becomes blasphemous for he thrives on chaos and disorder. The end result is that man loses his sense of morality and has succumbed to the abyss of degradation. Many religious leaders preach religion but how many in reality actually practice it. For example, how many Christian priests actually practice love and forgiveness? Or how many Buddhist monks actually practice the giving up of desires? Or how many Muslim *ulema* (religious teachers) actually practice solidarity and brotherhood? Preaching has become commonplace, while practice has become their object of disdain. Hence, man is depraved, not for want of truth, or on account of religions, but for the lack of genuine followers of these principles and religions.

Solutions for Reaching the Unity

For genuine unity to be achieved, the self must exhibit the moral virtues of patience, forbearance, fortitude and tolerance. We can know truth and live truth, but we cannot imprison truth. The prevailing challenge for humanity is how can the finite mind of man achieve a logical, true and corresponding unity of thought? To begin with, solutions to drive home the unity are first and foremost to encourage the truth. Respecting the rights of others by cooperating with and complementing each other. Listening to each other's point of view as well as opening lines of sound and fruitful communication best achieves complementation. Reconciling differences is best achieved by exhibiting empathy.

In order to reach unity, we must make further progress to understand each other by overcoming our prejudices and preconceived notions. We must learn to respect one another by recognizing the good in each other. We must care and love each other and work together toward the common goal of unity. We need unity of action, unity of time, and unity of space. Trying to change each other does not win the unity. Trying to understand each other gives us a better chance of reaching not only the unity but also the fulfillment of our obligations.

Need for Islamic Unity

Many people are incredibly happy not because of the city or town they live in, but because of the community that composed it. The atmosphere of support, helpfulness, and neighborly good cheer is what makes that city or town great, and that atmosphere transcends into the community, people, and social cohesion.

The Muslim population in the world is growing by leaps and bounds. This rapid increase in numbers is fueled by both births and conversion trends. But what can we learn from these numbers and how can we use them to benefit the entire community? First of all, we need to become more unified. In the United States, for example, the Muslim community seems to be a more fractured one than that of other ethnic minorities. We often spend too much time figuring out who belongs to what nation or village or tribe. We preoccupy ourselves with classifying the people in our community. We are so busy categorizing ourselves into so many separate little groups that sadly we forget that we are all part of the same family. It should not matter from what country or village we immigrated to the United States, but, rather, we should be proud of our faith, our heritage, and our diversity. In the realization that we have a common lineage, it is essential that we get past our differences and appreciate each other for what we are.

Often times, we are quick to blame others in the society for our problems. Almost daily, we read, view and hear negative overtones against the Arab and Muslim people around the globe. We witness the racism and prejudice against Muslims in America. But do we ever take time out to look at ourselves inside out? Do we ever stop and think that perhaps we are not so sensible even with our own people? Are we not exhibiting this type of prejudice when we introduce and nurture provincialism in our own community?

So the question becomes not only how to become unified but equally important what does unity mean. Unity involves being able to function cohesively with one another, for generating mutual support, and for strengthening community ties. How this is accomplished is from the basis of unity, which is love for one another.

Each community has their heroes and role models. We find the common thread that makes these superstars successful is that they didn't forget their roots, that they learned from their heritage, and that they invested their time and efforts back into the community from which they were bred. True, these luminaries had their struggles; yet, they faced adversity with an open heart and mind. They confronted the many challenges with earnestness for hard work and patience. Communities are built upon such stalwarts as these who view that empowerment makes a better community and affords the cornerstone of that community, its youth, the chance and hope to also succeed. We are of the same heritage, so we need to support one another, be good role models for others to follow, be civil, strong and united.

Definition of Islamic Unity

Islam is a universal concept that comprehends man and the Cosmos. Islam is based from beginning to end on *tawhid* (oneness) for Allah is One. Unity is a process of synthesis, a means of becoming whole and comprehending the absolute oneness of all existence. Every facet of Islam revolves around the principle of unity. The basic faith that lies behind the ideal of unity is that the existence of life and humanity has meaning. Islam is essentially a way of knowledge that integrates our being and makes us know who we are as well as our purpose in life. In return for Allah's Blessings, man must remember his real nature, and who he is and where he is going.

The definition of Islamic unity is not that we work together on the same cause or that we totally agree on all issues. We do not all have to think alike, or conform, in order to have unity. Unity is bridging the gap between people of different views in such a way that enables them to complement each other, to be more complete, and to concentrate on the bigger picture. True unity transcends differences. In reality, true unity comes out of diversity. When true unity exists, dialogue becomes productive. The source of unity comes in accepting one another, and its purpose is that we remember Allah. We demonstrate unity by accepting, honoring and respecting one another, by impacting one another, and by forgiving, caring and being kind toward one another. How we cement this unity is by genuinely loving one another and striving in the way of Allah:

"Truly Allah loves those who fight in His Cause in battle array, as if they

were a solid cemented structure." (Qur'an 61:4)

A community, which holds together as a solid cemented structure, will foster cohesion and order in the society. Each individual, family or institution contributes strength in its own way, and the sum of the parts makes a more meaningful whole. The end result is peace and harmony and a meaningful existence.

Unity is the state of being one or united. It is the quality of being one in spirit and purpose, in harmony, and in feelings. It is unity in diversity. Different ethnic and racial groups blend together in sharing food, cultural and religious activities. They exercise tolerance and respect for one another. They understand each other and work together for the common good. Prophet Mohammad had said:

"Unity is mercy, while disunity is punishment."

The political and social ambience that reigns in the world today emphasizes disparity, disarray, and devastation rather than the qualities of unity, creativity, and positive dynamism that are required to sustain human societies. Unity in diversity is the highest possible attainment of a civilization. By encouraging diversity, each society ensures a rich source of ideas and techniques for its own future. Despite the vast diversity of creation, there exists in nature a deep underlying unity. This implies that there exist universal values that lie at the foundation of religions and cultures. These religious and cultural values are imbued in the human persona such as brotherhood and commonality. True unity exists when each participant becomes an active and integral part of the whole community. Interfaith dialogue provides opportunities for different racial and religious groups to learn more about each other, thus nurturing increased awareness and understanding of the diversity within the society.

In a *Peanuts* cartoon Lucy demanded that Linus change television channels, threatening him with her fist if he didn't. *"What makes you think you can walk right in here and take over?"* asks Linus. *"These five fingers,"* says Lucy. *"Individually they're nothing but when I curl them together like this into a single unit, they form a weapon that is terrible to behold."* *"Which channel do you want?"* asks Linus. Turning away, he looks at his fingers and says, *"Why can't you guys get organized like that?"*

Often times, our Muslim communities appear to be just like that. We cannot seem to get organized. To set aside our own concerns for the benefit of others is a real strength. We may not agree on a lot of issues, we may not even think alike, but we must be united in purpose, vision and design. We need to care about each other. When we are united, it pleases Allah, and it is pleasing to others because they sense Allah's Love in our midst. There are a number of ways to be united. For example, we can be frozen together or we can be melted together. Some people feel that they are frozen together out of duty and obligation. But let us be melted together as a family, institution and community in the direction of love and forgiveness. When love of unity resides in the community, even the most fragile of things, like snowflakes, will stick together.

Definition of Islam

Achieving the unity can be attained by way of understanding and practicing our Islam. And to understand Islam, we need a definition that is all encompassing and workable. Imam Ali (first cousin and son-in-law to Prophet Mohammad) eloquently described Islam by stating:

"Islam is submission; submission is certainty; certainty is believing; believing is acceptance; acceptance is adherence; adherence is action."

As a student of Imam Ali, and guided by his maxims and sermons, I have included the words attitude, endurance, behavior, and patience in this definition:

"Islam is the attitude, the zenith of which is endurance; endurance is submission; submission is certainty; certainty is believing; believing is acceptance; acceptance is adherence; adherence is action; action is behavior, the essence of patience; Patience is an Attribute of Allah, the Compassionate, the Merciful."

Before one can submit, he or she must first have the attitude or frame of mind to be ready to take hold of the banner of Islam. All the other criteria in the definition of Islam will now fall into place. When we have the attitude to endure as Muslims, and action translates into patience by way of behavior and example, the end result is a bulletproof, impregnable definition. And Allah is the Patient, the Compassionate, and the Merciful.

Without unity, we are like a ship lost at sea never knowing which direction to turn. Unity is the compass that directs and guides us to the straight path. In the next chapter, we will explore the Universe and the cosmic compass that directs it.

CHAPTER 3: CONTINUITY OF UNITY

"Knowledge is light, while ignorance is darkness."
(Tallal Turfe)

The prevalence of ignorance over knowledge is a common dilemma for people with convictions of all types, not only in religion but also in every area where our knowledge is not put to the test of reality. Allah made the laws of nature, and we are surrounded by many of its miracles, such as the Universe. These miracles provide the means by which we are able to emerge from darkness into light, from ignorance into knowledge, and from evil into good. Notwithstanding the enormous progress that has been made in the study of the Universe, we still wonder in amazement as the Universe of life continues to broaden our eyes to its astounding complexity, beauty and mystery. Truth emerges out of our ability and readiness to confront our own ignorance. For mankind, this ignorance has been the reason to pursue knowledge.

Cosmos

The Cosmos is a complex and orderly system, such as our Universe. It is a well-ordered and unified system that is perfect in order and arrangement. In Islam, the concept of the Cosmos is one whereby there is movement in all that exists, and that this movement continues to advance until Judgment Day when the Cosmos is transformed into a new creation.

There is unity within the Cosmos. Everything in nature follows an orderly design. There is consistency and harmony in the marvels of nature, for example the growth and decay of plants and animals. For this to happen, nature has to be created and planned. This plan entails a comprehensive design that has to be conceived from intelligence beyond our comprehension. Therefore, the Cosmos was created by an eternal existence, an existence that always was and always will be forever as Allah.

Cosmologists, or scientists who study the Universe, adamantly state that in the beginning the whole Universe was just a cloud of smoke. The Qur'an reveals the following verse:

"Moreover He comprehended in His Design the sky, and it had been as smoke: He said to it and to the earth: 'Come ye together, willingly or

unwillingly.' They said: 'We do come together, in willing obedience.'" (Qur'an 41:11)

Since the earth and the heavens were shaped from this single smoke, then they must have been linked together as one entity. Again, the Qur'an gives us the answer:

"Do not the unbelievers see that the heavens and the earth were joined together as one unity of creation, before we clove them asunder? We made from water every living thing. Will they not then believe?" (Qur'an 21:30)

How could Prophet Mohammad have known this to be so when, in fact, cosmology in his time was in its infant stage? This is the miracle of the Qur'an, the Ultimate Revelation of Allah. In pre-Islam, ignorance prevailed. At that time, illiteracy was the norm, and education was reserved for the privileged few. The Qur'an was revealed, and the wonders of creation were illustrated. During the Age of Ignorance, creative and innovative thoughts were virtually non-existent, and no one was able to perceive and understand the mysteries of the enormous Cosmos. The Qur'an changed all that, as it discloses facts that only the Creator of the Cosmos could know. In Islam, the Universe is not static. Allah is steadily expanding the Universe, and again the Qur'an gives the explanation:

"And among His Signs is the creation of the heavens and the earth, and the living creatures that He Has scattered through them: and He Has Power to gather them together when He Wills." (Qur'an 42:29)

This means that life, in whatever form, is scattered throughout the Universe. This means that life in some form or other exists in the galaxies. This Universe is an entity that was created and sustained by Allah. It is Allah Who created man, so that man can harvest the land and seek out knowledge and meaning to his existence. Towards this end, Allah made the earth and the heavens submissive to man. Allah gave man a free will in order for man to be responsible for his actions. It is this free will that gives meaning to humanity, and the concept of reward and punishment in the hereafter manifests itself in the accountability of man's actions on earth. To attain ultimate bliss, man must live a life of virtues such as piety and knowledge. As man's knowledge expands, he sees more and more how unity is dominant in the Cosmos. In his progress, man's role is a perpetual quest for knowledge. It is in this manner that we must constantly seek Allah's Benevolence and Mercy and to remember Allah as we submit our will to the Will of

Allah.

How man increases his understanding of the unity in the Cosmos is by obtaining more knowledge and wisdom about the physical world:

· Impact of the moon on the ocean tides.
· Affect of the Earth's magnetic field on the migration of birds.
· Harmony in solar system as caused by gravitational and centrifugal forces.

In reality, the unity of creation continues to exist allowing for multiple forms of creation to maintain their linkage to the initial *"Oneness"* of the Universe. The Qur'an points to the continued expansion of the Universe:

"With power and skill We constructed the Firmament: for it is We Who create the vastness of Space. And We have spread out the (spacious) earth: how excellently We do spread out! And of every thing We have created pairs: that you may receive instruction." (Qur'an 51:47-49)

Even the structure of the Universe is consistent with modern scientific findings:

"He Who created the seven heavens one above another...." (Qur'an 67:3)

In addition, the linkage of the speed of light with the concept of relativity is yet another example of the unity of the Cosmos. The premise here is that time is not absolute in the Universe:

"He rules (all) affairs from the heavens to the earth: in the end (all affairs) will go up to Him, on a Day, the space whereof will be (as) a thousand years of reckoning." (Qur'an 32:5)

Balance of Nature

There is integration of nature's phenomena within Islam. This integration helps reinforce and strengthen our lives, whether spiritual or moral, political or economic, social or cultural. Each of these aspects is uniquely integrated, as they do not separate from one another. In balanced form, these aspects fit and flow with the nature of man. Humanity is interconnected with natural phenomena, as it is located at the center of the Cosmos. This interaction of human life within the Cosmos is the channel by which light enters the world of nature. We see ourselves reflected in nature, as we penetrate into nature's inner meaning by probing into our own inner depths. Despair within us can lead to disorder, while harmony can bring about the best in character. What brings about the unity within us is Islam. It is Islam that is the universal order, for it affords us the vehicle by which to gain peace and happiness. By submitting our will to the Will of Allah, Islam brings us into harmony with nature.

According to Islam, it is Divine Guidance that is the only source of knowledge. The Cosmos is a moral order, and the unity of mankind is that which reflects the essence of spirituality and piety. Our knowledge of unity leads us to understand its process, i.e., Unity of Allah, Unity of the Cosmos, Unity of Creation, and Unity of Purpose. In essence, Islam means conformity to the natural law.

As the Universe is a Cosmos, everything in nature follows a carefully structured and precise balanced order. There is a consistent order or reliability and permanence of laws governing the mechanism of the Universe. Allah created everything in the Universe with a perfect plan. The Qur'an reveals that there are Signs of Allah in the natural world, such as its balances and the rhythms of life. Some of these are the cycles of life and death, the seasons of the year, the orbits of the planets, and the mysteries of the human body. This perfect order and balance are neither haphazard nor accidental. This order and balance extend to how humans should relate to their natural world. Humans are an integral part of the natural world and as such they should fulfill its needs without being indulged in its desires. For example, humans should not pollute the environment or destroy plants or kill animals for sport. Rather they should respect the natural milieu and take from it only that which is needed to sustain their lives. Islam encourages us to discover and observe the natural world as Signs that point to Allah. Allah has given mankind the capacity to reason. As we reason, we realize that the natural order works because it is in submission to Allah.

Prophets

All the Prophets had a role to perform, and the foundation of their mission was to preach Divine Unity. All the Prophets concentrated on the basic principle, as stated in the Qur'an:

"...O my people! Worship Allah: you have no other god but Him...."
(Qur'an 11:84)

Many Prophets were sent to convey this message of Oneness to the people. While many Prophets came at different times in the course of history, they all agreed on a single premise, which is that God is One. The principle of unity means that all the Prophets conveyed to mankind the single Divine Plan directed by God. The summation of their spiritual works became fully realized with the Final Revelation – the Qur'an. There are twenty-five Prophets listed by name in the Qur'an of which five are Major Prophets. Each of the five Major Prophets (Noah, Abraham, Moses, Jesus, and Mohammad) delivered the Message of Allah. They delivered to mankind the spiritual works by which we can perform good deeds. There were many other Prophets whose names were not cited in the Qur'an, but are alluded to.

Allah alone decided who is to be a Prophet. What distinguishes a Prophet from others is that he performs miracles and is infallible. The Qur'an is replete with revelation of miracles performed by Prophets. For example, the miracle of Noah surviving *The Deluge* with his Ark; or the miracle of Abraham walking in an extremely scorching fire untouched; or the miracle of Prophet Moses who turned a staff into a serpent; or the miracle of Prophet Jesus who spoke in the cradle; or the greatest miracle of all whereby Prophet Mohammad delivered to mankind the Qur'an. And each of these miracles is covered in the Qur'an with precision and depth.

The Qur'an is replete with stories of many Prophets and of Mary. The mother of Prophet Jesus is the only female mentioned by name in the Qur'an, and a chapter is named in her honor. Each Prophet mentioned in the Qur'an had a purpose, whether it was to address the ills of the society, oppression and tyranny, disbelievers, or a moral condition. Each Prophet was sent by Allah to guide mankind. Some of the Prophets had greater responsibility and importance, thereby being called Major Prophets. All the messages focused on the One Allah and the unity of brotherhood. Each Prophet was gifted with a kind of supernatural power by means of which he worked one or more miracles to prove his credibility as a Prophet.

As each Prophet performed miracles, each was also infallible or incapable of committing sin. They were immune to sin. As they were free and protected from error, they were also unyielding to error and sin. In addition, they were gifted with great intellectual and supernatural powers and revelation as well as perfect moral virtues. The lifestyle of each Prophet is the direct result of Divine teachings and guidance. Each Prophet was the continuation of the Prophet that preceded him, except for Adam who was the first Prophet. This continuation is like a rope extended with each knot representing a Prophet. As the Qur'an is often referred to as the *Rope of Allah*, then each of Allah's Messengers provides a certain strength and intensity to that *Rope*.

Imams

Muslims believe that the concept of Divine Unity is based on the Qur'an and recognition of the Unity of God in all His Attributes, in particular that God alone must be worshipped. Based on their belief in the Divine Unity, the Shi'as maintain that while God is Just in the obligations He imposes on His worshippers, He does not impose obligations on mankind beyond their capabilities. That man is essentially free to choose between right and wrong, and his choice to be good or bad is of his own free will. The Twelve Imams expounded upon the concept of the free will and volition. The Twelve Imams that succeeded Prophet Mohammad were men of purity, excellence and were equally sinless and infallible. The Twelve Imams are manifested in the Divine Light of guidance, as this Light passed from one Imam to the next. For Shi'as, the Twelve Imams are unified strands within the *Rope of Allah*.

Picture the *Rope of Allah* as having two ends. At one end is the Qur'an and at the other end is *Ahl al-Bayt*, the Members of the Family of Prophet Mohammad. Just as the Prophets were a continuation of the previous Prophet, the Members of the Family of Prophet Mohammad are a continuation of the root of Prophet Mohammad. They are called the Twelve Imams. They, as well as Fatima, the daughter of Prophet Mohammad and wife of Imam Ali, were infallible and immune to sin; however, they were not Prophets. Prophet Mohammad was the seal of the Prophets. Nonetheless, these Imams possessed similar qualities to those of Prophets. The first Imam is Imam Ali, the first cousin and son-in-law to Prophet Mohammad. The last Imam is Imam Mohammad al-Mahdi who is still alive in his occultation.

Since man is not self-sufficient to guide himself in terms of faith and religious doctrines, the necessity for Imams arises. While patients may be able to read a book on medicine, they still need a physician to help diagnose and administer a cure for their ailment.

Similarly, Imams are needed to continue the work of the Prophet in explaining what the many verses in the Qur'an mean. Centuries have followed since the passing of Prophet Mohammad, and the world has had a dramatic change owing in large part to technology and space travel as well as easy access around the globe. The major role of Imams is to guide the people from ignorance, tyranny and disputes, to mention just a few. After the death of Prophet Mohammad, the Imam was entrusted with the guardianship of the Prophet's accomplishments and the continuation of the Prophet's leadership. In short, the Imam's role was to guide mankind in all aspects of their existence.

The Twelfth Imam is in his occultation until he returns back to Earth with Prophet Jesus, at which time they both will be in unison with each other as they address the ills of the societies around the world. In the interim, another channel of religious teaching and training is needed. These are the *ulema*, or religious teachers, who are not infallible but are schooled in the philosophy and jurisprudence of Islam making them qualified to impart knowledge on their constituents.

The Prophets and Imams provided guidance and understanding of Islam to their constituents, and these are illustrated quite vividly in many verses in the Qur'an. The Qur'an also describes the Cosmos and balance of nature.

CHAPTER 4: UNITY IN THE QUR'AN

"The panacea for ignorance is knowledge."
(Tallal Turfe)

Divine revelation has given mankind the means to acquire true knowledge and understanding. The essence of unity is manifested in the fact that divine revelation must derive from a single author. In addition, the foundation for this revelation must originate from a single unadulterated moral code. Furthermore, the revelation must have historical credibility, and it should stand the test of evaluation by scholars for its accuracy, consistency and reliability. One such test is the criterion of miracles. Divine revelation should be replete with historical and future accounts of miracles. Muslims believe in the Books that Allah has sent down to mankind through His Prophets. These Books all had the same source, which is Allah, and all were revealed in truth in their original form. Of all of these Books, only the Qur'an has been preserved in truth, and it has not been altered since it was revealed. Muslims believe that Allah sent a final revelation, the Qur'an, through the final Prophet of Allah, Mohammad.

Allah's Books

The Books (*Kutub*) of Allah are revealed in the Ultimate Book (Qur'an). The Books were sent for the express purpose of unifying the various sects, to teach the right conduct, and to guide man towards salvation. The sects had fallen in disarray and were leading a very dangerous path. The Books of Allah – the Torah (*Taurat*), the Psalms (*Zuboor*), and the Gospel (*Injeel*) and the Qur'an - were revealed in stages:

"It is He Who sent down to thee (step by step), in truth, the Book, confirming what went before it; and He sent down the Law (of Moses) and the Gospel (of Jesus) before this, as a guide to mankind, and He sent down the Criterion (of judgment between right and wrong)." (Qur'an 3:3)

"We have sent thee Inspiration, as We sent it to Noah and the Messengers after him: We sent Inspiration to Abraham, Ishmael, Isaac, Jacob and the Tribes, to Jesus, Job, Jonah, Aaron, and Solomon, and to David We gave the Psalms." (Qur'an 4:163)

The Qur'an was revealed to Prophet Mohammad through the

Angel Gabriel, to reassure Allah's Benevolence and Mercy and to correct the misinterpretations of His previous Books revealed to other Messengers:

"This is the Book; in it is guidance sure, without doubt, to those who fear Allah." (Qur'an 2:2)

"Those to whom We have sent the Book study it as it should be studied; they are the ones that believe therein: those who reject faith therein - the loss is their own." (Qur'an 2:121)

"And We sent down the Book to thee for the express purpose, that thou should make clear to them those things in which they differ, and that it should be a guide and a mercy to those who believe." (Qur'an 16:64)

Qur'an - A Book of Unity

The Qur'an is a book that is the bedrock of unity, as it reveals that there is only One Allah as well as the creation of the Cosmos, humanity and all creatures. Muslims can reach unity only by affirming and believing in the Qur'an. The unity of the Qur'an is admittedly superior to that of any other sacred book:

"Do they not consider the Qur'an (with care)? Had it been from other than Allah, they would surely have found therein much discrepancy." (Qur'an 4:82)

How we account for this unity of the Qur'an is through the unity of Allah. When we analyze the structure of the Qur'an, we see how its various pieces unite together better than a jigsaw puzzle even when arranged without any regard to chronological order. When the Qur'an is recited those who listen to it immediately become unified within themselves. Unity is a recurring theme in the Qur'an. The verses and chapters of the Qur'an are arranged in a superb and immaculate order and jointly form a complete unit that has remarkable integration and symmetry. It is this integration and symmetry that makes the meaning of the verses apparent and comprehensible.

The 114 *surahs* (chapters) of the Qur'an fall into seven groups. Each group has a principal theme that permeates through all the *surahs* within that group. When the themes of all groups are interwoven together, the result is one cohesive unit. Each *surah* has a number of *ayahs* (verses). Each *surah* has a central idea of its own, and all the verses converge around that idea. The verses are organized in an immaculate arrangement with extraordinary integration and balance. Each verse, each *surah*, and each group are tied and linked together just as the strands and knots of a rope are tied together. The Qur'an itself is referred to as the *Rope of Allah*. The Qur'an contains a pattern of a complete way of life for mankind. The Qur'an is replete with verses that cite the principles of belief, moral virtues and a legal system transcending all facets of human behavior. The Qur'an is an entity, and each *surah* and verse within it is coherently linked. In addition, the different approaches to the Qur'an, albeit philosophical, spiritual, juristic or political, must be regarded as components of a single tapestry.

There are verses from the Qur'an that emphasize the concept of unity. Following are selected verses:

"And remember when We took your covenant to this effect: Shed no blood amongst you, nor turn out your own people from your homes: and this ye solemnly ratified, and to this ye can bear witness." (Qur'an 2:84)

The covenant (agreement, treaty or pledge) refers to the laws of morality. Once a covenant is made, it must be abided by and not broken. This requires a great deal of cooperation, courtesy and protection between the parties. This verse relates to the covenant between the Muslims and Jews in Medina at the time of the Prophet Mohammad. Unfortunately, the Jews deviously broke the treaty by joining forces with the pagans and idol worshippers against the Muslims.

"Say: We believe in Allah and in what has been revealed to us and what was revealed to Abraham, Ishmael, Isaac, Jacob, and the Tribes, and in the Books given to Moses, Jesus and the Prophets, from their Lord: We make no distinction between one and another among them, and to Allah do we bow our will in Islam." (Qur'an 3:84)

Muslims consider all people to be equal, and that they do not claim to have a religion unique to just them. In fact, Islam is a way of life rather than a religion. There is no racial or ethnic preference in Islam. Since Islam is defined as the submission of one's will to the Will of Allah, then all of the Prophets preached Islam. Therefore, there has been equanimity among the teachings of the Prophets through the ages whether by Prophet Abraham or Prophet Mohammad.

"And hold fast, all together, by the Rope which Allah stretches out for you, and be not divided among yourselves; and remember with gratitude Allah's Favor on you; for ye were enemies and He joined your hearts in love, so that by His Grace, ye became brethren; and ye were on the brink of the Pit

of Fire, and He saved you from it. Thus doth Allah make His Signs clear to you: that ye may be guided." (Qur'an 3:103)

Holding fast to the *Rope* takes a great deal of commitment in the earthly life. Muslims are required to ward off evil by enjoining good deeds as they struggle to perfect themselves morally and ethically. Allah has given us guidance with His Books (Torah; Psalms of David; Gospel; and Qur'an) and Prophets, so we can live in peace and harmony with one another.

"Be not like those who are divided amongst themselves and fall into disputations after receiving Clear Signs: for them is a dreadful Penalty." (Qur'an 3:105)

This implies a unity within oneself as well as unity of the family and community. Striving for perfection in unity by way of happiness, prosperity and brotherhood is the ideal and should be pursued.

"Allah did indeed fulfill His Promise to you when ye with His Permission were about to annihilate your enemy, until ye flinched and fell to disputing about the order, and disobeyed it after He brought you in sight of the booty which ye covet. Among you are some that hanker after this world and some that desire the Hereafter. Then did He divert you from your foes in order to test you. But He forgave you: for Allah is full of Grace to those who believe." (Qur'an 3:152)

Unity is a test, and our purpose in life is to pass the test. In this verse we find that the test is one of discipline. Victory was in sight for the Muslims until some became attracted to the booty and left their military posts. This division caused defeat for the Muslims at the *Battle of Uhud*, and acted as a constant reminder that division is a weakness and disease and must be overcome with discipline of mind and discipline of heart.

"O ye who believe! Obey Allah, and obey the Apostle, and those charged with authority among you. If ye differ in anything among yourselves, refer it to Allah and His Apostle, if ye do believe in Allah and the Last Day: that is best, and most suitable for final determination." (Qur'an 4:59)

Authority is derived from Allah, Who is the Ultimate Authority. In order for discipline to be effective, Muslims must seek cooperation with governments that are righteous, irrespective of whether it is a religious government or a secular government. Even when there are disputes relative to a secular government, still the Muslims must respect its authority and attempt to work towards righteousness in light of differences between law and morality within that government.

"As for those who divide their religion and break up into sects, thou has no part in them in the least: their affair is with Allah: He will in the end tell them the truth of all that they did." (Qur'an 6:159)

Fragmentation of Islam into sects is forbidden in Islam. While Muslims can adhere to the teachings of various schools of thought, they must remain united.

"And moreover He hath put affection between their hearts: not if thou had spent all that is in the earth, could thou have produced that affection, but Allah hath done it: for He is Exalted in Might, Wise." (Qur'an 8:63)

The self-realization of affection is heightened when two parties in dispute find the means to reconcile their differences. For example, nations at war find the means for peace. Yet, another example is when husband and wife search their hearts for affection to resolve their disputes. How this affection unfolds is a miracle from Allah.

"The unbelievers are protectors, one of another: unless ye do this, protect each other, there would be tumult and oppression on earth, and great mischief." (Qur'an 8:73)

To preserve the good and prohibit the evil, we must find the way to protect one another. Husband and wife should protect each other; brother and sister should protect each other; and parents and children should protect each other. The community must protect each other from the unbelievers by finding the means to live in mutual harmony and tranquility. This protection of one another strengthens and reinforces the unity.

"Mankind was but one nation, but differed later. Had it not been for a Word that went forth before from thy Lord, their differences would have been settled between them." (Qur'an 10:19)

Allah created mankind as one nation, and as they began to dispute and became belligerent with one another they went astray. Allah sent Messengers to guide them back on the straight path. While egotism erodes the soul and causes disunity, truth and unity will prevail thus fulfilling Allah's Message to mankind.

"The same religion has He established for you as that which He enjoined on Noah – that which We have sent by inspiration to thee – and that which We enjoined on Abraham, Moses, and Jesus: Namely, that ye should remain steadfast in religion, and make no divisions therein: to those who worship other things than Allah, hard is the way to which thou calls them. Allah chooses to Himself those whom He pleases, and guides to Himself those who

turn to Him." (Qur'an 42:13)

The source of unity is the revelation from Allah. And this revelation was the same for all the Prophets. The message was not to break up into sects but, rather, to be united in steadfastness and faith and to guard against false worship and false conduct. Just as the Qur'an is one and unified, the Muslim community should be one and unified. It is the example of the Qur'an that provides the guidance for Muslims to achieve unity from every aspect and fiber of life. The means toward achieving the Muslim unity should begin with an understanding and appreciation for the Qur'an, and to be grateful for that Blessing from Allah.

Relevance of the Qur'an

Over a period of twenty-three years, Angel Gabriel revealed the verses of the Qur'an to Prophet Mohammad. The Qur'an is the cornerstone of the Islamic faith. The Qur'an is the Word of Allah, and it was preserved in the Prophet's lifetime, both orally and in written form. Prophet Mohammad considered ignorance a disease and presented the Qur'an as its treatment:

"...Say: 'It is a guide and a healing to those who believe....'" (Qur'an 41:44)

"We send down (stage by stage) in the Qur'an that which is a healing and a mercy to those who believe...." (Qur'an 17:82)

The Qur'an is a cure for the diseases of ignorance and doubt. It is full of remedies that bring the mind and soul into balance. The Qur'an contains the most important criteria, fundamentals, branches, and anything that has to do with the connectivity to the motion of life. For example, the belief in the absolute Oneness of Allah, the Articles of Faith, and the Branches of Faith are derived from the Qur'an. There are three major categories of the Articles of Faith:

· Belief in Allah
· Belief in the Prophets
· Belief in the Hereafter

The Belief in the Unity of Allah, the Justice of Allah, the Angels, the *Imamah* (succession of Prophet Mohammad), and the Books of Allah derive from these three categories. For example, the Books of Allah are revealed to the Prophets who in turn deliver Allah's Divine Revelation to mankind.

The Branches of Faith are many. The more important ones are:

- Prayer
- Fasting
- Alms (*Zakat*) and Charity (*Sadaqah*)
- Pilgrimage
- Struggle (*Jihad*)

These Islamic fundamentals are interconnected into a complete and unified system. The spirit of unity is embedded within the Islamic way of life. These Islamic fundamentals inspire and elevate the *Ummah* (community), both individually and collectively, so that they can fulfill their obligations in Islam. A Muslim's well being lies in his character being in harmony with these fundamentals.

Branches of Faith
Prayer

Here, faith is a requisite for prayer. Faith alone is not enough. Faith and prayer are justified when we worship and submit to Allah alone. This is accomplished by being steadfast and patient. To merely pray, for example, without steadfastness and self-restraint in our prayer weakens our resolve. *Sabr* (patience and endurance) becomes the essence of prayer. With *sabr*, one can pray the daily requirement of seventeen *rikats* (parts) and come away with more piety than one who lacks *sabr* and prays 1,000 *rikats* daily. Habitual prayer, with patience, brings us closer to Allah. Through prayer, believers are able to express their faith in words.

The mental attitude one practices in prayer manifests itself in our daily activities. To seek help only through prayer falls far short of ensuring that we will behave accordingly in our daily activities. *Sabr* guards the dignity of the prayer and ensures that our behavior will reflect the true essence and meaning of prayer: Allah stresses the impact of patience by giving it great importance in relation to prayer. So be thorough with your prayer and do not be hasty. Our spiritual well being is enhanced through prayer:

Haste makes waste. Be patient and perform each of the five prayers. To start on the right path each day, pray the Dawn Prayer (*fajr*) on time for it sets the stage for the rest of the day. With the Dawn Prayer, we are reminded of our obligation and duty to Allah. We end the day with the early Night Prayer (*'isha*) by thanking Allah for His Blessing having watched over us by warding off evil and guiding us toward the good deeds.

Once each week we meet at a mosque to perform the Friday Prayer. This Friday gathering of Muslims at a mosque further strengthens their unity via steadfastness in their prayer. At that Friday gathering, one can readily see how patient the Muslims are as they stand side by side, in unity, as they prostrate in prayer. Prayer behind the religious leader is the symbol of unity. If Muslims follow the example of unity in prayer, then their social and political life will be united to a common purpose. Even during the pilgrimage, notice how patiently the millions of Muslims stand in prayer. It is patience that makes the unity prayer or individual prayer a success.

There are the five daily prayers, which are obligatory and incumbent upon every Muslim to observe and perform:

1. Dawn Prayer (*al-fajr*)   two parts (*rikats*)
2. Noon Prayer (*al-zuhr*)   four parts
3. Afternoon Prayer (*al-'asr*)   four parts
4. Evening Prayer *(al-maghrib)*   three parts
5. Night Prayer (*al-'isha*)   four parts

The total number of parts (*rikats*) in the five prayers combined is seventeen. In addition to these daily prayers, there are several other prayers, among which are the prayers for the dead and the holiday prayers.

We must be active in our search for truth through prayer. With patience one can reach a higher level of understanding in his prayer, thereby setting him on the path of truth as he confronts the tumultuous world that is full of discord and disenchantment.

Fasting

Fasting (*siyam*) is referred to as self-restraint:

"O ye who believe! Fasting is prescribed to you as it was prescribed to those before you, that ye may (learn) self-restraint." (Qur'an 2:183)

Fasting means to abstain primarily from eating, drinking, smoking and sex from dawn to sunset. Ramadan, according to Prophet Mohammad, is:

".... a month of endurance (sabr), and the reward for endurance is Paradise.... a month in which a believer's provisions are increased."

It is incumbent upon Muslims to fast during the month of Ramadan, the ninth month of the Islamic lunar calendar. Muslims, for example, who are sick, traveling, or frail due to old age, are exempt from fasting. However, missed fasts must be done at another time when the Muslim restores his health or completes his travel. There are severe penalties for violating an obligatory fast. The type of violation will determine the extent of the penalty. There are other recommended fasts outside the month of Ramadan, such as the fast during the first and third days of the month of Muharram, the months of Rajab and Sha'ban, and the first and last Thursday of every lunar month, just to a mention a few.

One of the ways to practice *sabr* (endurance) is to recite the entire Qur'an during the month of Ramadan. All Muslims, rich and poor, come into balance during Ramadan, as all are equally engaging in the same type of abstention. During this month, the Muslim becomes healthier due to a balance in the diet, a more balanced character due to self-restraint, and a reward from Allah for abstention and submission. *Sabr* permeates both aspects of self-denial and repentance.

The principle of self-denial by fasting is not new. As Muslims, we differ in the way we fast from those who preceded us; we differ in the number of days we fast as well as the time and manner of fasting. Self-restraint here is in the manifestation of piety (*taqwah*). Not only do we control our natural physical desires but we also abstain from satisfying our carnal desires. With piety we can achieve self-restraint. Ramadan is the month in which the fast is practiced. During the month of Ramadan, we practice endurance (*sabr*) in our fast and reflect upon the words of Allah by reciting verses from the Qur'an, the Book sent to mankind during this holy month. We guard against our temptations and frailties of character by offering ourselves in deep meditation as we cement our metaphysical relationship with Allah. Fasting and prayer are the means by which this is accomplished as we struggle (*jihad*) in our quest for unity.

There are many passions, carnal desires, and temptations that threaten the dignity of man. How we thwart off these weaknesses is through fasting. It is fasting that increases our resolve and self-restraint, resulting in patience and perseverance against evil. Fasting becomes our struggle and resistance against evil, and with prayer we are guided to the straight path of purity.

Repent and work righteousness before it becomes too late. Do not put off repenting until tomorrow for tomorrow may never come as we may find ourselves resting in our graves awaiting the Final

Judgment. Reforming oneself immediately is true repentance. Prophet Mohammad is instructing us to repent for our sins. Repentance reassures one's faith and increases that person's resolve. It is patience that makes repentance a realization, since it gives the proper direction for the soul to adjust and reform. Fasting places the repented in a controlled self-environment, and because of this it plays a far more effective role in the liberation of man from the bondage of sinful acts.

Here, the linkage between fasting and repentance leads one to achieve piety by way of patience. True repentance is achieved when a person feels ashamed of what he has done and is willing to reform. Prophet Mohammad had made a speech during the month of Ramadan where he states that Ramadan is the best of all months, its days the best of all days, its nights the best of all nights, and its hours the best of all hours. He reminds the Muslims to pray, read the Qur'an, refrain from what Allah forbids, repent, and ask for Allah's Forgiveness.

To repent for a sin means that one's faith is sound, since that person can still distinguish between right and wrong. Fasting during the month of Ramadan is not just self-restraint of food, water and sex during the prohibited portion of the day but also self-restraint at all times against some of our weaknesses: backbiting, slandering, gambling, and alcohol consumption. Here, fasting becomes fully attained as we achieve our major struggle against ourselves. As fasting affords us the opportunity to think about others and their needs, it draws us closer to brotherhood and solidarity. This in turn helps cement the unity.

Alms (Charity)

Unity within oneself is strengthened by practicing *zakat*, which is an Islamic tax that must be paid on certain kinds of products (for example, produce and livestock) and on gold and silver. *Zakat* may be given to the needy and poor; religious leaders; non-Muslims attracted towards Islam; travelers experiencing hardship; Muslims having difficulty repaying debts; or on anything considered in the way of Allah. In fact, the economic unity and prosperity of the Muslim community is based on *Zakat*.

Additionally, we are required to pay one-fifth (*khums*) of surplus income; lawful portion of wealth or property mixed with unlawful wealth or property; riches from mining, treasures, and the seas (for example, pearls); and booty obtained in holy wars. The distribution of this *"fifth share"* is that one-half of the amounts belong to the descendents (*sayyids*) of Prophet Mohammad who are poor and in need, while the other half belongs to Imam al-Mahdi (the final Great Imam) and is allocated to his renowned Islamic scholars (*mujtahids*).

Charitable deeds are of value when they are done without any self-serving motive. *Sadaqah* (charity) for our relatives, the orphans, the poor (especially those who do not ask for charity), and other people or institutions in need are the responsibility of each and every Muslim. Charity and alms are complementary and are often considered the same.

Practice alms and charity as often as we can. While charity is usually associated with monetary gestures, it can be fulfilled with non-monetary considerations. Do not frown upon the one who receives charity; one day we may be the recipients. Above all, practice patience whether in wealth or in poverty. Charity without patience will not last. Be charitable in whatever we give.

Do not wait to fulfill the requirement of charity. The very little we give still means a great deal to the one who receives. Never underestimate the effect of a small contribution, for that mere gesture may be the spark that sustains the life of the needy. Be spontaneous in our generosity. Spontaneity that comes from patience humbles the giver and enlightens the receiver. We feel good and our spirit is cleansed because our patience in giving was ample reward for the good we performed. The good deed resulting from charity endures and lasts as long as the giver maintains his silence. Be habitual in charity, and do not seek a purpose for doing it. Do not give charity for the purpose of getting back more than what was given, for surely we will lose the reward and our efforts will be in vain.

When Muslims practice charity with one another, this helps solidify their brotherhood. An example is voluntary charity where non-monetary deeds are performed. The giving and receiving can be a kind gesture, smile or warm embrace. The giver of charity practices patience in his giving, and the receiver of charity practices patience in his receiving. Allah grants the giver patience as he reflects on the needy. At the same time, Allah grants the receiver patience as he reflects on his need.

Pilgrimage

Brotherhood and solidarity come full circle in the performance of the pilgrimage (*hajj*). The complete pilgrimage (*hajj*) is performed during the first ten days of the month of *zul-hajj* (last month of the Islamic calendar), while a less formal pilgrimage (*'umra*) is performed at any time of the year. The complete pilgrimage is obligatory on every Muslim once in their lifetime as long as they fulfill the conditions of age, health, sanity, and affordability. In addition, if there are travel restrictions to Mecca or if the area of Mecca is unsafe due to war, for example, then there is no obligation to perform the pilgrimage at that time. Should future conditions change for the better, the Muslim, if able, should perform the pilgrimage.

Pilgrimage is a place and time when one expresses his gratitude to Allah for His Blessings through submission to Him. Muslims from all over the world gather together in unity and in humility to purify their faith through prayer. They seek to cleanse themselves of their worldly weaknesses that inhibit their steadfastness and self-sacrifice to Allah. The annual assembly of Muslims at the *hajj* is a vivid manifestation of Islamic unity in its objectives and practices. The Muslim identifies himself as a vital unit within the larger and consistent body of the *Ummah*. The dress code is one and the purpose of *hajj* is one. These underscore the uniformity and symbol of unity. As there is equanimity among all pilgrims, this equality of status strengthens and reinforces their unity.

At the pilgrimage, they have the opportunity to express their solemn sacrifice to Allah and to ask for His Forgiveness and Guidance in order to perfect themselves as Muslims; thus they will be better able to serve Islam. What the pilgrimage teaches us is to strive and fight in defense of truth, a struggle that first comes from within oneself. This test of self-sacrifice (*sabr*) continues after the pilgrimage where the person is expected to practice Islam in all its beauty and manifestations.

One aspect of unity is in the sharing of food. By sharing food with other fellow Muslims during the pilgrimage, particularly, the sacrifice of meat that is eaten for food and distributed to the poor and needy, one becomes truly thankful of Allah, the Sustainer. We are instructed to take our trials with patient perseverance and not to be afraid of the afflictions of this mortal life. Pilgrimage is a form of worship (*ibada*) that covers all aspects of human life. It trains Muslims to sacrifice all their wealth, time, and energies in the way of Allah. The course to follow is the straight path, and to follow that path with faith, righteous deeds, truth and constancy.

Muslims go to Mecca and perform the circumambulation (*tawaf*) around the *Ka'bah* (Holy Shrine). This truly brings out the unity, as they perform this circumambulation in solidarity with one another. Whether in nice weather or inclement weather, Muslims perform this ritual with love and devotion. During the pilgrimage, Muslims visit many holy shrines in Mecca and Medina. These visits leave an everlasting impression in the minds and hearts of the Muslims, and they pray to achieve tranquility (*sakina*) to increase their faith. How wonderful it is to see millions of Muslims lined up together in prayer at the *Ka'bah*, as if there were an imaginary rope clinging them altogether in unity.

There is no distinction between race, color, sex, rank, or nationality as all are equal, and each has the opportunity to express their gratitude and love for Allah. This annual gathering brings Muslims from all over the world closer together and closer to Allah. How they become closer is through their perseverance (*sabr*).

Struggle

What drives home the unity is how well we are able to contain our inner self. It is the containment of the self that helps purify our inner desires thereby allowing us to fulfill our solidarity. In Islam, there are two forms of struggle or *jihad*: minor and major. The minor *jihad* is a two-fold concept in Islam that means to (a) defend Islam against all aggressors; and (b) to enjoin good by prohibiting evil. *Jihad* essentially means the endeavor towards sacrifice or struggle for the sake of Allah. Self-sacrifice may require fighting in Allah's Cause. Here, *sabr* becomes the spirit of *jihad*. To serve Allah is the cause, and worldly possessions and motives dissipate.

Defense is an aspect of *jihad* for the cause of righteousness and justice. Defending Islam by way of physical activity against the oppressor is one aspect of *jihad*, while scholarly work, charity, or a contribution of some sort are other aspects. *Jihad* is not always physical; quite the contrary, it is primarily non-physical and the self-sacrifice one makes may be in terms of wealth, property or forgiveness. For example, to reconcile differences with each other is at the pinnacle of *jihad*.

Man in his struggle is often confronted with opposition. Disputes or fights may result. A Muslim who is struck a blow is entitled to return a similar blow to his attacker. With *jihad* one reaches *sabr* by turning the other cheek, which sets an example of the highest form of conduct and behavior. He walks away from the dispute or fight or he tries to console his adversary with kind words or gestures. With *sabr* he will find the way to resolve the conflict peacefully. Allah protects the patient ones no matter how distressful a situation may be.

A wife who is faithful to her husband and, likewise, a husband who is faithful to his wife is yet another aspect of *jihad*. Each has a duty as a spouse, and the fulfillment of that duty is the forbearance they have for each other. Each must set aside their egos and work towards a unified marriage.

Here, *jihad* against egoism is the major *jihad*, a *jihad* of self-restraint. To fight against one's own wild passions and egoistic pleasures is the best *jihad*. Men and women are each other's garments and as such have mutual interaction in terms of support, comfort and protection. Garment (*libas*) symbolizes the mutual relationship of husband and wife. Each spouse develops an Islamic personality, a personality in which consciousness, love and fear of Allah predominates. This Islamic personality results in a *jihad* against egoism and those elements within the self that are at opposition to fulfilling this personality.

Worship

In order to achieve the unity, we must be steadfast in preserving and maintaining our Islamic beliefs. These Islamic beliefs must be fulfilled not only in practice but in action as well. In other words, these beliefs must be lived. By self-actualizing in our Islamic beliefs, Muslims will come closer together in peace and stability. For example, worship as a belief means more than just praying and fasting. Rather, worship is everything one says or does for the Pleasure of Allah. In Islam, a Muslim is viewed in the context of totality and mandated to submit completely to Allah. Worship transcends into many ways; for example, seeking knowledge is considered a high priority. In fact, Prophet Mohammad made it a point to inculcate into the minds of the believers that seeking knowledge is a religious duty of every Muslim. Other high priorities of worship are extending kindness, being courteous and cooperative, and performing acts of charity. When looking at worship from a macro level, we see that it is a comprehensive concept that includes many obligations and actions.

Submission of one's will to the Will of Allah represents the essence of worship. Ignorance is manifest when one worships the creation instead of the Creator. The message of Islam is to worship only Allah and to avoid the worship of creation. One aspect of worship is prayer. Prayer is the cornerstone of ritual worship, and it is the bedrock of the practical aspects of Islam. Other criteria for ritual worship are fasting, charity, pilgrimage and struggle. Islam is a way of life and requires its followers to model their practices after that of Prophet Mohammad and his progeny.

Islam presupposes a unity of body and soul. This unification necessitates purification (*taharah*) by means of regular ablution before prayers (*wudu'*) and bathing from physical impurities (*ghusl*), as a religious requirement linked to the very notion of worship. As water is a gift from Allah, it is therefore pure. *Wudu'* and *ghusl* are both components of worship. With ablution Muslims also invoke their intention to pray (*niyyah*), which is the manifestation of submission to Allah. As water purifies the body, the mind is concentrating on the remembrance and love of Allah. *Taharah* brings the Muslim into focus and harmony with the Islamic principle of *tawhid* (oneness). For example, the body and mind are united in fulfilling the obligations and responsibilities in Islam by worshipping Allah. When Muslims surrender to Allah, they do so with body and soul. The body and soul are linked together, as the body is the mirror of the soul.

Rope of Allah
Functions of A Rope

The concept of a rope has many meanings and interpretations, among which are dreams. Although unsubstantiated as realistic, dream analysts have rendered interpretations of dreams on a number of levels. In many psychology books, we find discussions dealing with the concept of dreams. For example, to dream of seeing or handling a coil of rope signifies the successful completion of a difficult task or assignment. To uncoil rope predicts the beginning of a new chapter in one's life. If the dream featured making of rope, the dreamer will soon learn the reason behind a long-standing mystery or puzzling situation. A rope noose indicates an unfortunate personal entanglement, which will entail some unpleasant moments. To dream of walking a rope signifies an auspicious period of speculation. To see someone else walking a rope is a sign of gain through influential friends.[7]

Even the properties and uses of ropes are numerous. Information from an encyclopedia reveals that nylon is the strongest rope available, and it is ideal for anchor lines and commercial fishing. Polyester rope is not quite as strong as nylon, but it has excellent resistance to abrasion, chemicals and weathering, and it is recommended wherever minimum stretch, high strength and durability are needed. Polypropylene is the lightest, most widely used, most economical rope on the market, has long life, ease of handling and is flexible in cold temperatures. It is suitable for a wide variety of marine, farm and general purpose applications. Manila rope is made from natural fibers, lubricated to increase resistance to abrasion and wear, and to retard water absorption that is a major cause of rot and mildew. Applications include oilfield-spinning lines, industrial and marine applications. Sisal is an excellent low cost general-purpose rope, and it is commonly used for truck tarp tie-downs, tarpaulins, tent ropes and general farm, home and industrial requirements.[8]

Rope has great elasticity. Fibers are made into rope by machinery. First the fibers are prepared by separating them, laying them straight, and combing them into ribbons. Combing reduces the width of the ribbon for spinning into yarn. Two or more yards are twisted into strands. Then the strands are twisted, or laid together to form the rope. Most ropes are made of three strands. The number of yarns varies. Strength of the rope depends on its size and the material from which it is made. The greater the number of strands the stronger the rope.[9]

Concept of the *Rope* in Islam

Just as a rope in this life has many strands, great elasticity and strength, it also has similar characteristics and significance in the hereafter. The Qur'an says:

"And hold fast, all together, by the Rope which Allah stretches out for you, and be not divided among yourselves…." (Qur'an 3:103)

The essence of our existence and our purpose in life is to abide by, adhere to, and cling to the *Rope of Allah*. So what does the *Rope of Allah* mean?

Symbolically, the *Rope of Allah* consists of many threads, with each thread representing a virtue. These threads, or virtues, are interwoven and represent the basis for unity. Some of these virtues are kindness and gratitude. Reinforcement is strengthened when many threads or virtues connect together to form a unified whole. The beauty of the *Rope* is that it intertwines and absorbs each person within its fold, particularly, when Muslims seek unity in congregational prayer, unity in family, and unity in the community. Each Muslim has to make a concerted effort towards the realization of these virtues in order to hold firmly to the *Rope*.

Significance of the *Rope of Allah*

We achieve self-actualization when we reinforce and strengthen our grip to the *Rope*, as we adhere to the fundamental virtues of Islam: the Articles of Faith and Branches of Faith. Some of these virtues are the essential precepts of Islam, such as the belief in the Oneness of Allah, the belief in the prophets, and the belief in the hereafter. Other basic virtues deal with prayer, fasting, alms, pilgrimage and struggle (*jihad*). Yet, other virtues interweave with these founding principles, such as tolerance, generosity, righteous deeds, truth and patience. Reinforcement and strengthening of these virtues are accomplished by way of cleanliness both of the external self as well as of the internal self.

And what do we reference and follow in order to understand the nature of these virtues as well as how to conduct ourselves accordingly? To begin with, we have the Qur'an, which is the *Rope of Allah*, and it is extended to include the *Sunnah* (traditions and lifestyle of Prophet Mohammad) and the *Ahl al-Bayt* (Household of Prophet Mohammad). This transcends into the proper attitude and behavior for Muslims to follow. The end result of the *Rope* is the truth of certainty for unity must prevail. The *Rope* becomes fully executable, for example, when Muslims at the *hajj* (pilgrimage) meet and pray in unity, or when they bind together in their struggle to enjoin good and prohibit evil, or when they congregate at a funeral to bury the deceased. The *Rope* is the vehicle that determines if one is to go to heaven or to hell. The stronger the *Rope* the easier it is to drive on to heaven. The weaker the *Rope* the more difficult it is to find heaven's road. The symbolism is that of a *Rope* hanging down from heaven to earth so that by holding it, believers may climb up to heaven.

There is even a kind of rope that starts with conception. Babies receive nourishment and oxygen in the womb through the placenta, which is connected to the inner wall of the mother's uterus. The placenta is connected to the baby by the umbilical cord through an opening in the baby's stomach. After the baby is born, the umbilical cord is clamped and cut close to the body in a painless procedure, leaving an umbilical stump. Within a few weeks, the stump will dry up and drop off; leaving a small wound that may take a few days to heal. The meaning of the *Rope* here is that it begins from conception to birth to life's journey of trials and tribulations. For each of us is tested on how well we cling to that *Rope* and prepare ourselves for the hereafter. A major test is that of prayer, which is nourishment for the soul like the umbilical cord is nourishment for the fetus.

Selected Examples of the *Rope of Allah*

Here are some examples of the application of the *Rope of Allah*:
·   People aligned in unity at the congregational Friday Prayer or holiday prayer asking for Allah's Blessing.

Fasting is yet another example of the *Rope*. Deep concentration is needed to complete each day of the fast. Great concentration is needed as we pray the obligatory five prayers each day to remind us of our commitment to Islam. Refraining from idle gossip, backbiting, profane language, and pessimism helps strengthen that *Rope* and complete our fulfillment to Islam.

·   In the string of charitable undertakings, Muslims should not boast about their good deeds. Rather, concentration should be on seeking additional ways to partake in charitable causes. In this way, Muslims strengthen and secure their grip to the *Rope*.

·   The circumambulation at the Ka'bah during the pilgrimage is like a *Rope* that Muslims cling to. If their faith is strong, they will have no problem in holding fast to the *Rope* as they encircle around the Ka'bah unified as one. If their faith is weak, the *Rope* will feel slippery and their hands will slide away.

·   Our struggle (*jihad*) is also part of the *Rope*. As we struggle to do well and prohibit evil, and as we struggle to suppress our ego, we are doing so in order to hold fast to the *Rope of Allah*. Division within ourselves occurs when we compromise our Islamic morals and values or when we substitute materialism for spirituality. Unity with each other occurs when we are steadfast and put our reliance on Allah for His Gratitude, Generosity, Gentleness and Patience.

In short, we are in harmony with each other when we have unity within ourselves, unity within the family, unity in congregation prayer, and unity in the community.

Adherence to the *Rope of Allah*

What do we mean by holding firm onto the *Rope of Allah*? The Qur'an, and every injunction therein, is a fiber or strand in the *Rope of Allah*. Total adherence to every verse of the Qur'an, to the traditions or *hadiths* of Prophet Mohammad, and to the lifestyle and behavior of Prophet Mohammad and the Twelve Imams, will create unity and harmony among its adherents.

Adherence to the Qur'an and the *Sunnah* of Prophet Mohammad and his *Ahl al-Bayt* is the only basis for unity, because they are the bedrock upon which the unity of the *Ummah* (Muslim community) can be sustained. As stated in the Qur'an, Prophet Mohammad did not speak of his own accord:

"It is no less than inspiration sent down to him." (Qur'an 53:4)

The Qur'an and the *Sunnah* of Prophet Mohammad and his *Ahl al-Bayt* do not change in their decrees. They are constant, absolute, and there can be no compromise. For example, homosexuality was unlawful during the time of Prophet Mohammad and, therefore, there is no question of gay rights being outlawed in Islam. Here, the truth of certainty becomes manifest as the Qur'an is protected by divine promise from all distortions.

Rope of Allah - Strengthens the Unity

Prophet Mohammad had said:

"I leave behind me among you two Ropes; if my people hold them fast after me, never, never shall they be led astray. One of them is greater than the other, the Book of Allah, i.e., the Rope, hung from Heaven towards the earth, and my issues, my Ahl al-Bayt. Be it known that never, never shall any of them

74

be separated from the other until they both meet me at the cistern of 'Kauthar.'"

Unity is the basis of Islam. The Unity of Allah, the unity of brotherhood, the unity of purpose, and the unity of action are often mentioned in the Qur'an. Unity makes it possible to create strong ties with each other in order to achieve Allah's Blessing. To achieve this unity, it is patience and wisdom that make us realize that we have many more things in common than we have differences. What we may dislike in the community and the hardship of obedience is better than what we may like in division.

It is through education that we become self-actualized in Islam. On the other hand, ignorance is a way of life that has its own faith and lifestyle that it totally opposite of Islam. The Age of Ignorance, pre-Islamic times, was one where people lived in a most decadent and perverse manner. The Age of Ignorance was full of chaos and corruption, as deviation from truth and justice became the hallmark of the society. Islam provided the panacea for people to remove the shackles of deviation and chaos by offering them a better life, one that is based on truth and justice. In doing so, Muslims caught hold of the *Rope of Allah* and persevered in their daily activities.

Prophet Mohammad had said:

"Allah likes three things for you and hates three things for you. He likes for you that you should worship Him; that you should not associate any partner with Him; and that you should hold fast to the Rope of Allah all together and not be divided among yourselves. He dislikes for you to have much talk and arguments; the plentiful questioning and asking; and the waste and destruction of wealth or property."

Holding fast onto the *Rope of Allah* is to maintain Allah's Obedience, to observe His Commands, and to seek His Pleasure and Reward.

Meaning of Holding Fast to the *Rope of Allah*

Holding fast (*I'atisaam*) to the *Rope of Allah* protects us from misguidance and destruction. Holding fast also protects us from deviation. Holding fast is to attain the Shelter and Protection of Allah.

There are degrees of holding fast. One degree is to submit to and comply with the Qur'an and the *Sunnah* of Prophet Mohammad and his *Ahl al-Bayt*. Muslims believe in the Promises and Warnings of Allah. They adhere to Allah's Commands and Prohibitions. Their total reliance on Allah is based on faith that does not know doubt or suspicion.

Holding fast is to self-actualize in spirituality and to deny any attachment to materialism. To achieve the Islamic personality and morality with the best of manners and conduct is purification of the soul that strengthens the grip of the *Rope*. And what better way to achieve this than to prostrate in prayer in order to be nearer to our Lord.

A major artery of the *Rope* is prayer. There is no substitute for prayer. No matter how many good deeds are done in one's lifetime, the combined weight of all these good deeds will not equal the weight of one prayer. How each person fares with respect to good and evil will determine their strength within the *Rope*.

Holding Fast During Ramadan

For true unity, let us all hold fast onto the *Rope of Allah*. During the month of Ramadan, we must become more focused and our senses heightened towards virtues such as piety, humility, forgiveness, generosity and forbearance. We must practice self-restraint on that which is against Islam. Fasting becomes our struggle and resistance against evil, and with prayer we are guided to the straight path of purity.

Every obligation in Islam is, therefore, a building block in the quest for unity. Being ignorant or unaware of certain obligations weakens the struggle for unity. Neglecting certain obligations does exactly the same. And being lethargic and unenthusiastic about any of our obligations retards the process of unity.

Mosques, Islamic centers, and Islamic schools are places where we heighten our remembrance of Allah. They are places for unifying in prayer, gaining knowledge about Islam, and spreading the message of Islam. At these places, all Muslims start with the same ideals and values.

Fasting during the month of Ramadan affords us the golden opportunity of focused reflection and action. We need to reflect on how to unite the *Ummah* (Muslim community). We need to be nurtured with the ideals of discipline and sincerity as we move towards activating the unity. Without unity we lose sight of Islam and the community becomes lost. With the individual, there is unity of interaction with virtues. With the family, there is unity of trust and tolerance. With peer groups, there is unity of gentleness and understanding. With the community, there is unity of working together to build a better society. With the nation, there is unity in diversity. With the world, there is unity of security and peace. With the Universe, there is unity of the Cosmos.

We need to have unity of purpose, which can only be achieved through knowledge and understanding. We need to have unity of expression by working together, complementing each other, and bringing the community into harmony with one another. We need to demonstrate our commitment to Islam by achieving our Islamic objectives.

Unbreakable *Rope*

Holding fast primarily means an intense spirit of attachment and devotion to the Qur'an and the *Sunnah* of Prophet Mohammad and his *Ahl al-Bayt*. They represent the strong unbreakable *Rope*. Holding fast to the *Rope* means remaining closely united identifying with Prophet Mohammad and his progeny whose lives are the best examples and the perfect mold of the practical aspect of the Qur'an. *"Be not divided among yourselves,"* means do not differ from or do not leave the path shown by Prophet Mohammad.

Islam aims at the establishment of peace, unity, and harmony not only between people of any particular family, community, race, or country, but also between mankind as a part of the Universe as a whole. As Muslims, it is absolutely imperative that we unite together in goodness for the sake of establishing the true religion of Allah. However, this will never happen, unless we learn to support one another in our good works, causes and efforts.

Applications of the *Rope of Allah*

How can we apply the concept of the *Rope of Allah* to our everyday practices? By clinging to the *Rope* we can build stronger families and stronger communities. The *Rope* serves as a catalyst to engage families and communities in a process of change.

Interconnectivity between family and community by supporting one another impacts everyone within these environments. How this unfolds is when we witness parents getting involved with their children by making sound and meaningful connections through shared experiences. Or by getting parents and children to engage in mutual problem solving, effective communication between one another, and facing the myriad of challenges that come of age within a family. Husband and wife relationships are strengthened when each realizes that they are the garments of the other. When husband and wife place themselves in the shoes of the other, they create stronger ties to one another.

The community can cling to the *Rope* by approaching the problems of the society in a cohesive manner. Here connectivity and caring become the hallmarks of an effective society as they share experiences together. Teachers and students need to establish a better mentor to student relationship, in order for the student to establish a stronger bond and attachment to education. When viewed in totality, these binds or ties are like strands, and each strand becomes reinforced as it cements itself to other strands. Toward this end, while each is strengthening their own *Rope*, they are also helping others to strengthen theirs. And that translates into charity, a major pillar of faith.

Overcome Obstinacy by Holding Fast to the *Rope of Allah*

In order to cling to the *Rope of Allah*, we should set free our narrow perceptions and biases and overcome obstinacy. We need to contain our ego in order to set free our suspicions, doubts and fallacies. We need not have predetermined notions of what should be or what should not be but, rather, to let our hearts and innermost self speak out.

The self-will and obstinacy put us in a state of confusion, as they overpower the heart and lead us into temptation and misery. We need to hold steadfast to truth and love in order to achieve self-fulfillment. If we are to cling tenaciously to the *Rope*, then we must find the way to energize ourselves and hold fast to each strand and to each knot. This energy must allow the heavenly flow of creativity and wisdom into our hearts and minds. Holding fast to the *Rope* unleashes our innermost fears, anxieties and weaknesses. People oftentimes demand respect from others rather than earning it. They insist on being respected even to the point of overpowering others to get it. Respect cannot flourish in a clogged-up system that detonates from mistrust, power and falsification of truth.

As long as we know that this life is temporal, then we have a better chance of overcoming our innermost fears and letting go of our self-will. If we view this world to be the end of our existence, then we will fall into an acceptance to being powerless and miserable. That is why people prefer the status quo as opposed to the frail struggle of containing the self-will.

Trust and faith cannot be built on the festering basis of suspicion and lack of faith. In order to trust, there must be a linkage to those we love and who are tranquil and pious. This connectivity forms the attachment to a state of a sincere and optimistic expectation of life, where there are no pressures and anxieties. Instead there is the deep faith that Allah is Benevolent and Merciful and that we can have the very best on all levels of existence. With an open energy system we can positively create fulfillment and enrichment within ourselves.

People do not need just a mosque; they need a unity-committed mosque. To become a unity-committed mosque, we must fulfill the requirement of humility in order to rethink, that which is important for us to self-actualize as Muslims. We need to rediscover our passion for the Islamic doctrine of the unity of all believers. One of the great strengths of our brotherhood is our pledge to the Authority and Commandments of Allah. Our challenge is that we must pursue Islamic jurisprudence and the passion for unity. It is high time that we recognize that our passion for issues and our willingness to reject each other over them are not virtues. They are not an indication of security. Rather, they are evidence that we are too often controlled by our self-will.

Unity is not something we create; it is a Gift and Blessing from Allah. Sometimes we will fail in our pursuit of unity, but let our disappointments come only after our most genuine efforts have been exhausted. And let our disappointments be manifested not with accusations, but with the sweat of uphill struggles and the tears of heartaches.

We need a unity-committed mosque, and may Allah give us a passion for that unity. We need to allow for some diversity in our dealings with other members of the mosque. If we cannot learn to allow for diversity of opinion, then we do not have any hope for unity. Uniformity allows no room for personal opinion because the slightest deviation destroys it. The Qur'an nowhere orders or envisages such uniformity. Instead, the Qur'an calls those with differing opinions to be united in a common identity and a common hope in Allah. We weaken our demeanor when we preach unity and practice division. If we are going to make any sort of a positive contribution toward the unity of all our community, we must learn to reach out.

We need to find ways to engage in meaningful dialogue with each other. Dialogue is not debate rather mutual exchange of ideas and discussion. Listening to each other with openness and empathy creates an atmosphere of understanding. Each participant must come to the dialogue with complete integrity and sincerity so as to allow others to genuinely express their points of view. Each participant must come to the dialogue with no rigid assumptions as to where the points of disagreement are. Effective dialogue can only be achieved when a foundation of mutual trust is first established. Therefore, our commitment to unity must begin with each other. Then, we may begin to extend our reach to others who share the same common principle and common ground with us. As we reach toward them, let us do it with an open mind, an open heart and an open hand, inviting peaceful dialogue.

As we meet, let us seek to understand before we seek to be understood. We become better motivated when we recognize who the real enemy is, and the enemy is Satan. Our failure to recognize the enemy and to engage in the struggle against the enemy only leads to the weakening of the self and the fragmentation of our brotherhood.

Every light has its shadow, and the truth is differences among one another arise out of their aloofness toward each other, growing out of their mutual ignorance and intolerance of each other. Unity comes full circle when denominational sects are broken down and the true faith, as Prophet Mohammad revealed it, is once again cemented together as one. Only then can Muslims stand tall and realize that their blessed unity will truly rouse the spirit and courage of man towards self-fulfillment.

Unity in diversity is the highest possible attainment of a community, an attainment made possible through passion and trust. For unity to work, a great deal of effort needs to be made in order to put away traditional rivalries, provincialism and fragmentation. When tribalism is the order of the day, tension mounts giving rise to conflicts. Prophet Mohammad preached against the intolerance and radicalism that can emerge from tribalism, provincialism and nationalism. He promoted a universal diversity that breeds harmony and serenity.

CHAPTER 5: UNITY OF COMMUNITY

"If a community is to survive, it must cultivate knowledge and uproot ignorance." (Tallal Turfe)

To really unify our community, we have to live up to the cultural diversity that Islam teaches. We have to focus on the basis of Islam, accepting one another, accepting our diversity and understanding that we can agree to differ on certain things and allow Allah to bring clarity to our hearts and minds through our trust and faith in Him. We have to make efforts within our community to find real unity based on our Islam, not disunity based on culture, race, and historical differences. Perhaps what will motivate us to find that unity today is to engage with each other on the common problems that we face, as Muslims in the world; problems and issues, however, which are not limited to the Muslim community. For when we look around us, we see that non-Muslims are seeking solutions to the same problems: bigotry, prejudice, poverty, an inadequate educational system, crime, and the excesses of materialism. All who believe in one community come to realize that they are one. [10] Knowledge sustains the unity within the community, while ignorance fragments and destroys the society.

Concept of Community

The Muslim nation, or *Ummah*, is comprised of many communities and is a special name given to Muslim brotherhood and unity. These communities share the same common values and characteristics of the *Ummah*, which are (a) the belief in the Oneness of Allah; (b) the belief in the Prophets; and (c) the belief in the Hereafter. The Qur'an states the following:

"Thus have We made of you an Ummah justly balanced, that ye might be witnesses over the nations...." (Qur'an 2:143)

There needs to be a balance within the society. When disputes arise between two parties, impartial witnesses need to intervene for the purpose of justice. In Islam, it calls upon the *Ummah* to maintain an equitable balance between extremes, pursue the path of moderation, and establish the middle way. Justice must even be rendered in such matters as excessiveness. This means that everyone, including individuals and communities, should avoid excessiveness. Islam abhors extravagance, and the *Ummah* must always strive towards this balance with justice. The concept of *Ummah* means that all Muslims are members of a single nation that transcends tribal, ethnic, racial and national divisions.

There will never again be a time of absolute ignorance after the coming of Prophet Mohammad, because righteous people will be present to avoid it. The Muslim *Ummah* will never be devoid of righteous people. However, ignorance can still manifest itself through sins. While ignorance will still be prevalent among the *Ummah*, it will not be pervasive. Ignorance directly affects every aspect of our lives. Furthermore, we cannot unite in the absence of knowledge, which should be advanced by accurate beliefs and understanding. How we remedy the disease of ignorance is by asking or inquiring about the principles of Islam.

The *Ummah* is the bedrock of our heritage, of our identity as Muslims. It must be representative and act as a role model for its constituents. To work towards moderation is the true test of the *Ummah*, a trial whereby each member within the community is tested for their resolve and patience. The Muslim *Ummah* must have unity of vision, unity of purpose, and unity of design in order to justly strike this balance of moderation.

Meaning of Community

A community is a unified body of individuals that interacts and has joint ownership and participation. It is a group of people with a common characteristic of living together within a larger society. Members of a community become integrated and recognize that community as a valuable source of information. Members of a community encourage and support one another. Members gain self-esteem by providing something of value to the community. Therefore, a community is a group of people who share social interaction and common ties with other members.

The Islamic community likewise has certain traits, such as its purpose, its uniqueness, and its permanence. The basis of the community in Islam is the tenet whereby each member completely submits his will to the Will of Allah. In a nutshell, an Islamic community is viable only when it is nurtured in the ideals of Islam. Each Muslim within that community must continuously seek the straight path and uphold Islamic virtues and morality, resulting in the ideal Islamic personality. As each member seeks unity with other members in that community, the end result is brotherhood and solidarity at its finest. Just as there has been continuity of the Prophets and Imams throughout the ages, there must also be this continuity of the members of the community. To lead by example as role models instills within the community this continuity and, as such, strengthens the unity.

Concept of *Ummah*

The Muslim *Ummah* is founded on two important criteria. The first criterion is *taqwah* (piety), because when Muslims have *taqwah* they will avoid anything that displeases Allah. In addition, with *taqwah*, Muslims will fulfill their obligations and duties toward other Muslims. The second criterion is unity among Muslims, because division and discord are characteristics of disbelievers. Division and discord are the major problems for a fragmented *Ummah*. Here Muslims ignore the straight path that is requisite for unity. Instead they follow the path of Satan, which fragments the *Ummah* into factions and sects.

The *Ummah* consists of believers in Islam whose daily activities are modeled and governed by the Qur'an. A unified *Ummah* makes it possible for Muslims to truly live out the Qur'an, as the Qur'an addresses every aspect of our lives. The *Ummah* is not just a religious community but also an economic, political, social, cultural, technological and moral community as well. From generation to generation, the *Ummah* represents the values set forth in the Qur'an, and it carries out Allah's Commandments. Allah has given us clear and unambiguous principles of faith as well as laws and practices.

The center of the Islamic *Ummah* was never a state or a nation. The center of the *Ummah* is Mecca, for all Muslims turn to it in prayer and fulfill their pilgrimage obligation as well. Within the concept of *Ummah*, the affairs of Muslims are governed not by the state or nation but, rather, by the morals, character, and justice that come from a state or nation.

Significance of *Ummah*

The Qur'an reveals the following:

"You are the best of peoples, evolved for mankind, enjoining what is right, forbidding what is wrong, and believing in Allah...." (Qur'an 3:110)

Islam exists for mankind, and the Muslim nation is the best among nations. This Muslim nation is called the *Ummah*, which is distinct from other nations, in that it has been created specifically to enforce the canons of Islam. Its mission is to bring Muslims to the straight path by doing righteous deeds and warding off evil. Islam merged all nationalities and tribes collectively into one *Ummah*. Islam transcended all types of nationalities, languages and ethnic backgrounds and hence established a global community committed to the faith:

"O mankind! We created you from a single (pair) of a male and a female, and made you into nations and tribes, that you may know each other (not that you may despise each other)...." (Qur'an 49:13)

This verse deals with the national brotherhood of man. The concept of *Ummah* can be viewed as an interpretive community of Muslim believers, as it symbolizes the very notion of the Islamic community. In the early years of Prophet Mohammad's mission, the concept of *Ummah* was first instrumental in the transformation of various tribes into an Arab society of Muslim believers. As Islam extended to non-Arab nations, the concept of *Ummah* transformed its followers into a single Muslim community with no distinction made as to race, ethnicity or nationality. The requirement for becoming a member of the Islamic *Ummah* was one based on faith, without any other prerequisite or constraint. The concept of *Ummah* transcended into a consciousness of belonging thereby bringing about the universality of Islam. Over the course of history, Muslims became immersed in the concept of *Ummah*. With a sense of social consciousness, Muslims were united and practiced the faith of Islam as a complete way of life.

Establishment of A Way of Life

The establishment of a way of life is referred to as *iqamat-ul-deen*, which guides the *Ummah* to strive towards the best attitude and best behavior in their daily lives. [11] For example, the establishment of prayer or the establishment of fasting is a necessary requisite for fulfilling our obligations in Islam. This fulfillment not only necessitates the practical establishment but the intellectual establishment as well. *Iqamat-ul-deen* requires the *Ummah* to be completely obedient to Allah in the fulfillment of its obligations, and to be aware of such obligations as well in their practical and intellectual activities. *Iqamat-ul-deen* requires that the *Ummah* implement the commandments of the *shari'a* (law).

Iqamat-ul-deen is a system of life in which Muslims consciously surrender to Allah. It is a system whereby Muslims live a life of total obedience to Allah. One's faith must be more than just expression; it must be truly lived. While we surrender to Allah in total obedience, at the same time we are devoted and grateful to Allah for His Blessings. As such, we strengthen the *Ummah* by spreading and teaching the *iqamat-ul-deen* to others by calling them to the light of Islam.

Historical Perspectives

Prophet Mohammad enforced the concept of *Ummah*, as he integrated Muslims of different races, ethnic groups and social classes into one brotherhood. As Islam expanded, the *Ummah* absorbed a mixture of people from diverse cultures integrating them into a collective union. It engendered an open society for all to excel. Based on Quran'ic commands, Prophet Mohammad stressed the significance of unity, and authorized harsh admonishments and reprimands for those who intentionally assailed the unity of *Ummah*.

The human ego of arrogance and conceit led to conflicts among the followers of the *Ummah*. These conflicts immediately led to insults against each other. Contingent on the state of affairs and historical events, arrogance and conceit exhibited numerous forms – individual, economic, political, social, cultural, ethnic, racial, regional or geographical. Needless to say, whatever form it took, it produced the identical consequence – separation of the *Ummah* into unproductive and destructive sectarian groups disputing with each other. Rather than creating peace and justice for everyone, the separation added to the problems of the *Ummah*. As a result, this divided *Ummah* was infested and dominated by those who instituted tyranny, injustice and oppression. The history of mankind is full of examples of such repression of the *Ummah* by tyrannical and oppressive communities – the repression of the Palestinians by Israel is just one example.

Throughout centuries of difficult periods, the Muslim *Ummah* survived, notwithstanding changes in philosophies and jurisprudence as well as scientific developments. During these difficult times, Islam continued to flourish and the *Ummah* maintained its solidarity. When outside forces attacked Islam, this only strengthened the resolve of the *Ummah* and Islam became stronger.

Islamic history is full of examples where the *Ummah* was threatened. During the period of the Umayyads and later the Abbasids, there had been many attempts to disintegrate and disunite Muslims. But these attempts were futile, and the *Ummah* survived. The Muslim *Ummah* suffered many physical calamities, but always managed to prevail over each one. The *Ummah* arose persistently to resume its mission with resolve and steadfastness, irrespective of how great the adversity. Islamic scholars had a great deal to do with the survival of the *Ummah*. The excellent and sincere work of Islamic scholars had an impact on the disintegration of sects such as the Khawarij. While there were intellectual differences of opinion among the scholars of Islam, the *Ummah* remained intact.

As time marched on, Muslims began to defend and expand the boundaries of the *Ummah*. With cultural diversity and compliance, the *Ummah* became the structure whereby its followers maintained the unity. By prevailing over ethnic and cultural disparities, the Muslim world became engrossed in a fervent awareness of unity that pervaded and encompassed their daily lives. Here the *Ummah* is viewed as a spiritual, non-territorial society differentiated by the shared beliefs of its members. As such, the *Ummah* integrates religious, political and ideological dialogues. The very structure of the *Ummah* is predicated on the basis of the Qur'an. For it is the revelations in the Qur'an and the teachings of Prophet Mohammad that are the guiding principles by which the *Ummah* prospers and flourishes.

Challenges

According to Islam, differences of opinion (*ikhtilaf*) are a mercy. Differences of opinion are natural and unavoidable, especially since the companions of Prophet Mohammad had differences among themselves. *Ikhtilaf al-Fuqaha'* refers to the divergence or difference in the positions of the jurists. [12] Agreement is worthwhile only if it is the outcome of a process encompassing all aspects of diversity. Genuine universalism means recognition of differences. The Qur'an states:

"If your Lord had so willed, He could have made mankind one people: but they will not cease to dispute, except those on whom your Lord has bestowed His Mercy...." (Qur'an 11:118-119)

As man was imbued with a free will, this made differences inevitable. This verse plainly stipulates that Allah has left man to cultivate his innate gifts at his own free will. Allah did not compel man towards any particular way of life, as there will be differences of opinion exclusive of those who have submitted their will to the Will of Allah. In addition, we seek Allah's Blessings and Mercy for which we have been created. The concept of *ikhtilaf* establishes the notion of freedom of belief and thought in Islam. These differences in beliefs and thoughts represent the fundamental reason of human existence. Here our challenge is to develop clear ethics and morals and to find the means to cope with these differences. This is the challenge of religious diversity. This is the challenge of the *Ummah*.

In today's global society, we see a great deal of fragmentation in the ranks of the *Ummah*. One reason is attributed to the impact of information technology and communications, as the Muslim world has been deficient relative to scientific and technological advancements. Additionally, the Muslim world is beset with political, social and cultural problems. Some of these problems are the result of economic underdevelopment, colonialism and exploitation of resources. For this reason, the challenge for the *Ummah* is one of intellectual discourse. This intellectual discourse will heighten the awareness and consciousness of the Muslim brotherhood to be a viable and persevering entity within the Islamic *Ummah*. Rest assured, the Muslims of today are strong in their faith and commitment to Islam, but they have lacked the intellectual skills to move forward in the economic and political streams of life. As a result, they have fallen prey to outside influences that are insidiously working towards further fragmenting the *Ummah* and driving a wedge between various Islamic nations and their communities.

What we see in the Muslim world today is a preference for material possessions and self-interests such as wealth and power. Deviation from the straight path has led some Muslims to place self-interests over righteousness. By being content with worldly success, the Muslim *Ummah* has weakened. Some political leaders of Muslim nations have opted to undermine Islamic unity by inflicting tyranny and oppression on their citizens. In addition, the Eastern and Western powers are aiding and abetting the disunity of the Muslim *Ummah* with colonialism and exploitation.

The *Ummah* of today have been demeaned and humiliated. Witness the occupation of Kuwait by Iraq and Iraq's destruction by the Western powers. Furthermore, the genocide of Bosnian Muslims was a humiliation exacerbated by the neglect of Muslim nations to come to their aid. This indifference by the political leaders of Muslim nations not only was shameful but further eroded the *Ummah*. Even the plight of the Palestinians in their constant quest for survival and autonomy has met with little assistance from Muslim nations.

The challenge is for Muslims to regroup and trek the path that is righteous in order to fulfill the mission of Prophet Mohammad. We must catch hold of the *Rope of Allah*. While it is true that within the Islamic *Ummah* there are groups with different histories, courses and perspectives relative to the aspects of Islam, they are nonetheless solidified as genuine believers. The *Ummah* exists; it just needs to be reawakened and nurtured in the ideals of Islam. We must evoke the breadth and unity of the Islamic *Ummah*. We must lead by example. We have the duty to uphold the rights of Muslims, even when we are not in front of them. We should be kind to one another and avoid backbiting and slandering against our Muslim brothers and sisters. Not only must we study the Quran'ic principles of peace, forgiveness, tolerance and brotherhood but we must also apply these principles as well. Only in this way can the *Ummah* be strengthened and return to the path that Prophet Mohammad had established, a path in which the code of behavior is based on the *shari'a* (law).

Some of the major elements or characteristics that the *Ummah* would require in order to mediate the needs between and individual and society are: (a) sense of community; (b) sense of permanence and social structure; and (c) sense of belonging.

Sense of Community

The community must be flexible, and it could be small or large. There can be many communities within the *Ummah* of Islam. Within each of these communities that constitutes the *Ummah*, Muslims must feel that they are part of the larger social order. The sense of community is heightened when all members submit their will to the Will of Allah and obey His Commands.

The Islamic community thrives on adherence to the precepts of Islam. The Islamic way is to live as a community. Muslims must be intertwined into the fabric and structure of the Islamic community. They must act and function as a team whereby all members have the same goal in mind. The sense of community is where Muslims come together as one with the same goal or purpose in mind; otherwise, their sense of community is weakened. We need to put Islam as our top priority in life instead of the amusement of this world. Holding fast to the *Rope of Allah* is the means whereby Muslims cling to and share the same goal. And the means is the Qur'an, which is the *Rope of Allah*. The Qur'an has to be our guideline for living, and it needs to be our central focus. The Islamic sense of community and of the brotherhood of all Muslims is both political and religious at the same time. What this means is that Islam is not just a religion but also a way of life. It is not only a system of faith and worship but a community as well.

Sense of Permanence and Social Structure

Within the Muslim *Ummah* there must be social order. Creation of institutions, such as religious, political, social, cultural, economical, educational, and scientific is deemed basic to all societies. From the vantage point of Islam, all of these institutions must focus their efforts toward a unified *Ummah*. Members of each of these institutions must feel their sense of worth of the larger community, and they must feel that they are making a contribution to the welfare of that community.

There must be permanence or stability as well as social structure within the *Ummah*. Brotherhood and solidarity must be the order of the day. Muslims must interact with each other on a communal and spiritual basis. What matters is the well being of each of the members transcended into the well being of the *Ummah*.

The *Ummah* must be more than just survival. It must survive on the basis of enjoining good and forbidding evil. Today there are many divisions among Muslims based on nationalism, tribalism, or some other ideology. When Islam is divided into sects, there can be no continuity, only discord. Muslims must adhere to the Qur'an and unify; otherwise, chaos will set in and erode into the structure of the *Ummah*. The mosque must play a key role in community development and the affairs of the community. We should not seek to replace the mosque in these roles, and we should be careful not to marginalize the mosque by an erroneous distinction between religious issues and secular issues. As Islam is a complete way of life, then every issue is a religious issue. The *Ummah* must be strong and united in order to flourish and sustain itself. When Muslims cling to the *Rope of Allah*, they free themselves of hatred and disputes.

Sense of Belonging

There must be significant interaction among Muslims within the *Ummah*. Whether interaction is primary or secondary, there has to be accountability. Muslims must function in the society with the utmost respect for one another as they fulfill their obligations and virtues. Whether they are members of a scientific organization or are attending a social gathering, they must interact on a level consistent with Islamic behavior and feel hospitable and welcomed. When there is consistency and equality in behavior, the *Ummah* is strengthened. Mutual consideration for one another is a hallmark of a viable and continuous *Ummah*. Just as there is continuity in Islam, there must also be continuity among the Muslims within the *Ummah*. A strong bond of brotherhood holds the Muslims together. In this way, each Muslim has a sense of belonging to one unified *Ummah* characterized by the same faith, the same purpose, the same vision, and the same Qur'an.

The Muslim *Ummah* must protect itself and its members. There must be provision for social services, ensuring a reasonable standard of living, and facilitating community needs such as education, employment, senior citizen programs and business development. The *Ummah* must raise its children in an Islamic way in both Muslim and non-Muslim societies. We must support our mosques, so that they keep providing all the different services and programs necessary to build a strong *Ummah*. Supporting our mosques and Islamic centers is done by our participation in programs and activities both individually and collectively. Unity projects strengthen friendships, create bonds between neighbors, bridge everyday misunderstandings, and foster mutual respect and increase everyone's sense of confidence in the safety of the *Ummah*. Other activities could be to promote the understanding and appreciation of Muslim values and culture; seminars on community issues; lectures on health care; and youth development programs.

An analogy relative to the sense of belonging in the community can be drawn from the relationship of mother and child. Just as the fetus is tied to the mother's womb for nourishment, the Muslim *Ummah* must be tied to each other in order for the society to be nourished and to flourish. The Arabic word *Ummah* is closely related to the word for mother, *Umm*. Just as our mothers cared for us when we were young, the *Ummah* likewise cares for us from the cradle to the grave.

Basis for Unifying the Community

Unity is on the lips of every Muslim scholar, whether it is written in articles and books or spoken in lectures and sermons. Yet, in spite of this, Muslims are drifting and being further divided. Why? It is because Muslims are confused as to what principles and ideologies unite them. Holding fast to the *Rope of Allah* is the only true solution. We must fulfill all our obligations in conformity with Islam. When we forsake the tenets of the Qur'an, we become victims to division and conflict. The Qur'an is the center of our life, and we must understand the meaning and significance of the Quran'ic revelations in order to be united in true spirit and brotherhood. We must have true faith by clinging to the *Rope of Allah*, which is the Qur'an. We must reflect on the passages from the Qur'an and understand their meanings with clarity of vision and remembrance of Allah. The basis for unifying the Muslim *Ummah* is the establishment of a system of social justice as prescribed in the Qur'an.

"Let there arise out of you a band of people inviting to all that is good, enjoining what is right, and forbidding what is wrong: they are the ones to attain felicity." (Qur'an 3:104)

The ideal Muslim *Ummah* is one that is prosperous and united. It is a community that is content and undisturbed by quarrels or suspicions. It is a community that is sure of it and passionate. It is all of these, because it invites to all that is good, enjoins the right, and forbids the wrong. This Quran'ic verse presents a challenge and command to Muslims. They must fulfill this command and obligation with assertiveness and a sense of fraternal order so as to effect positive change in the structure of the *Ummah*. To enjoin good and forbid evil is the basis for unifying the *Ummah*.

CHAPTER 6: UNITY OF FAMILY

"When knowledge triumphs over ignorance, the family dwells in harmony." (Tallal Turfe)

The family is the foundation of each and every society. Family unity is based on those things that define a family – birth relationships, genetic factors, and social factors. The ideal society is one where people live together in trust and harmony as one unified family. This can be accomplished by developing within individuals an awareness and knowledge of the underlying unity that connects all members of the human family. Strong family development aims at increasing awareness, knowledge and practice of a healthy, stable and harmonious family life.

Today, the Muslim family institution is beset by many problems, particularly in Western societies. These problems can erode into the Muslim family to the point of destruction, not only for the spouses but also for the entire family. This could mean the destruction of the Muslim society and the failure to transmit Islam to the next generation. What are these problems? First, many Muslims are ignorant of the Islamic laws that govern the family. Second, we find many Muslims succumbing to the influence of desires and a way of life that is in direct conflict with Islamic customs and traditions. Third, many Muslims take the attitude that they just don't care and have fallen into complacency relative to their lifestyle and family practices.

Relative to the Muslim family, the husband and wife play an important role in a shared relationship that unifies the family, particularly if there are children. This shared relationship extends to providing the necessary means to sustaining the family. Each family has a pivotal role that constitutes the society in general. Therefore, families are the units of which the society consists. Strong and unified families make the society strong and unified, while weak and disorderly families make the society weak and disorderly. From an Islamic perspective, the Muslim family is one unit in the chain of units. The family relationship is one of partnership and mutual collaboration, which is the Islamic view based on the Qur'an. The Qur'an provides the framework and set of laws by which a family can unify and sustain itself whether in marriage, parenting or some other function in the family unit.

Community and Family

The Muslim community is made up of many parts. Some of these parts are institutions that are social, cultural, business, educational, and political as well as family. Members within each of these institutions cooperate with each other towards the betterment of the society. The ideal community is one where its members can coexist together in peace and harmony, as their hearts and lives are intertwined with a mutual passion and zeal to be better Muslims. In an atmosphere of cooperation and commitment, they can enjoy the fruits of a viable community both personally and physically. Each person in the community is like a piece of thread that intertwines into a mesh, which eventually forms a quilt connecting all members together as a cohesive entity. Removing psychological and social obstacles in order to build and establish cordial relations within families avoids conflicts. It breaks up intolerance, suspicion and other differences of ignorance and changes them into human values and lawful objective considerations.

Muslims within a community have a common cultural and historical heritage. In the past, the bonding aspects of the community had to do with external threats, family bloodlines and cultural heritage. In the post-Industrial Age, communities are formed intentionally around shared intrinsic values rather than common threats and obligations. In today's mobile society, such as in the United States of America, the Muslim community does not need to be defined entirely by where its members live. Shared values are a rallying point of community. Commitment is an essential ingredient along with trust, honesty, compassion and respect. Muslims look to the community for social support, meaning, identification, interaction and a setting where one is accepted as a separate entity with the society. A community is larger than the sum of its parts, and Muslims will create it wherever they can. Lately, we have seen more focus on social connectedness as a means to link Muslims as individuals to the larger society. When cohesiveness results, these Muslim communities hold its members together despite their diversity and what appears to be a lack of social organization.

The focus of our discussion is on the family institution within the broader framework of the Muslim community. It is the sum total of all the families within that framework that constitutes the community. By cooperating together, these families can draw upon the values that Allah has bestowed upon them, for the purpose of creating a more perfect society.

Strengthening Family Ties

In today's society, people are often under a great deal of stress. As a result, family relationships are severely impacted. With a full load of daily activities, people are hard-pressed to find time for anything else. Although family matters are a priority, they are often set-aside until a future time. This back burner approach has caused havoc in the family, since issues and problems in the family need to be resolved as they occur. Families begin to break apart as problems mount and personalities clash. Nonetheless there are uncomplicated ways to strengthen family ties and resolve issues and problems.

Time needs to be set aside to hold family meetings or family dinners, and these should be held at least twice a month. There needs to be mutual exchange between all family members at these meetings. Respect for one another's point of view must be honored, and all discussion should be considered vital even though it may appear to be mundane. At these regular meetings, rules can be established and personalized, activities planned and scheduled, and issues and problems worked out. There is a sense of connectivity and cohesiveness when holding family meetings. Keep the meetings fun while at the same time serious. Hopefully, these meetings will generate positive action resulting in a personalized outlook for all participants. Staying connected with our spouse and children is often not an easy task, but is necessary in order to have a viable and strong family relationship.

Promoting Family Strengths

There is no set family structure in today's society. Family structures take on many different forms; however, most of them accomplish similar tasks. Family tasks such as social engagements, child rearing, providing for basic needs and wants, and delegating responsibility are both challenging and time-consuming. Fulfillment of these tasks manifests the way a family functions in a society. There is a great amount of diversity across families in any given society. The conventional family has undergone many changes in American society, such as increases in the rates of divorce, teen pregnancy, substance abuse and suicides as well as transformation of social values.

Social change has distorted traditional family patterns, resulting in the rise of many family problems. Principal causes of these problems stem from dissimilar perceptions and lack of family time and interaction. As a result, emotional gaps set in between spouses, between parents and their children, and between siblings. The problem of generation gaps between family members is escalating. For example, the working mother has posed a problem as to who rears the children while she is at work. Lack of motherly attention widens the generation gap between mother and child.

As the erosion of traditional family continues, the family structure is severely impacted by social problems that continue to soar and intensify. Resilience to these pressures is becoming necessary and vital. How this resiliency unfolds is when family members exhibit and display such actions as self-assurance, sincerity, collaboration and forgiveness. By sharing experiences with members of the family, stresses and strains can be minimized. Having shared experiences with respect to family traditions, for example, holiday celebrations, can help strengthen the ties among family members. When a family member loses his job, or there is an untimely death in the family, these impose severe stresses on family members. Recovery in the way of coping with these stresses is needed to bring the family back into focus.

Following is a template on how to develop and preserve healthy family relationships:

·   Promote open communication that is action oriented. Demonstrate the understanding of another's point of view. Foster good relationships with other relatives to generate support.

·   Preserve and reinforce relationships in the family. Establish family rules and priorities, encourage accomplishments, share responsibilities, and acknowledge and extol the efforts of others.

·   Manage time effectively. Face and understand crises and conflicts with the objective of resolving and reconciling issues on a collective effort.

While each family member's actions are imperative, strengthening family relationships necessitates the dedication and collaboration of all family members. By working in unison, family members can develop and maintain close relationships during the good times as well as the stressful times. Strong families appreciate each other. They have the ability to show love and support and acknowledge others for their individuality. Strong families spend time together. A pious connection, by way of Islam, helps unite a family. Communication and shared thoughts are important to strengthening family ties, as are good listening habits. A hallmark of a strong family is when its members encourage others, build teamwork, and keep criticism at a minimum. One of the most stimulating, exhilarating and satisfying discoveries we can make as human beings is finding that our emotions are actually reflections of our awakened enlightened potentialities.

By overcoming ignorance, strong families can appreciate the individuality and contributions of each family member, and that each is special in their own way. This appreciation is sometimes neglected as we are caught up in the frenzy of day-to-day activities. We often take each for granted, and fail to express our appreciation for each other. One way to solidify a family relationship is to give a family member a card or gift expressing our appreciation. We must find the time to spend with family members, irrespective of whether or not we are tired or bad tempered. We need to reach out and enjoy our family, and a way to do this is by exhibiting humor and amusement.

Patience and tolerance are values that make for cementing family ties, and these attributes bring out the best in us. A kind word, touch or embrace goes a long way in solidifying family ties. It is a pleasant feeling to know that others understand our emotions and look beyond our faults. Having confidence in airing one's thoughts in the open goes a long way towards resolving a dispute or issue. Family members must display positive commitment as they share in the kinds of experiences that help promote happiness and make families strong. When was the last time we put our arms around our mother or father and thanked them for all they do? Parents do most of the nurturing, but they need to be nurtured too. Prayer is the panacea to strengthening the family, and prayer must be done on a regular basis. Prayer will protect us from the enemy and render peace and tranquility and love within the family.

Example of Unity of Family

My parents, Haj Alie Turfe and Hajjah Hassaney Turfe, had a profound sense of faith and justice. Very early in our childhood, we were nurtured in these values. My parents instilled a great sense of religion within their family. For example, they taught us that Islam is more than just a religion; that it is a way of life. They also taught us about the importance of loyalty and respect. For example, loyalty and respect for parents are tantamount to loyalty and respect for the Prophets and Imams. These ideals cannot be separated, as they are linked together in the true meaning of unity. My parents emphasized that keeping an open mind and an open heart in our relations with Muslims and non-Muslims were essential for fostering unity among our neighbors.

At the same time, my parents inculcated within the minds and hearts of their children the importance of civility and justice as personified by good citizenry. Being good practicing Muslims was more than just prayers and fasting. There was a profound linkage between beliefs and practices. For example, my parents were devout Muslims and constantly espoused humanitarian principles. In addition, they were so totally immersed in the affairs of their community that they took a personal interest in establishing a shared relationship within that environment. How they resonated within their community can be traced back to their faith and religious convictions. These in turn shaped their ardent zeal for the pursuit of peace and justice for all. My parents were good examples of what is meant by the *Rope of Allah*, for faith and justice were the hallmarks of their lives as they were cemented together in unity and harmony.

Filled with a sense of importance and enthusiasm, my father, for example, adroitly and skillfully approached the problems of his community brethren with a spiritual heart and open mind. With vision and purpose, he could quickly see where and how problems emerged in his community. And with each problem he was a good listener, did not take sides, and applied justice to it's fullest. That was the mark of a leader, and my father exhibited the many qualities of leadership. He spoke to his fellow brethren in a language they understood, whether oral or tacit, as the foundation for any discussion was predicated on faith and morality. My father's sense of justice was the result of his faith and upbringing. In Islam, the formation of justice entails the reinstatement of a person's right to which he is entitled.

CHAPTER 7: UNITY OF SELF

"Knowledge frees the self from ignorance and brings it into harmony with the soul." (Tallal Turfe)

What adversely affect the self are the ego and its army of bandits: lust, greed, anger, pride, violence and envy, to mention a few. The dense forest of ignorance is infested with these bandits who occupy hidden holes and traps as they inflict pain and suffering on its victims. As long as the self is under the spell of ignorance, it is unable to find its way out of the forest. The remedy for ignorance is knowledge. As knowledge clears the path in the forest, the self is enlightened and escape is within reach. Enlightenment derives from divine knowledge, which armors the self from the deadly venom of ignorance. To completely overcome ignorance, the self must make a connection with the deepest parts of its inner being; it must touch its individual soul consciousness. When connecting with the inner being, the self moves away from an ego state toward a more permanent connection with the soul placing it at the entrance of the vast and immense knowledge accessible to it at any moment.

Family Unity and Self

Strong families recognize that there are benefits and pleasures to be gained from time and activities together. By spending time together, families build a reserve of good feelings and are able to cope with personal and family crisis more effectively. Strong families are deeply committed to the family unit and to promoting the happiness and welfare of each other. Family commitment comes from an active involvement in setting and carrying out family goals. Family unity encourages families to create daily routines as well as special traditions and celebrations that affirm members, connect them to their family roots, and add fun to ordinary family events. Family unity includes time that family members spend together. Family unity means maintaining family identity and togetherness and balancing family priorities with support for individual needs. Family unity produces strong family bonds and freedom for individual self-expression.

Families are products of the community that weaves them, and they transmit the social strengths and weaknesses of those larger social institutions. Family experiences shapes development of individual and collective consciousness. Persons and family systems carry within them the roots of identity that involves genetics, culture, spirit and emotion. At least these four core elements are keys to self-knowledge. The resulting construct of identity, for both families and individuals, is the lens through which human existence and experience is filtered and defined. Beginning to learn about one's heritage can help facilitate self-awareness as a member of a family. This provides the bridge to a cultural base, empowering individuals and family systems to confirm or reweave their values, identify patterns, and make changes in personal, family and cultural activities.

Each individual is a self that has a role to play within the family. Whether the self is a parent or child, the collective unity of these members in terms of cooperation, respect and accountability makes that family strong and prosperous.

Enlightenment

In Islam, we are to question and use our faculties of reason in order to find absolute truth. There is no blind following or imitation. One must always question his values to make sure they are in accordance with the Divine Law as stated in the Qur'an. It is impossible for reason to extend beyond the boundaries of Islam, because there is no contradiction between reason and Islam. On the contrary, reason of the mind leads one to the path of Islam.

As Muslims, we are encouraged to overcome ignorance by seeking knowledge from the cradle to the grave. Before Islam, man was to limit himself and his mind. When faced with a contradiction in dogma, he was told to follow the law strictly by faith and negate reason. This imprisoned man's soul. Islam opened the gate to reason, stating that all knowledge and truth emanate from Allah; therefore, an unbiased search for truth and knowledge leads one directly to the path of Islam. Islam does not place a boundary. Islam is the epitome of reason. It is Allah Who is the Giver of Enlightenment. To be enlightened in Islam means to gain spiritual insight and knowledge in the search for truth, understanding and wisdom. This search takes on a commitment in one's mind, and it can only come about through one's endurance and patience. Enlightenment is not ignorance. Enlightenment is based on free will and independent intellect. Ignorance, on the other hand, is darkness. The religion of Islam gave us a new perspective of enlightenment. This allowed man to better understand himself while at the same time liberating him from ignorance and confusion. Therefore, man was now able to restore his self-dignity and self-identity.

Cowardice and impatience are vices of deficiency in relation to courage and patience. Let us look at the example of a man who grows blind in the prime of his life. There is nothing that can bring back his sight. The potential for a good life, however, remains. He is healthy, prosperous, and surrounded by the people who love him. However, he is fearful of how others will regard him now that he is blind. He always pitied the blind, and the thought of being a pathetic spectacle to others is terrifying. His fear of humiliation makes him hide from the world. Although others reassure him that independence and competence can be regained with effort and flexibility on his part, he doubts his own capacity to learn a new way of life. Trying and failing to learn is more frightening than failing by not trying at all, and so he drifts helplessly.

In this example, this blind man has no patience for the moral task his blindness has set him, and no amount of courage or fortitude can compensate for the absence of that virtue. Enlightenment by way of patience is what he needs because it entails a discipline of those particular emotions that threaten to loosen or destroy one's hold on the good in circumstances of this kind. In courage, there is discipline of the fear that would make us cowards and the overweening confidence that would make us reckless. In patience, anger and despair are the things to be controlled if we are to cleave to the good against the temptations of impatience or a dejected passivity.

Self-Concept

The self-concept has a powerful influence on one's behavior, perhaps, the most powerful influence. Man has a basic tendency to strive, actualize, maintain and enhance himself:

"Man gets only what he strives for." (Qur'an 53:39)

The person develops this self-concept in order to gain confidence and feel good about him. There are boundaries that one must not extend beyond. The danger of enhancing one's self-concept outside the parameters of Islam, for example, an egotist, miser, gambler, drunkard, to mention just a few, renders that person a failure in his faith. Therefore, man's self-concept is one that strives toward the goal of patience and perfection in Islam, and one of the ways this is achieved is by performing good deeds:

"As for those who strive for Our Cause, We will definitely guide them to Our Paths...." (Qur'an 29:69)

Self-Esteem

Controlling self-esteem shapes and molds one's self-concept. Developing positive self-esteem means to regard life and its surroundings with respect and affection. We become more positive about our feelings for ourselves. As our opinion of ourselves improves, we become better Muslims as well. People with high self-esteem take risks, and each risk they take teaches them something. Risk, however, requires patience.

Self-esteem is an extremely powerful factor in our growth and development as Muslims. To grow in Islam, we must practice endurance. Part of that endurance and power comes from its uniqueness. It operates as a mechanism for maintaining our inner consistency. It helps determine how our experiences are interpreted. It provides a set of expectancies - what we do in situations and how we interpret what others do in situations.

Self-Fulfillment

Becoming the best we can, as Muslims require a commitment and the patience to succeed. We need to be committed towards working up to our potential to learn and understand the concepts of Islam. This results in self-fulfillment and self-satisfaction. Knowledge and understanding give direction for one to realize his objectives and goals, while wisdom enhances one's self-fulfillment to its fullest potential:

"...For Allah has sent down to you the Book and Wisdom and taught you what you knew not...." (Qur'an 4:113)

And truth is the light that enlightens one's mind and keeps him on the straight path. When self-fulfillment comes into balance with the self-concept the end result is self-esteem, the ultimate in happiness. Just as man needs to come into balance with his society, so does self-fulfillment need to come into balance with the self-concept. The way to achieve this balance is by way of self-esteem, the basis of which is intellectual enlightenment and the zenith of which is patience. This balance gives the person an integrated self, a higher standard of perfection. What emanates from this integration is the value of truth. And this truth allows one to fulfill his submission to Allah. Those who accept the guidance of truth will purify their minds and bodies:

"Say, O you men! Now Truth has come to you from Your Lord! Those who receive Guidance do so for the good of their own souls; those who stray do so to their own loss...." (Qur'an 10:108)

Criteria for Developing Islamic Self

When we come to learn and understand this balance, we gain an entirely new perspective about ourselves. We begin to understand the meaning of unity within the self. So how can we create, nurture, and then effectively use this perspective to help us be what we want to be - better Muslims?

· *Be patient*: Self-discovery, self-development, self-awareness, self-esteem, and self-confidence take time to acquire. One thing we can do is to try giving away of ourselves. Instead of pulling everything towards ourselves, allow things to go out from us. When we make important connections with others through our commitments, attention, time, respect, and attitudes toward them, we will be defining ourselves by what we are giving to them. Patience will help us be what we want to be, because attainment is within reach if we persevere. But, remember, patience is not passive; on the contrary it is active; it is concentrated strength.

· *Be purposeful*: Have a goal; have a set of goals. Plan and have alternative plans as well. But be true to us. What we do while in the process of becoming not only can influence what we become, but it can provide a clearer definition of the perspective that we seek. So plan our work and work our plan because the person, who fails to plan, plans to fail!

· *Be persistent*: Stick with our perspective. In today's society, we want instant gratification. Why? Because everything appears to be instant - instant coffee, instant potatoes, instant winners, and instant rewards. Self-fulfillment through one's perspective is not instant. Becoming who we want to be is not instant. The only thing about it that is instant is when we can start. We cannot do everything at once; but we can do something at once!

Controlling the Islamic self is not an easy task. It requires control of one's inner thoughts and actions. Becoming enlightened in Islam is to understand one's self-concept, control one's self-esteem, and attain self-fulfillment by way of patience, purposefulness and persistence. Control is achieved by way of order and harmony within the self. The Cosmos is the systematic order, harmony, and unity within the Universe, as well as within a society, institution, and family and above all within oneself.

Ego - Threat to Self

From various dictionaries, we find many meanings of the term ego. Ego is the conscious mind and the consciousness of one's own identity. Egoism is the doctrine that the supreme end of human conduct is the perfection of happiness of the ego, or self; and that all virtues consist in the pursuit of self-interest. It is the habit of valuing everything only in reference to one's personal interest. It is the ethical doctrine that morality has its foundations in self-interest. It is the ethical belief that self-interest is the just and proper motive for all human conduct. It is the excessive preoccupation with one's own well being and interests, usually accompanied by an inflated sense of self-importance. It is the tendency to evaluate everything in relation to one's own interests, that is, self-centeredness.

Egotism is the habit or practice of thinking and talking much of oneself, or the spirit that leads to this practice, for example, self-exaltation. It is the tendency to think only about one's self and to consider one's self to be better and more important than other people. It is an exaggerated opinion of one's own importance and an inflated feeling of pride in one's superiority to others. It is the concept in which a person is so possessed by the ego that he becomes convinced that he is the center of the Universe.

Whether one is egoistic or egotistic, he is morally depraved and suffers from false impressions of himself. This self-centeredness and self-absorption within himself immensely diminishes his chances of ever reaching moral fulfillment and self-respect. Keeping occupied with thoughts and actions of materialism, greed, center of attention and conceit, he continues to fall deeper and deeper into a spiral pit of which he cannot escape. This obedience to his self further erodes his soul, as he commits every act of transgression, deception and sedition in order to achieve his superiority or authority over others. In a nutshell, he begins to worship himself thereby becoming totally impervious to spirituality and the common good.

The person who is continually boasting about himself is someone whose self-worth is meaningless, and he feels the necessity to tap other avenues or sources to restore his self-esteem. This need for replenishment is vital since the ego functions out of fear. The ego operates in such a way so as to give the egotist a sense of loneliness and separation from the world. The egotist feels he is obliged to act the way he does since no one really cares about him. This leads him constantly seeking approval in any way he can get it. His addiction to his inner self makes him even more anxious to not only seek approval from others but to demand it as well. The end result is that the egotist finds himself rejected by others. Still the egotist revitalizes himself and seeks other means for acceptance, even if it means engaging in corruption and immoral acts to achieve it.

How a Muslim fulfills his needs is by devoting himself to spirituality and not to vanity and conceit. Spirituality helps mold one's personality and sets the individual on the right track. Vanity and conceit severely limit the person's strive for self-worth, thereby resulting in humiliation and disgrace. With humility and self-sacrifice, one can recover his sense of worth and regain his spirituality free of pride and complacency. There is no room for selfish ambition or vain conceit or self-delusions. Those who have a superior attitude that they are always right portray this kind of approach. They confront others to prove their point, and they must have the final say in all matters. Rather than recognizing their mistake, they keep on pressing forward against those who support truth. For the egotists, they feel that those who oppose them are rivals. But the real rival is the rival within them.

With a lack of unity within one's self, the egotist becomes weak, suffers from low morale, and consumes his energy focusing on trivial issues and problems. This in turn leads to personality clashes and enmity. The egotist is ignorant about his obligation to strive for unity within himself and within others. The love of this life and the propensity to control others are reasons for discord. To combat egotism, we must have a strong sense of solidarity and brotherhood whereby we better understand one another and work towards the common good. We must cling to the *Rope of Allah* with every ounce of energy and determination to succeed.

Self-Forgiveness

Forgiveness is an attribute that has received much discussion in Islam. The self-realization of forgiveness is when one is willing to forgive when he has the power to take revenge. Forgiveness is an acknowledgment of a person's pledge to not inflict any more harm on anyone, and to make a concerted effort to remedy his inner self towards one of peace and harmony. Toward this end, forgiveness benefits both the one who harms as well as the one who is harmed. Prophet Mohammad had said:

"The best deed before Allah is to pardon a person who has wronged you, to show affection for relatives who have broken ties with you, and to act generously towards a person who has deprived you."

One of the Attributes of Allah is that He is Forgiving. This Attribute takes on different names in the Qur'an. For example, Allah is mentioned in the Qur'an as *Al-Ghafoor* (The Most Forgiving); *Al-Haleem* (The Clement); *Al-Rahman* and *Al-Rahim* (The Beneficent and The Merciful); *Al-'Afuw* (The Restorer of Forgiveness); and *Al-Tawwab* (The Acceptor of Repentance). Various sources reveal different occurrences of these Attributes in the Qur'an. From these sources, it is estimated that collectively these six Attributes are mentioned over 270 times in the Qur'an.

As Allah Forgives, it is necessary for humans to forgive as well. When we pardon others for their inequities and harm against us, we reach the highest level of forgiveness. We cleanse and emancipate ourselves from the evils of Satan. Forgiving one's enemies is a hallmark of self-respect.

Self-Criticism

Self-criticism (*muhasaba*) is a necessary requirement for one to bring his thoughts and actions in harmony with righteousness. [13] A righteous Muslim constantly evaluates his actions and seeks improvement in order to bring him closer to Allah. The Muslim becomes unified within his self by overcoming his inner weaknesses of sins and deviant behavior. Through self-criticism, one can seek and discover his spirituality. By reaching the spiritual level, one can make amends for past mistakes and seek forgiveness from Allah. Self-criticism is one of the most difficult deeds to perform. It takes an enormous effort to evaluate and take account for one's own deeds. Repentance follows the awareness of one's mistakes. This awareness is a direct result of constant self-criticism, which is a prerequisite for achieving piety:

"O you who believe! Fear Allah, and let every soul look to what (provision) he has sent forth for the morrow. Yes, fear Allah: for Allah is well acquainted with (all) that you do." (Qur'an 59:18)

This verse commands us to practice self-restraint and avoid committing sins. We should always strive to please Allah by evaluating our inner selves so that we can be righteous. Self-criticism brings us closer to Allah, as it intensifies and heightens our piety. Self-criticism acts like an alarm system. It can alert a person as to whether something is good or evil. Hopefully, the person engages in self-criticism in order to avert committing an evil action. Through self-criticism, one is able to attain peace and tranquility.

Before one criticizes someone else, he should first criticize himself. Perpetual self-criticism allows one to move closer to perfection in his faith. Self-criticism may precede an action or it may follow an action. For example, one may evaluate his inner self before making his intention so as to commit a good act. If it is not a good act, then he rejects it. Even if the act is a good one, the believer will always consider if that act will please Allah. *Muhasaba* detects impurities of intention. If the person determines the act to be evil, then he will not make his intention to pursue it. Always the believer holds the self to be accountable for all actions. This, of course, requires the believer to be sincere, obedient to Allah, and to follow the example of Prophet Mohammad. Islam encourages self-criticism in order for us to call ourselves to account before Allah does. As self-criticism is the first step in repentance, we need to constantly evaluate and re-evaluate how we have spent our time each day.

Islamic Personality
Self and Personality

Within our personality structure, we have individual selves. Each of these selves has a unique system. For example, the self has its own goals and priorities. Each has its own perceptions and motives. Each has its own style and developmental cycles. Each has its own limits of tolerance and emotional sensitivity. Dynamic and interactive, our sub selves can communicate with each other to form a decision. When making decisions, the sub selves condition our true basic self.

We are not born with a personality. Our personality is formed, shaped and developed in the framework of our relationships with our family and environment. Personality is consistence of individuality, as we behave in a manner consistent within each of us. It is this consistency of our behavior that defines the kind of personality we are associated with. Our personality is a product of our genetics and environment. For example, our personality may be one of tolerance or aggression. Nonetheless, while personality traits may be acquired from parents at birth, our environment is a major influence as to how these traits unfold. A child may be born into a Muslim family; however, his environment may influence whether he develops into a good Muslim. Character traits form the personality pattern, which is a product of heredity and learning available in one's environment. Therefore, while genetic makeup may serve as the foundation of one's personality, relationships within the environment shape his personality.

People often see themselves differently from how others perceive them. How one sees oneself is what is referred to as the self-concept, which can be either positive or negative. A positive self-concept results in one feeling good, while a negative self-concept results in one feeling bad. The self-concept consists of one's thoughts, attitudes and feelings about himself, i.e., his perceived self worth. Like the personality, the self worth is also a product of one's heredity and environment. What have a bearing on one's self-concept are such factors as education, religion, family background and overall health.

The basic self-concept is the person's concept of what he is. The person arrives at this after considering such things as his physical appearance, strengths or weaknesses, position in a community, values and aspirations. The ideal self-concept, however, consists of ideas of what one would like to be or what he believes he ought to be. It may be realistic in the sense that it is within reach or unrealistic if it is out of reach. For example, he may want to be a physician but has not prepared academically for that career. Or he may want to be a professional football player but does not have the size, strength, speed and agility to become one.

Family influences the development of the personality both directly and indirectly. One direct influence is the deliberate effort parents make in molding the child's behaviors to conform to societal expectations. The parents use reinforcements such as rewards and punishments to make their teachings effective. One indirect influence is role modeling. Here the child identifies with and emulates the behavior of an older family member. As a result, the child is likely to develop desirable or undesirable personality traits as he tries to mimic the behaviors of the admired family member.

Development of the Islamic Personality

We need to develop unity within ourselves by holding fast onto the *Rope of Allah*. One of the ways in which we can achieve this is by developing an Islamic personality:

"Therefore, be patient with what they say and celebrate (constantly) the praises of the Lord, before the rising of the sun, and before its setting; yea, celebrate them for part of the hours of the night and at the sides of the day: that thou may have (spiritual) joy." (Qur'an 20:130)

Evil hovers around us. We must be patient and ask Allah for Guidance so that we can avoid evil. The Islamic personality makes the believer cherish his human dignity and prestige and accept his responsibilities as a Muslim. The best example of the Islamic personality is that of Prophet Mohammad and his progeny.

The justification of religious morality, that is, Islamic morality promises the continuance of life in the Hereafter for the morally good individuals. In Islam, there is no distinction between theoretical morality and physical morality. Morality deals with determining right from wrong. Morality is comprised of virtues. Faith, righteous deeds, truth and patience are the basic virtues of Islamic morality. Man gains eternal happiness through moral virtues. Prophet Mohammad had said:

"My religion is based on cleanliness."

Cleanliness here does not just refer to our daily washing and cleansing of our bodies. There is a higher meaning to this message, a meaning that attaches itself to the inner purity of the soul. We must cleanse our thoughts and our hearts in order to attain ultimate and final perfection. In striving towards perfection through self-purification, Allah will guide us:

"And those who strive in Our (Cause) - We will certainly guide them to Our Paths: for verily Allah is with those who do right." (Qur'an 29:69)

And the path is the straight path (*sirat al-mustakim*). We must free ourselves from the spider's web of this frail world. We must walk the path of struggle against immoral tendencies. All that we can do is to strive in the way of Allah. With firmness of purpose, determination and patience we can attain the Mercy of Allah.

In addition to cleanliness, there are other traits that help nurture one's Islamic personality. For example, while the ideal Islamic personality is one of moral excellence, it is also the preservation of self-respect and dignity by way of piety. It is one of righteousness and faith. It is one of adhering to the beliefs and practices in Islam. For example one studies the rules of *hajj* before making the pilgrimage. When he returns from the *hajj*, his awareness is heightened, his soul is purified, and his lifestyle exemplifies that of a Muslim.

The ideal Islamic personality is one who believes his sole purpose in life is to worship Allah, and to seek the Pleasure and Guidance of Allah. The ideal Islamic personality is one where faith leads to good deeds and good deeds lead to faith. By helping others he is in effect helping himself become a better Muslim. He sincerely concentrates on every aspect of his life, as he continues to understand the beauty and wisdom of Islam. He reads the Qur'an so that he can be enlightened, and he is grateful for the bounties and blessings Allah has bestowed upon him. Therefore, he continues to remember Allah and to win the satisfaction of the Creator.

Other examples of the ideal Islamic personality are when the spouse becomes the garment of the other spouse in the path of mutual responsibility and respect. In addition, the ideal Muslim is one who is truthful, does not cheat, is not envious, is sincere and keeps his promises. He is gentle towards people, compassionate and merciful. He is tolerant, forgiving and patient. He refrains from backbiting and slander, and avoids suspicion. He is humble and modest and strives for reconciliation between Muslims.

Revolving Hierarchy of the Islamic Personality

As a guideline, the author has formulated the Revolving Hierarchy of the Islamic Personality, which begins with faith (*iman*) and ends with endurance (*sabr*) and then proceeds back to faith (*iman*) by way of cleanliness. This is based on the four virtues in Chapter 103 of the Qur'an, which inculcates within man the four primary virtues of faith, righteous deeds, truth, and patience or endurance. Imam Ali said:

"…Practice endurance and patience; it is to faith what the head is to the body. There is no good in a body without a head, or in faith without endurance." (Nahjul Balagah)

Tantamount to this circular effect is the analogy of proceeding from theory to fact and then back to theory again. The Revolving Hierarchy of the Islamic Personality is comprised of six groups:

(1) *asas an-nafs* (self-foundation)
(2) *aman an-nafs* (self-security)
(3) *waee an-nafs* (self-awareness)
(4) *tahkeek an-nafs* (self-achievement)
(5) *retha an-nafs* (self-satisfaction)
(6) *idrak an-nafs* (self-realization)

There are at least two theories as to how we absorb these criteria. One theory given by a number of religious scholars is that Allah makes these and other criteria prior to our existence. And that in our lives we practice the criteria that Allah has already given us at birth. Another theory postulated by several philosophers is that we are not given these criteria at birth but, rather, we develop these criteria as we progress in our lives. What this means is that we choose during our lives whether to develop some or all of these criteria. What is important in either theory is that we can practice these criteria according to the values given us by Allah. As we search for meaning in our lives, it is these values that make for a better Islamic personality.

These criteria of the Islamic personality are intertwined with each other. Self-foundation is the basic need, while self-security and self-awareness are deficit needs. Self-achievement, self-satisfaction and self-realization are growth needs. As these needs are dependent on each other, they cannot be separated. They comprise the total Islamic personality. For example, assume that we have progressed to the growth need of self-satisfaction and suddenly the deficit need of self-security is threatened. Therefore, we have to regress back in the hierarchy and fulfill the deficit need of self-security. Growth needs must be pursued once the requirements of the lower needs are fulfilled.

With faith as the self-foundation, we proceed upward until we attain self-realization by way of endurance, and then we proceed back to faith. We always need to reinforce and strengthen our Islamic personality by absorbing ourselves in these criteria.

Having faith leads us to practice and be secure in at least the five requirements of prayer, fasting, alms, pilgrimage and struggle. With this we become aware of truth as we seek knowledge, understanding and wisdom. The straight path via worship and piety results in the self-achievement of righteous deeds, respect and prosperity. Prosperity or salvation occurs when man has freed himself from selfishness and basic desires. Prosperity emanates from man's self-achievement. One who is purified through worship and is humble and patient will attain prosperity and success:

"But those will prosper who purify themselves, and glorify the name of their Guardian Lord, and (lift their hearts) in prayer." (Qur'an 87:14-15)

"O ye who believe! Persevere in patience and constancy; vie in such perseverance; strengthen each other; and fear Allah; that ye may prosper." (Qur'an 3:200)

Tranquility and happiness are the levels of self-satisfaction arising from self-achievement. At the zenith of the fulfillment of these needs is self-realization through endurance. Similarly, moving from endurance downward through each of the six categories makes us more cognizant of our role as Muslims and of our contribution towards Islam.

Moral judgment is applied to all activities of man, which results in a single undivided Islamic personality. Through prayer, we can strengthen our Islamic personality and resolve in order to grapple with evil and overcome its dastardly venom. Struggle (*jihad*) manifests itself in prayer:

"Enjoin prayer on thy people, and be constant therein. We ask thee not to provide sustenance: We provide it for thee. But the (fruit of) the Hereafter is for righteousness." (Qur'an 20:132)

True, Allah provides sustenance for all, just and unjust, in this ephemeral world. But this is a transient existence that ends almost as soon as it begins. So be prudent and wise in how we utilize that sustenance, and exercise our patience and struggle in the way of Allah by doing good and prohibiting evil:

"So persevere in patience; for the promise of Allah is true: and whether

We show thee (in this life) some part of what We promise them, - or We take thy soul (to Our mercy) (before that), - (in any case) it is to Us that they shall (all) return." (Qur'an 40:77)

The Muslim has to protect his external behavior and his deeds, his words and his thoughts, his feelings and his intentions. Truth and virtue are his goals. Justice will prevail. Every soul must return to Allah for His Justice and Judgment. Life in this world is very short; however, life in the Hereafter is eternal. Allah provides sustenance to the righteous in the Hereafter. The unjust are doomed to a dark and ghastly world of punishment. The Muslim's relationship with Allah is one of love and obedience.

Case Examples of the Evil Personality

At the time when Prophet Mohammad was spreading the message of Islam, there were evil people who tried to discredit him. These people were malevolent, as they were transgressors with satanic whims. One example was Prophet Mohammad's uncle, Abu Lahab, who was a vile and ruthless person who disbelieved in Allah and was a constant threat and enemy to Islam. In addition, Abu Lahab's wife was just as evil. Chapter 111 in the Qur'an states the fate of Abu Lahab and his wife. Their penalty is one of eternal damnation and fire.

Abu Lahab, also known as the *Father of the Flames*, was a person of burning temperament. He and his wife, Umm-i-Jamil, a sister of Abu Sufyan (another enemy of Islam in its early years), did much damage to Prophet Mohammad.[14] Abu Lahab was a wealthy man, and he used his wealth against Islam. His wife was equally bad tempered and evil. She and her husband worked hand in hand to try to derail Islam. As an example of her wickedness, she used to tie bundles of thorny branches with ropes of twisted palm leaf fiber, carrying them and scattering them about on dark nights along the paths that Prophet Mohammad was expected to take, with the expressed intention of wounding his feet and causing him bodily injury.

The story of Abu Lahab and his wife has yet another meaning. First, there is no preferential treatment for people who deviate from the straight path, even if they are related to the Prophet. Second, the revelation of this Quran'ic chapter condemns Abu Lahab and his wife to eternal Hell, and that is one of the miracles of the Qur'an.

Abu Lahab and his wife were still alive when the revelation took place. Had Abu Lahab and his wife professed their declaration of faith and loyalty to Islam, and then Islam would have been destroyed right then and there. However, Allah knew that Abu Lahab and his wife would never convert to Islam, while other enemies of Islam did in fact later convert.

Muslims seek to hold fast to the *Rope of Allah* by pursuing unity in all respects. The rope that Abu Lahab and his wife chose to hold on to was one of fire. On the Day of Judgment, a rope of fire will be placed on her neck to make her taste the punishment of Allah. The reason being that she had sold her necklace and used the money to harm the Prophet. As she supported her husband in disbelief and persecution of the Prophet and his followers, she will share with her husband the same fate, an eternal Hell.

History is replete with other examples of the evil personality, such as Genghis Khan, Joseph Stalin and Adolph Hitler. Each of these individuals inflicted tyranny and oppression on their citizens, and the atrocities they committed were catastrophic and satanic. These individuals personified the antithesis of the ideal personality representative of their faith. They ruled empires with total force, with no restraints. Their regimes were composed of masters and slaves, in which gentleness, kindness, pity, respect for the law, and freedom were no longer virtues, but inexpiable crimes. It was an environment where people exterminated for pleasure and where the murderers were treated as heroes. Their egomania and paranoia eventually contributed to the near destruction of their nations. As these vicious tyrants were the embodiment of the evil incarnate, they are prime candidates for the *Hall of Flames*, along with Abu Lahab and his wife.

SECTION II: INSIGHTS

CHAPTER 8: SOCIETAL WEAKNESSES

"To understand ignorance requires knowledge to perceive its weaknesses." (Tallal Turfe)

Social problems within the society have a negative impact on the human persona. Some of these social problems can range from crime and juvenile delinquency to teen-age pregnancy and abortion to unemployment and divorce. As Muslims, we strive towards perfecting our Islamic personality by overcoming these social problems. The Islamic personality is self-actualized when Muslims make it their duty to reach out into the society and carry on the struggle against all forms of evil and corruption. The Islamic personality must be instilled with the determination to fight against injustice, tyranny and oppression as well as pessimism, hatred and envy. The Muslim society should be one that is as ideal morally as it is possible. But where is such a society? Islam can be effective only to the extent that Muslims practice it. It is essential to maintain a clear distinction between what Islam is and what Muslims are, between the religion and the Muslims who profess it.

Many Muslims are losing sight of the true reality of Islam by immersing themselves into the societies in which they live. For example, outside influences, such as Western nations, have made a major impact on the Muslim society by introducing their lifestyles that are not compatible with Islam. As a result, the products and services of these nations have fascinated Muslims as a means toward modernization and progress within their own societies. Unfortunately, by accepting the lifestyles of the West, Muslims began to weaken their Islamic personality. The appeal to modernizing the Muslim society has been so strong that few Muslims have yet grasped the fact that material advancement is not necessarily the road to genuine self-respect and satisfaction. What has in fact happened is that the Muslim society is best with many social problems, because it has been divorced from the spiritual and moral dimensions of Islam.

The current state of affairs in the Muslim world is that Islam continues to be a target of attack both externally and internally.

Externally, Muslim leaders are being influenced and manipulated by the world powers for the purpose of exploitation, plunder and colonialism. In addition, the genocide in Bosnia, Kosovo and Iraq has left the Muslim world in a state of uncertainty and grief. Part of the reason is that those who commit these acts of genocide are taking advantage of the disunity within the Muslim world. Internally, rogues have appeared within the Muslim world, and they have distorted Islam by painting an untrue picture of that faith.

A major cause of discord is that many Muslims are ignorant about their obligation to seek and achieve the unity. When ignorance prevailed in pre-Islam, the people were disunited and suspicion and jealousy were widespread between them. When Prophet Mohammad brought the knowledge of Islam to his community, they accepted it and implemented it. As a result, they became united. The Age of Ignorance had been replaced with a state of unity and bonding among the Muslims, which led to one *Ummah* (community).

Today, the enemies of Islam are insidiously working hard to discredit the Qur'an, because without the Qur'an the Muslims become disunited and return to a state of ignorance. Within the Islamic society today there are many obstacles that impede the pursuit for unity. These obstacles have major impacts on the human mind and cause a great deal of animosity and distrust within the community. Some of these obstacles are pessimism, hatred and envy.

Pessimism

Pessimism is the tendency to emphasize or think of the bad part of a situation rather than the good part, or the feeling that bad things are more likely to happen than good things. Pessimists look at the worst side of a situation and take the opposing view in any positive conversation. Pessimists turn conversations into griping and complaining. They ridicule attempts to rectify a dysfunctional situation.

Pessimism is a dangerous spiritual illness. It is the cause of many losses, defects and disappointments. Pessimism is a painful calamity that torments the human soul and leaves irreparable defects on man's personality that cannot be expunged. Why this erratic behavior on the part of pessimists? Pessimists feel they are isolated or abandoned as well as deceived, resentful and uninvited. Pessimists lack friendly interaction with others, because they are adamant and one-sided in their views. Other reasons for this erratic behavior on the part of pessimists may be due to tragic events in their lives. These tragic events can range from the loss of a family member to affliction with a permanent disability. They may be shameful of having done something wrong and are unable to seek atonement and forgiveness for their transgressions. When pessimists are continually reminded of their shortcomings, they become very resentful and seek revenge. When undergoing pain or annoyance they tend to become overly responsive by exhibiting adverse emotional outbursts as they revolt against those whom they see as their enemies.

Pessimism inflicts anxiety and pain to its victims, and ultimately denies them of hope and optimism. The damaging effect of pessimism harms the body and corrodes the soul. Pessimists experience seclusion and distrust when interacting with others. How does one overcome pessimism? There needs to be a reassessment in their lives. They need to reassess their behavioral patterns with those with whom they interact. This requires recognition and identification of their deficient behavior and attitude as to how this negatively impacts them as well as others. They must rejuvenate their spirituality and reconnect with faith. The Qur'an clearly counts pessimism among the sins and evil deeds and cautions Muslims about thinking negatively of each other.

When Prophet Mohammad came on the scene, he was confronted with pessimism from every direction. During the pre-Islamic Age of Ignorance (*jahiliyah*), people were overly pessimistic, even to the point of being absorbed by superstitions. One example was the Islamic month of Safar. In a *khutbah* (sermon), entitled *Superstition*, which can be accessed from Alminbar.com on the Internet, there are examples of superstitious practices during the month of Safar. At the time of Prophet Mohammad, disbelievers strongly felt that month was taboo. As a result, marriage ceremonies, trade transactions, and endeavors in general were forbidden. Disbelievers actually felt that to engage in these activities during that month would inflict hardships and disasters upon them. When Prophet Mohammad appeared, he instilled within the community a sense of reliance on Allah.

Prophet Mohammad abhorred with great distaste any act of

pessimism. All forms of pessimism are unacceptable in Islam. Prophet Mohammad exercised all possible endeavors in explaining the evils of pessimism. He made it unmistakable that we need to purify our hearts from thinking evil or being pessimistic. Social order and unity benefit from optimism, while decay and disintegration of the society are the consequences of pessimism.

Hatred

Hatred is a pervasive emotion and socio-psychological problem. As defined in a dictionary, hatred takes on many forms. It is enmity, hostility, antagonism, animosity, rancor, antipathy and animus. Enmity is hatred such as might be felt for an enemy. Hostility implies the clear expression of enmity. Antagonism is hostility that quickly results in active resistance, opposition or contentiousness. Animosity often triggers bitter resentment or punitive action. Rancor suggests vengeful hatred and resentment. Antipathy is deep-seated aversion or repugnance. Animus is distinctively personal, often based on one's prejudices or temperament.

How does hatred manifest itself in the human persona? People who are imbued with hatred feel that they have been unfairly treated, unjustly accused or betrayed. Perhaps their honor was questioned; or their needs were never understood; or they never received recognition. As a result, they begin to hate and harbor the most extreme level of anger against those who hurt them. They become agitated and antagonistic towards others. In addition, they become inflamed, rude and belligerent towards others. Reasons for this hatred against others may be that they feel they had been victimized by lies, cheating, rejection and condemnation. They may feel that they had been used and abused. Because of this enmity, those who hate are never fully content. Rather, they are bitter, hostile, sarcastic, embittered, paranoid, suspicious and defensive. They are irrational in their behavior, as they feel there is no hope for tolerance; just despair and distrust. Hatred stems from the power of anger and destroys man's spiritual balance.

To overcome hatred, those who hate must be able to assess and analyze their own irrational behavior. They must identify how others react to them. When they evaluate the causes of their own hatred, is it a figment of their imagination or is it real? Were they intentionally being mistreated or neglected? Or were they just wrapped up into their own ego?

There is much concern about hatred in the world. There is concern that people have become disinclined to be intolerant of hatred. Is each diverse culture too myopic and autonomous to look outside itself at other cultures for workable insights and solutions? Are we too wrapped up in the evolution of technology and change that we are incapable of effectively dealing with hatred? Hatred has no single location, for it permeates through all aspects of national, ethnic and religious spheres. And within these spheres, hatred often erupts into violence and war. Hatred is often nourished by ignorance. Ignorance breeds hatred, as it closes one's eyes to what is actually happening. Ignorance isolates people from the rest of humanity. Lack of knowledge is the ultimate barrier. Ignorance enslaves and leads to the enslavement of others. At the core of the struggle with hatred and ignorance are issues of the lack of community involvement.

Here in America we are confronted with the disease of xenophobia, or fear and hatred strangers or foreigners. It is fear of that which is different. It is fear that leads to hatred and a desire for control over those who are different. Xenophobia is based on ignorance. Ignorance breeds fear. Fear brings about intolerance. Intolerance gives rise to hatred. In America, people are ignorant concerning information about the cultural beliefs and practices of other nations. Unlike many other countries, most Americans speak only one language – English. In America, we find many people who are ignorant and naïve regarding other cultures and nations, and the foreign policy of the American government at times is representative of this unjust reality. For example, the American government's lack of a genuine even-handed policy in the Middle East has severely tarnished its credo of democracy and justice.

There is a lack of trust, partnership and shared values among people within the same community. To be sure, reconciliation in resolving religious disputes, in resolving ethnic quarrels, and in resolving marital problems is indeed a great challenge if brotherhood and solidarity are to be effective. Hatred, in all forms, not only offends the dignity of man but also is an offense against Allah. In overcoming hatred, Muslims must seek ways to foster the vitality and moral well being of the society. Islam offers us the way to enlightenment. When hatred appears, Islam provides the solution to overcome this evil. Islam provides the necessary and trustworthy values, norms, motivations and ideals, all grounded in an ultimate reality. To overcome hatred, we can extend a helping hand to one another, by being compassionate and understanding. Above all, we must be forgiving, even of those who hate. We must overlook the mistakes of others as we learn how to forgive.

Envy

Envy is a feeling of discontent or covetousness with regard to another's advantages, success or possessions. It is often referred to as one of the *Seven Deadly Sins*, the others being pride; gluttony; lust; anger; greed; and sloth. Envy is a common sin and the perpetual tormenter of virtue. Envy is treacherous because it draws people to its venom. Envy renders its victims miserable and unhappy. Envy is associated with hypocrisy, hatred and discord. Envy is like a vampire who feeds on others. Envy pollutes the heart.

Envy is a complex and puzzling emotion. According to the Greek philosopher, Aristotle, envy is pain at the good fortune of others. Envy is a frustrated desire turned destructive. In envy, the impulse to make contact with others becomes the impulse to destroy others. An envious person wants to destroy the morals and ethics of others. An envious person works to demoralize others so as to adversely impact their lives. Envy distorts and then insidiously works towards devouring the thoughts and views of others.

While jealousy is directed toward the possession of values, envy is directed toward the destruction of values. Envy works out of fear and resentment toward others. Survival for those who envy is fed by an insatiable diet to consume the values of others. Ignorance breeds suspicion and suspicion breeds envy, all of which are incompatible with the essential attitude of sympathy and love. In addition, greed also breeds envy and hate. Imitation is the result of envy. Many social structures are based on envy and imitation. One of the main causes of division in a society is envy and the craving for success; each is imitating the one above him. Envy spreads between Muslims differentiating their hearts and making them hate one another. Envy transcends in to selfish transgression, which is one of the causes of disunity and division among Muslims.

The remedy for envy is love. Envy is born in hate, and is cured in love. In Islam, the word envy is called *hasad*, which is the desire towards destruction of something good that belongs to someone else. *Hasad* is the most destructive and greatest obstacle toward establishing and cementing relationships between Muslims. Envy can be overcome by the spirituality of Muslims in the direction of cooperation, comfort and confidence. Remember we are the members of the same *Ummah* (Muslim community). We can strive for unity in the community if we overcome ignorance, allay our fears and suspicions, and combat envy with love and respect for one another.

Causes of Disunity

In a world full of disarray, dissension and discord, there have been futile attempts to unite because the basis for unity has been, and continues to be, distorted. For example, if material wealth, and whatever means are necessary to increase that wealth, are the precepts under which to live, then the end result has been, and always will be, chaos. In this earthly life there appear ropes of various twists and thickness, and by them are represented various methods of conjunction, where cords of vanity denote combinations of untruths through which there is iniquity or evil of life.

Other causes of disunity, such as greed and apathy, interplay with ignorance. Greed, apathy and ignorance are mutually reinforcing. Greed depends on the absence of empathy, and it benefits from ignorance about a social problem. Ignorance has its origin in greed. As greed grows, ignorance also grows; as greed decreases so does ignorance. Ignorance exists where greed exists. The root cause of greed is loss of judgment. Greed is both the cause and consequence of ignorance. Apathy can be curtailed if there is less greed and less ignorance. Ignorance is strengthened by apathy, particularly when some people do not seek knowledge in order to decrease their apathy. Greed thrives on the ignorance of those who do not have sufficient empathy to counteract greed. To resolve these societal weaknesses, replace greed, apathy and ignorance with charity, empathy and knowledge.

Ignorance about our Islamic obligations is a major cause of disunity. Consequences of disunity are all detrimental to Islam. We become weak. We suffer from low morale. We waste time and energy addressing minor problems. Personality conflicts arise. Factual problems are ignored. More attention is paid to attitudinal problems. And while all of this is happening, the enemies of Islam are rejoicing. The Qur'an states:

"Be not like those who are divided amongst themselves and fall into disputations after receiving Clear Signs: for them is a dreadful Penalty." (Qur'an 3:105)

Everlasting order and the basis for unity can only come about by adhering to the verse from the Qur'an:

"And hold fast, all together, by the Rope which Allah stretches out for you, and be not divided among yourselves...." (Qur'an 3:103)

In these few words the Qur'an proclaims the injunction of being united, together with the formula for achieving it. Here the cords of firmness and truth are conjoined. In simple terms, if everyone holds firm onto the *Rope of Allah*, everyone will be united. How we do this is mentioned in the Qur'an:

"O ye who believe? Fulfill all obligations...." (Qur'an 5:1)

We need to fulfill our divine obligations by strengthening our spiritual nature. We need to fulfill our mutual obligations by fulfilling our promises. We need to fulfill our tacit obligations by conducting ourselves with civility. These obligations, divine, mutual and tacit are interconnected and interwoven as they strengthen the *Rope*.

Some of the causes of division and disputes among Muslims are: [15]

· Deviation from the straight path by fragmenting into separate groups, each group thinking they are following the straight path. This fragmentation may be based on nationalism, regionalism or tribalism.

· Abandoning or dismantling parts of the Islamic tenets, therefore, causing animosity and hatred among Muslims. Some Muslims pick and choose which Islamic rules fit their objectives.

· Selfish transgression leading to envy and hatred between Muslims.

· Disputes among Muslims are signs of missing the Mercy of Allah.

Aspects of Tribalism and Nationalism

The terms tribalism and nationalism are called *asabiyyah* in Islam.[16] The Qur'an says:

"O mankind! We created you from a single pair of a male and female,

and made you into nations and tribes, that ye may know each other (not that ye may despise each other). Verily the most honored of you in the sight of Allah is he who is the most righteous of you, and Allah has full knowledge and is well acquainted with all things." (Qur'an 49:13)

True, Allah made people into nations and tribes so that they may come to know one another, but he did not create them to boast and have pride over one another. Rather, Islam calls for modesty, humility and solidarity. As mankind is descended from one pair of parents, nations and tribes, therefore, this verse is a call to all mankind. This verse underscores the importance of establishing social relationships and cooperation with one another.

Let us look at an example in the automotive industry. General Motors Corporation is an automotive company that has several divisions. Each of these divisions is divided into staffs, and each of these staffs is further subdivided into departments and so on. At the helm is a board of directors who oversee the macro policy of the entire firm. One of the policies is to establish a standard set of duties, responsibilities and relationships across all segments. Segmenting the firm into divisions, staffs and departments is not for the purpose that each of these segments should despise and feel hatred towards each other, or to antagonize each other. True, there is competition for sales between each of the divisions, but this is done in a systematic and orderly fashion, under the direction of the firm's board of directors. Similarly, a Muslim nation, in a sense, is like the automotive company. The Muslim nation is divided into tribes, villages, towns, cities, or some other form of societal structure. Within each of these, are segments, activities and leaders. Tribes have numerous common factors and values that require their unity. For example, Muslims within the tribes all believe in the Oneness of Allah, the unity of the Qur'an, the unity of their nation, the unity of direction of prayer, and many more aspects of unity. Therefore, these common values transcend into mutual respect and complementation with one another. As a result, having tribes is not for hatred but, rather, for mutual cooperation and common objectives.

There are two aspects of nationalism. One form of nationalism, which is forbidden in Islam, is negative in that it breeds discord among tribes. For example, a tribe may have good people and bad people in their society. Negativism occurs when members of that tribe begin to boast that even the bad people in their tribe are better than the good people in another tribe. This type of tribalism is abhorred by Prophet Mohammad and rejected in the Qur'an. From an historical perspective, we find this type of negative nationalism occurred with the Umayyads who gave preferential treatment to their own constituents to the detriment of Muslims from other nations. This type of nationalism and tribalism only weakens the grip of the *Rope of Allah*, and those who follow this path are prime candidates for the eternal Hell.

What drives the negative *asabiyyah* is the corrupt feeling of being better than others. Here *asabiyyah* is a perilous circumstance for an individual and for the society. We must consider the consequences of such acts not only here but also in the Hereafter. *Asabiyyah* may direct one to perpetrate immoral acts such as backbiting, insolence and tyranny. Prophet Mohammad repeatedly declared that negative tribalism and nationalism are forbidden in Islam. This type of provincialism results in fragmentation, disunity, and the planting of seeds of hatred in the minds and hearts of people. Here ignorance and provincialism are linked together, and nationalism is out of realm of truth having its roots deeply embedded in prejudice. Negative nationalism is a call to transgression, conceit and egotism.

Another form of negative *asabiyyah* can be found among scholars. For example, if a professor imparts knowledge upon his students for his own personal benefit or gain without it being in the way of truth, then this results in negative *asabiyyah*. When a professor professes Islam, then he must regard his own purpose as trivial in favor of truth. In this way, the professor is free from ignorance as he moves in the direction of reality. Even religious scholars need to be extremely careful in their lectures so as not to utter an inkling of enmity or hatred towards other schools of thought. Other forms of negative *asabiyyah* are racism and sectarianism. In each of these forms, the negative *asabiyyah* destroys the individual, the family and the community as it breeds disunity and discord.

The other type of nationalism is positive, in that it breeds brotherhood and solidarity. Here we find tribes working together for the benefit of the entire nation. While this type of nationalism serves Islam, it does not replace Islam. What this means is that a viable and productive microcosm of brotherhood within the context of nationalism cannot replace the macro entity of Islamic brotherhood. The latter is the protector and sustainer of all the microcosmic brotherhoods within a community.

Innovation and Deviation

The Qur'an states the following:

"Verily, this is My Way, leading straight: follow it: follow not other paths: they will scatter you about from His Great Path: thus doth He command you, that ye may be righteous." (Qur'an 6:153)

Any invented act or deed without any evidence from *shariah* (law) is called *bid'ah* or innovation in Islam. It means to originate, introduce, devise, contrive, and improvise or to be inventive in a manner not done before. Sometimes a person engaging in *bid'ah* thinks it is a religious act, and continues practicing it never realizing that it is a sin. There is only one true path to follow, and that is the straight path of Islam. This path is that of the Qur'an and the *Sunnah* of Prophet Mohammad and his *Ahl al-Bayt*. The above verse does not refer to many paths but, rather, just one path. Therefore, any deviation from this one path is a violation of Islam. *Bid'ah* is something that has no precedent and, therefore, is deviation from the straight path. A prime example of *bid'ah* is dividing Islam into sects, which also results in deviation from the straight path.[17]

When a Muslim says it is not mandatory to fast during the month of Ramadan, this is a form of *bid'ah*. The rule mandating fasting during the month of Ramadan cannot be changed, as it is part and parcel of the *shariah*. Another example of *bid'ah* is when one wants to make that which is *halal* into *haram*, and that which *haram* into *halal*. For example, eating pork and drinking alcoholic beverages is *haram* and not *halal*. Similarly, eating a banana is *halal* and not *haram*.

Material and physical products cannot be called *bid'ah*. For example, the technical innovations or developments in the mode of transportation from horses and camels to automobiles and airplanes are not *bid'ah*. Rather, Islam encourages technical developments that make transportation more convenient. Allah revealed the creation of advanced transportation systems:

"And (He has created) horses, mules, and donkeys, for you to ride and use for show; and He has created (other) things of which you have no knowledge." (Qur'an 16:8)

Muslims who perform *bid'ah* may truly believe that their acts bring them closer to Allah. This is a very dangerous path to follow, and Muslims are well advised to follow only that, which has been commanded, the Qur'an and the *Sunnah* of Prophet Mohammad and his *Ahl al-Bayt*. For those who do not know they are committing *bid'ah* places them in a very precarious situation. To say that one is pleasing Allah with this act, even when he does not know it is a sin, is just as great as the sin itself. An example of *bid'ah* is claiming that Islam requires more than two people to witness a transaction, even though the Islamic law requires only two witnesses.

Bid'ah is not only a fabrication but also a weakness, since the one who engages in *bid'ah* does so believing there is a shortcoming in Islam's way of life. This is tantamount to saying that Prophet Mohammad was devoid in his teachings and left interpretations open to anyone who wanted to invent rulings. This is total blasphemy and a grave transgression. Being convinced of his practice as one of Islam, the person engaging in *bid'ah* loses awareness that he actually deviated, which makes repentance even more difficult for him.

Bid'ah causes many evils in the society. It breeds discord among Muslims causing fragmentation. It causes the traditions of Prophet Mohammad to be misinterpreted or replaced. It causes evils in the Muslim society. It endangers Islam by spreading false premises as to what Islam is thereby endangering the Muslim community on a global basis. Whenever Muslims separate from the true message, knowledge will decrease and ignorance will flourish. How to counteract *bid'ah* is by referring to true and genuine religious leaders who are imbedded in Islamic jurisprudence and philosophy. This requires Muslims to become educated in Islam and not to make Islamic decisions and rulings based on intuition and creativity.

Bid'ah was practiced not only at the time of Prophet Mohammad but also at the time of other Prophets. Evil idol worshippers and transgressors set a path of deception and deviation in order to distort the teachings of the Prophets. Throughout history, man has deviated from the straight path. Even today we find this kind of deviation among Muslims who believe that the perfection of thought could be attained by immersing the philosophies of Plato and Aristotle with Islamic beliefs, which have opened up avenues toward fragmentation as they invent their own orders and set their own criteria relative to Islamic laws.

Complacency
Selected Problems Giving Rise to Complacency

Imagine that we live in a Muslim community beset with the following problems:

· Completion of Islamic projects threatened by community's lack of participation and failure to meet bank loan payments.

· Divorce rate for Muslims doubles in the last five years.

· Substance abuse becoming more prevalent among Muslim teens and young adults.

· Muslims are placing more emphasis on entertainment and activities outside the realm of Islam.

· Crime and juvenile delinquency among Muslims are increasing at an alarming rate.

· Muslim family values have deteriorated considerably over the last decade.

These potential problems are just an illustration of what could happen if Muslims sit idly by doing nothing. In short, Muslims are becoming more and more complacent.

Attributes of Complacency

So what is complacency? Complacency is self-satisfaction accompanied by unawareness of actual dangers or deficiencies. It is a lack of care or interest. It is a feeling of contentment. The greatest menace in our lives is self-complacency or *ritha-a-nafs*. Complacency can interfere with taking action when it is needed. Complacency leads to the death of a community. An example of complacency is when one says that he will never need to see a physician because he will never get sick. Sometimes we are shaken out of complacency, particularly, when we are faced with adversity or hardship. Then, at that time, we begin to reengineer and reexamine our lives, our faith. Self-complacency generates ignorance:

"The blight of knowledge is self-complacency." (Prophet Mohammad)

"Self-complacency is the evidence of the weakness of one's intellect." (Imam Ali)

How can the Muslim community be motivated from the drowning depths of complacency when it is that complacency itself that most seem to desire? Is it irresponsibility that leaves the

Muslim community complacent? Apathy or laziness is a cause of complacency. The more we cling to apathy – the less we can do with our lives – because our minds will be too full of inactivity to do anything. We are not depressed; we are simply complacent. We are stubborn with complacency. In essence, complacency lessens the self and corrodes the soul.

One problem Muslims confront in the life of faith is complacency. Some Muslims don't respond to Allah because they are comfortable in their routines. They are not mindful of Allah because other things occupy their thoughts. They don't pray and fast because other things occupy their time. They fail to put their trust in Allah because they put their trust in other things.

Self-Righteousness and Complacency

Self-righteousness is a weakness of the human soul. If we feel that we are what we ought to be, then we will remain what we are. We will not look for any change or improvement in our lives. This will quite naturally lead us to judge everyone by what we are. This is the judgment of which we must be careful. To judge others by us is to create havoc in the community. Self-righteousness leads to complacency, a great sin. Some people have the attitude that if they are satisfied with their spiritual condition they need not concern themselves with helping others, and that Allah will be pleased with them and grant them Paradise. These people are just fooling themselves. It really boils down to self-deception.

Complacency in a Muslim community may lead to the erosion and eventual destruction of Islamic endeavors. Complacency robs a community of many energetic servants. Complacency robs Muslims of their joy here and their rewards in the hereafter.

Wherever there is complacency there is the seed of corruption, chaos, confusion and ultimate destruction. Complacency is not outside us, but inside us. This mentality leads both individuals and institutions to become estranged and disconnected from the realities of life. In this condition one has no vision and can only produce ineffective solutions. When people move in this mental atmosphere of complacency, they are essentially cut off from their real selves and fall into a monotonous routine, the same old thing day in and day out. Complacency is self-destructive, and a family, an institution, or a community can be destroyed by it.

Some people just attend Islamic functions or gatherings because it is the thing to do, or because it is good for their image in the community. The causes of complacency are numerous. In America, for example, we have been raised and live in the most affluent nation in the world. We are accustomed to a lifestyle that would be viewed as extravagant by most of the rest of the world. We pursue riches and things as if they will last forever. Some Muslims seldom stop to think about their relationship to Allah, as they place more emphasis and time on pursuing wealth and power.

Cure for Complacency

Is there a cure for complacency? Yes! The first step is to seek the Compassion and Mercy of Allah. We must contemplate the value of eternity, that is, we must begin to live for eternity rather than for now. We must pray and fast and seek Allah's Help. The solution is bringing the mind and self into harmony with one another. When a person enters a mosque, he feels peaceful and tranquil. The self experiences this, and the mind is no longer in confusion or turmoil.

We need synergy by working together. So let's kick down the door of complacency. See where we can add value to Islamic projects already in operation. Often there is a gap between implementation of a project and completion of that project. We can add value by volunteering our skills and time to fill that gap. For example, a school project needs tutors for the students. Using our interpersonal skills and expertise in coaching these students can help immensely towards further developing and nurturing that student's mind.

Look to create something genuinely unique, so as to advance the state-of-the-art. Search for untapped opportunities – find that niche.

Voluntary Charity - A Prescription for Complacency

To rid ourselves of complacency, we need to look to Islam. Among the many virtues in Islam is the concept of *sadaqah*, which is of two components: (a) obligatory as with almsgiving (*zakat* and *khums*) and (b) voluntary. Basically, *sadaqah* means charity, and the concept of *sadaqah* or charity is linked with justice.

Sadaqah is a very wide term and is used in the Qur'an to cover most kinds of charity. Its scope is so vast that even the poor who can have nothing tangible to give can offer *sadaqah* in the shape of a smile or a kind word. Good conduct is frequently termed *sadaqah* in the *hadith* (traditions). Planting something from which a person or animal later eats also counts as *sadaqah*. In this extended sense, acts of loving kindness, even greeting another with a cheerful face, is regarded as *sadaqah*. In short, every good deed is *sadaqah*.

Imam Ali (son-in-law and cousin of Prophet Mohammad) said:

"How nice it is for the rich to behave with humility with the poor for the sake of that which is with Allah! Yet, nicer is the proud dignity of the poor in front of the rich due to their trust in and reliance on Allah." (Nahjul Balagah)

Islam asks the wealthy to hold their hand low while giving, so that the needy person's hand is above while he takes, in order that he does not feel humiliated and crushed. They should also refrain from being proud and overbearing.

Prophet Mohammad said:

"It is obligatory on every Muslim to do an act of charity every day...if you remove troublesome stones and obstacles from the public way, that is also considered an act of charity." (Bihar al-Anwar)

Prophet Mohammad mentioned lifting of stones from the road as a charitable action, because that is the least that a man without any means can accomplish. Muslims must perform acts of charity in proportion to their capacity.

Good deeds and charity are not confined just to monetary help, or to providing relief from physical suffering and hardship. Rather, spiritual assistance, moral guidance, and correction of moral conduct and qualities have a higher and greater value than material charity. From the viewpoint of Islam, the most valuable act of charity is to help the deviant and deliver those bogged down in the mire of corruption and wretchedness.

One of the essential and useful principles that contribute effectively to man's progress and development is self-discipline. The month of Ramadan heightens our awareness and development of self-discipline. Prayer and fasting instill self-discipline within an individual.

While *zakat* and *khums* are obligations that must be fulfilled, Muslims know that payment is mandatory and cannot be compromised. All wealth and riches belong to Allah. It is entrusted to us by Allah, so that we may satisfy our needs and help our less fortunate brothers to satisfy their requirements. *Ihsan* or kindness and *sadaqah* go hand in hand and are linked together. It is voluntary charity that affords Muslims the opportunity to self-actualize in their Islamic personality. Voluntary charity takes a much deeper concentration of individual effort to perform than does *zakat* and *khums*.

When a person becomes ill, he consults a physician who diagnoses his sickness and oftentimes writes a prescription for the patient. The patient takes that prescription to a pharmacy so it can be filled. Once the medicine is taken, the patient begins to feel relief and his pain is eased. Likewise, the human soul has an ailment, such as complacency, and needs cleansing. But where can the human soul go to for help? The best avenue and cure for the human soul is achieved by way of prayer. In his prayer, the person reminds Allah of his love for Him and his remembrance of Him and asks Allah to purify his soul.

The manifestation of *sadaqah* is heightened in prayer and further elevated as one fasts during the month of Ramadan. The combination of prayer and fasting provides the means by which one can have deeper concentration in order to move the soul from consciousness to tranquility. As in the case of the ill person who obtains a prescription for his ailment from a physician, the prescription for a troubled soul is the ingestion of *sadaqah* or charity during prayer and fasting so that one can rid himself of complacency. This then fulfills one's *jihad* or struggle, as his soul is purified and set on the straight path. His course of action now established, the Muslim proceeds with an open heart and open mind as he embraces and fulfills *sadaqah* according to his capacity.

Let us look at how *sadaqah* can be the prescription or solution to an Islamic project. Suppose a community undertakes a project to build a senior citizen facility, which is projected to cost $4 million including the construction and furnishings of the facility. How can *sadaqah* help towards fulfillment of this project? We know that the community is replete with skilled and non-skilled people who can volunteer their time towards the completion of the facility. The Muslim community has skilled millwrights, skilled electricians, skilled pipe fitters, skilled carpenters, draftsmen and designers who can volunteer their services, free of charge. In addition, the Muslim community has business owners who stock and sell carpeting, hardware items, lumber, bricks and other material. These business owners can volunteer to supply the material for building the facility, either free of charge or at a reduced discount. The non-skilled in the Muslim community can also help by cleaning the debris at the site of the facility, or by helping the skilled technicians perform their job, or by hauling the materials from the business owners. There are also construction contractors in the Muslim community who can volunteer their time to help oversee the project. When all is added up, the $4 million cost can be significantly reduced.

All that is required is for Muslims to want to volunteer their time. Volunteering one's time for charitable deeds is a means of overcoming complacency. By being involved in an Islamic project, and feeling a keen sense of responsibility in that project, helps overcome complacency. In this way, Muslims increase the level of their Islamic persona while at the same time rendering their community a service. They, in effect, become better Muslims by working together for the same endeavor.

Ramadan is the month for harvesting the spiritual reward from Allah, not only for an individual Muslim, but also for the community as a whole. Fasting represents personal decision of self-surrender to Allah. Fasting rids our minds of complacency and prepares us for recovery by way of *taqwah* or piety, which is the root of all good deeds acceptable to Allah. Creation of empathy among Muslims in charity is imbued in the ritual of fasting. Together, we can make a difference in our community. We can rid ourselves of complacency. We can seek peace, harmony and justice by way of *sadaqah*. In the end, we will have become self-actualized in spirit; our families will be well cemented; our Islamic institutions will be unified; our community will be enriched; and Allah will be pleased.

CHAPTER 9: REQUISITES FOR UNITY

"A drop of knowledge can extinguish a blaze of ignorance."
(Tallal Turfe)

Man has continuously ignored his most fundamental problems until they reach the critical level. At present, our problems are becoming so dangerous and prevalent that we must either learn to resolve our problems or suffer absolute desolation. Usually we are ignorant of the things that we could actually control and make better. Rather than seeking solutions by way of knowledge, we seek forgiveness. We want to keep doing wrong but not suffer the consequences. Yet, we do wrong and eventually suffer. We are inclined to be involved in short-range pursuits and ignore the consequences of our own actions. We pursue our desires, often at the cost of our real needs. We live for today and suffer tomorrow. Societal problems are closely aligned with ignorance. Some of these problems are pessimism, hatred, envy and complacency that have eroded into the Islamic personality thereby weakening the Muslim *Ummah* (community). In order to overcome these societal weaknesses and to achieve unity in the Muslim community, there are certain requisites for this to come about. Unity does not occur by chance but rather by mutual interaction among the parties. This interaction takes a great deal of effort among the parties involved. Let us explore some of the avenues toward achieving this unity, for example, conflict resolution, art of negotiating and advocacy.

Conflict Resolution

Every group has had periods of conflict. These conflicts can be the result of political upheavals, social disputes or cultural biases. We often lack the confidence or vision of what is appropriate to do. Many of us are under the assumption that conflict is something to be avoided. Many people view conflict as an experience of failure.

Understanding similarities and differences, in an atmosphere free of bias, enables Muslim scholars and religious leaders to meet together in order to intensify their self-respect in the direction of equality and justice. Attitudes and behaviors as well as environmental pressures can work towards a positive tolerance or a negative intolerance. It all depends on the mindsets of these proponents and their willingness to work towards unity.

In order for conflict resolution to be effective, the parties must adhere to the following:

· Atmosphere of mutual respect and trust.
· Reciprocal communication.
· Promoting self-worth.
· Free expression of ideas and thoughts.
· Advancing scholarly questioning and methodical decision-making.
· Promoting open-mindedness and regard for different points of view.
· Deciding on an outcome after carefully considering alternatives.
· Differentiating between rational behavior and emotional behavior.

There have been attempts to incorporate the above criteria into societal conflicts. In any Islamic society, conflicts can be resolved by the formal method of the court system or by the informal channel of traditional and religious methods. For our purposes, let us summarize the three informal conflict resolution methods or procedures that still exist in different degrees in Islamic societies. These methods are: (a) arbitration (*tahkim*), (b) mediation (*wasata*), and (c) reconciliation (*sulha*).

In pre-Islamic times the institution of arbitration (*tahkim*) was widely used in tribal and clan disputes. After the introduction of Islam, pre-Islamic arbitration practices were incorporated into the Islamic Law. Arbitration was basically used in marital disputes, especially in divorce. An individual or a delegation of elders for a range of issues from marital problems to family feuds can implement the mediation (*wasata*) process. The success of the mediation process is based on the necessity and desirability of preserving and restoring ongoing relations in the community. The last component is reconciliation (*sulha*). Reconciliation is usually used in violent cases such as family feud, murder, and traffic accidents. The aim of reconciliation is to reestablish peace between the parties. Because of the importance of the cases, the process of reconciliation is more elaborate than that of mediation. As a solution is one of forgiveness, reconciliation takes more time, effort and skills to succeed.[18]

These problems are more than just one of ethics or morality. They have to do with a myriad of issues that are very complicated and difficult to resolve. However, what is at the center of many of these conflicts are the following:

· Preconception and narrow-mindedness.
· Opposition and antagonism.
· Absence of constructive criticism.
· Disrespect for others.

Preconceived notions result from ignorance and may be obstacles toward creating alternative solutions. Frequently, people do not get the chance to learn how to find alternative solutions or develop constructive ways of resolving their conflicts. Learning to manage conflict without hostility can induce people towards sound communication. Conflict resolution rescues us from ignorance, and it is an important way to help people understand each other. Conflict resolution encourages people to be proactive and face conflict, not avoid it. The objective is to reach a win-win situation with a remedy that is satisfactory to everyone involved. Fundamental themes in conflict resolution include collaboration, communication and confirmation.

Effective communication and social skills are the bases of conflict resolution. These skills include arbitration, conciliation, problem solving, and critical thinking. Generally, the process in conflict resolution is to (a) define the problem; (b) obtain a joint solution; (c) implement the solution; and (d) test the solution. Muslim groups can conduct workshops in order to employ this process.

Conflict resolution ascertains the causes and outcomes of behavior. In addition, conflict resolution takes into account the feelings and emotions of all the people involved in a conflict. In a conflict resolution setting, methods are used in order to identify and understand the conflict situation. One method is to recognize and confirm the frustration of the group participants. Another method is to encourage communication by exchange of ideas and thoughts. Successful conflict resolutions are the result of teamwork, interaction and tolerance.

Conflict resolution is a solution towards generating empathy, reconciliation, candidness and forgiveness. Reconciliation and conflict resolution initiatives require the identification of those Muslim leaders in the society who have the fortitude to seek social justice and peace. These Muslim leaders must move in the direction of unity, even if it means to take the ridicule visited upon them. Attitudes and behaviors of people are, in part, the reflection of their family values and state of mind. There needs to be a transformation of the inner self in order to resolve deep-rooted conflicts. Empathy and advocacy are critical in the process of conflict resolution.

Muslim brothers and sisters must build relationships by exercising empathy into their persona in order to generate a common bond between the parties. For example, dialogue between devout Shi'a and Sunni Muslims could focus on the concept of empathy as a vehicle for understanding the needs and concerns of each other. Walk in our shoes and see the perspective from our vantage point can help in understanding the feelings of the other party.

There have been great strides for Muslims to engage in conflict resolution and interfaith dialogue with Christians and Jews more so than has been the case of intrafaith dialogue between fellow Muslim groups. This, in itself, is a tragedy. While we encourage dialogue with all of the Abrahamic faiths, charity does begin at home. We first need to tackle and resolve the differences among Muslim brothers and sisters, if we are going to be effective in pursuing reconciliation of differences with other faiths. What needs to be dealt with is the issue of countervailing religious values that will on occasion supersede the appeal for unity. Powerful interests that do not want peace often influence this struggle of divergent values. However, that does not mean that the conflict of values is not an alarming realism for the Muslim believers and theologians who struggle with their existence. In a religious situation, recognizing and dealing with those struggles is vital for conflict resolution to work.

Art of Negotiating

Life is a process of negotiations. For negotiations to work, there must be mutual discussion and arrangement of the terms of a transaction, agreement or meeting. The basic steps in the art of negotiating are to (a) focus on a strategic plan for the meeting; (b) focus on the problems and the process; (c) focus on major issues; and (d) focus on win-win outcomes for all parties. All parties involved in the meeting should proceed with objectivity and openness. They should not point fingers at each other or blame one another. Assessing all aspects of an issue and prioritizing each party's objectives goes a long way to having a healthy meeting. The ideal outcome is when conflicts are managed so that all parties feel they have won. This is not easy, for it requires a great deal of effort of all parties involved in the negotiation process. It requires creativity and strategic initiatives. It requires collaboration on all sides.

Culture impacts the process of negotiation relative to the positions, interests and priorities of the parties involved. Culture affects the process and strategy of negotiation relative to confrontation, motivation, influence and information. For example, in order to build trust among the parties, information needs to be reciprocal. Multi-issue proposals need to be negotiated, rather than issue-by-issue. All parties must attempt to lessen the difficulties of the negotiation process by implementing an open-minded strategy. The strategy should be tailored whereby there is a push for high priority interests.

Common problems that occur in negotiations are: (a) attempting to negotiate issue by issue; (b) position oriented rather than goal oriented; (c) problem solving methods differ; (d) afraid of losing face and social identity; (e) lack of communication and understanding; and (e) outcomes differ from expectations. Successful negotiations are those that have an atmosphere of understanding and respect. While each party sets its own goals, it still respects the goals of the other party. Mutual agreement must be made on high priority issues, as all parties must be willing to make concessions on low priority issues. Trust can be built through questions and proposals, and by securing commitment to long-term reciprocity. Issues and tasks must be clarified. Tolerance and trust must be built. Positive norms of interaction must be developed and maintained.

Negotiations on philosophical issues are extremely difficult to handle. Each party's experiences make it necessary to develop channels of communication and understanding. Our expectations are a result of our own experiences and, therefore, conflict occurs in the interaction process. Negotiators must be competent in listening to the viewpoints of others. Good listeners do not have a predetermined response but, rather, have an open ear to hear and understand the other's point of view without argument. Good listeners are those who can feel with and comprehend what others are saying.

Build rapport and show consideration. Demonstrate expertise and focus on the issues. Clarify the problem, so each party has a clear idea about what is the real issue. Avoid predetermined solutions, by generating a mutual list of possible solutions. Be creative by mutually deciding on the best outcome acceptable to all parties. A relative balance of power is necessary for productive conflict management. Use decision-making skills, and do not try to coerce others. Once the solution is implemented, then periodically evaluate it for effectiveness.

Advocacy

Advocacy is a type of problem solving designed to protect personal and legal rights, and to ensure a dignified existence. Self-advocacy can help us avoid or solve problems with family and loved ones, friends, and fellow Muslims. Advocacy takes time and effort. Developing a clear and specific definition of the problem helps minimize frustration and waste. Additionally, defining the problem requires distinguishing major issues from incidental details. It means getting to the heart of the issue and figuring out what is causing it. With advocacy, the parties can reconcile their differences and proceed in the direction of working together for a common goal.

What Muslims need to do is to develop an advocacy plan that will serve as a guide for their actions. In the development of this plan, all Muslim parties seeking to resolve their differences must describe their starting point, their destination, and what they will do to reach their destination. The advocacy plan will also include a tentative schedule and timetable of when to expect the attainment of their goals.

Be realistic about the options that are available. Decide on some compromise solutions that are acceptable although not ideal. Think about the other party as to their needs and priorities. Finally, think about what should be done if the plan is not successful.

Obligations
Fulfillment of Obligations

Imagine that we just received disturbing news concerning our Islamic community:
· 15 teenage boys killed as a result of gang violence.
· Police raid took into custody 5 teenage girls involved in a sex orgy.
· 10 teenage boys and girls found dead from overdose of drugs at a local party.
· Over 50% of all marriages end up in divorce within the first year.
· Foreclosure on an Islamic project for inability to meet bank loan payments.

Now these statements are not only devastating but could become a reality. Let us focus on these types of problems within the purview of what is meant by the concept of obligations in Islam, and how fulfillment of these obligations forms the Islamic personality. A look at marriage, as a case example, will heighten our awareness as to the nature and importance of these obligations.

The opening line of the Quran'ic chapter entitled *The Table Spread* says,

"*O ye who believe! Fulfill (all) obligations….*" (Qur'an 5:1)

Just what are these obligations? There are so many; however, the following discussion relates to just a few.

An obligation is that which a person is bound to do as a result of an agreement or responsibility. Each of us have obligations to fulfill throughout our lifetime: obligations to our families, friends, school, mosque, employer, community, nation, and most of all, ourselves.

Divine Obligations

Islamic obligations imply so many things. To begin with, our metaphysical relationship to Allah results in divine obligations, such as prayer and fasting. The human spiritual nature is such that whatever we do should become *ibada* (worship). Human reason can find many infinite signs and truths of Allah's Existence. He created us and implanted in us the faculty of knowledge and foresight. Besides His Gifts of intuition and reason, Allah also made nature responsive to our needs and inner life. Furthermore, He sent Messengers for the guidance of our overall attitude and behavior.

Moral Obligations

As to moral obligations, such as avoiding backbiting and suspicion, we have to establish and maintain order in the society. While performing righteous deeds is emphasized in Islam, it is not considered sufficient. Our moral obligations are to strive for excellence in our lives as well as in the lives of our families and communities. Here *jihad* (struggle) comes full circle as we establish and maintain justice in the society. Moral excellence is heightened when we arrive at the realization that love for others is what we love for ourselves. Achieving moral excellence requires a great deal of patience and self-discipline.

The teachings of the Qur'an and the *Sunnah* of Prophet Mohammad and his *Ahl al-Bayt* lay much emphasis on moral virtues. By fulfilling our obligations we are fulfilling our promise. We have been encouraged to stay true to our promise. In our life we undertake mutual obligations, expressed and implied.

When we make a promise, such as a marriage contract, we must faithfully fulfill all obligations in that contract. Keeping the promise is one of the attributes of Prophet Mohammad who was true to his promise under any circumstances. We have to take into account our obligations to Allah and the Blessings He has bestowed upon us. We have to take in account our obligations to the teachings of Prophet Mohammad who brought light and happiness into our hearts so we can coexist in peace. As human beings, we have obligations to fulfill in our dealings with other human beings.

Tacit Obligations

There are tacit obligations, such as empathy, gestures, intuitions, attitude, behavior and unspoken knowledge derived from human experience. These obligations are expressed or carried out without words or speech, arising without expressed contract or agreement. If morally just, we must respect the tacit conventions of a civil society. There are tacit obligations as to husband and wife, parents and children, employer and employee, with whom every-one needs to fulfill. All these obligations are inter-connected, and the hallmarks of these obligations are truth and fidelity.

Linkage Between Obligations and Applications

There is a linkage between obligations and applications. How to apply an obligation takes a great deal of concentration, commit-ment and sincerity. Take the mutual obligation of love in the family. Love is a gift from Allah. Parents are to love all their children equally, and children are to love their parents equally. Spouses are to love each other and share in mutual respect for one another.

We even have the social obligation of gift giving and gift receiving. Someone presents us with a gift, and in turn we reciprocate by giving that person a gift or at least an extension of some form of hospitality. Can we be any less with respect to our obligation to Allah? Did not Allah bestow upon us the greatest gift of all – that of life? What gift can we give Allah in return? We are obligated to perpetuate the faith of Islam by giving of ourselves, of our wealth, and of our time in order to please Allah. Yet, we take Allah for granted and forget about His Gift. Non-committal we have become complacent and lethargic. There are many ways to repay the obligation to Allah. For example, we can repay Him by being kind to our parents and siblings, by having a sound marriage and by raising a good family.

We fulfill these obligations in the way of Islam by our remem-brance of Allah and by our actions. In our social and civil life, we raise a family, we work, and we become active members of the society. These obligations are integrally inter-correlated, as they compose our daily life. These obligations are natural consequences from the Blessings that Allah has fully provided to us. So truth and fidelity are parts of Islam in all relations of life. Should we not fulfill our obligations to Allah, we will have become victims of Satan and strayed from the truth.

The youth in our society is a classic example. Today's youth no longer enjoy the stable family structures that previous generations did. With the breakdown in family values and the society's morality, our youth have adopted the values and behaviors of media heroes they are constantly bombarded by. Distorted images and false representatives of reality have blurred their perceptions, beliefs and behaviors. Television, movies, music, video games and cyberspace contribute to their corruption. Reality, as adults once knew and taught it, is virtually non-existent for our youth. The order of the day is now anti-social tendencies. We need to teach our children about the real heroes – our Prophets and our Imams!

To be sure, family problems existed on a much smaller scale in previous generations, but families still stayed together. Seemingly, advances in technology and a higher standard of living in today's society have indirectly led to the disintegration of our moral values, and the effects of this are causing a significant amount of havoc.

Obligations in Contemporary Society

In today's society, people are constantly trying to slip into imaginary worlds, to forget about life and its problems. Life is so pressurized to the point that people are literally looking for some form of escape. People also become bored of their pastimes and constantly search for new ones. How different are the ways of the Qur'an from the trends of modern society. The Qur'an does not hide itself from reality, but faces it directly. The Qur'an puts meaning into life, and gives one a sense of accomplishment and satisfaction.

The main reason why there is so much complexity in our daily lives is that we gradually forget and ignore the Signs of Allah in nature. Almost without exception, many of our most serious social problems – including crime, youth violence, drug abuse, school failure, divorce and teen pregnancy – are due to the collective inability of families to adequately nurture, care for, educate and rear their youth. The overwhelming majority of Muslims in the world practice Islam. However, the grim reality is that many Islamic communities are ignorant of their Islamic obligations, as they do not fulfill them in their daily lives. Rather, here Muslims have deviated from the fulfillment of their obligations, as they have opted instead for all kinds of materialism including nightclubs, prostitution and other vile acts. They have in effect become lost. They imitate the actions of others in their communities who are ignorant and do not know discipline or do not even care about faith and righteousness.

Good Deeds as Driving Force

Developing a strong Islamic personality that is nurtured in the ideals of outer and inner cleanliness helps fulfill our obligations. Asking people to do good deeds must first begin with our own practice. While it is easy to talk about what is right in Islam, it is not nearly so easy for us to practice that right Islam. All good deeds revealed to us by way of the Qur'an and the *Sunnah* of Prophet Mohammad and his *Ahl al-Bayt* make it clear what is the right Islamic way of life.

It has been mentioned by Prophet Mohammad that every good deed must start from one's self. What we need is a community of Muslims who are motivated to do good deeds. And who work very hard to implement the teachings of Islam to the very best of their ability.

One way of developing and enhancing our Islamic personality is to practice *sadaqah* (charity). Prophet Mohammad once said that *sadaqah* is more powerful than *du'a* (supplication). The reason for this may be that in *sadaqah* we sacrifice something that is part of our wealth, whereas in du'a there is no sacrifice of wealth. Most of the time, it is very hard for us to give away any of our wealth. In fact, if *sadaqah* were to be practiced by all Muslims today, it would help to substantially reduce poverty, diminish the gap between the rich and the poor, and retire the debts incurred by Islamic projects. Let us take Allah into our hearts in every aspect of our lives and in every action we do. In our intentions, we must always remember Allah and fulfill our obligations to Him in every situation.

Guidance and Direction

We can see in the present day that many Muslims do not know which direction to follow. When we do not have right guidance and direction, we do not know how to overcome the multitude of problems that occur in the society.

Every Muslim is responsible for fulfilling their own individual obligations by purifying themselves and by creating a healthy body and mind so that the soul may return to Allah. In all their dealings, Muslims are required to honor their obligations with true intentions and to stand by their word and their pledge. Religion must be lived. Thus ethics and religion are inseparable.

Every Muslim is the recipient, guardian and executor of Allah's Will on earth. The responsibilities of Muslims are all encompassing. Their duty to act in defense of what is right is as much part of their faith as is their duty to oppose wrong.

Responsibilities, Rights and Privileges

There is a relation in Islam between individual responsibilities and the rights and privileges derived from membership in the community or an Islamic institution. Individual obligations must be met before one can claim a portion from the community of which he is part. Each member of a society must fulfill his own obligations and rely on others to fulfill theirs before that society can acquire the necessary reservoir of social rights and privileges that can then be shared by all. The notions of brotherhood and solidarity not only impose upon the community the duty to care for its members, but also require each person to use his initiative to carry out individual and social responsibilities according to his ability.

In our pursuit of Islamic objectives and projects, we need to stand firm even more when victory or completion is delayed, so that we will not go astray after being steadfast. Trials and tribulations can cause the heart to change. Trials of wealth; trials of power and authority; and trials of courage test our resolve. Whether they are the trials of ease or of hardship, only those who have understanding and whose hearts are filled with faith can remain steadfast.

Charitable Obligations

Consider the obligation of charity. The concept of ownership of wealth in Islam is that all wealth, after necessary personal and family expenses, belongs to Allah. It is up to the individual to decide how much of this excess wealth he should give back to the cause of Allah.

The problem before Muslim fund-raisers is how to motivate people to open their hearts and their wallets in the fulfillment of charity. This takes great effort and leadership. One of the greatest challenges today is being able to articulate a clear vision of the future of the Islamic institution that is attractive, inspiring and so compelling that we will want to participate in advancing its goals.

Sometimes we do not want to part with our wealth due to the

love of our family and children, so that they might not suffer from financial distress. But if we know that it is Allah Who is the Provider for all of them, we should not worry. It is like putting money in a savings account in this world and cashing it in the next world, multiplied many times. What goes wrong at times is that donors do not have a clear vision of how their money was spent. The best way to solve this issue is in the old adage, *"a picture is worth a thousand words."* Take the donors to the site of the project and let them see for themselves. This will increase the confidence of the donors and will incline them to give more, since they will know that their money has been well utilized.

There is still another dimension relative to the parting of wealth. We are reminded by the proverb, *"putting the cart before the horse."* In some communities, the order of the day is to raise as much money as possible for Islamic endeavors. Yet, we find in these communities donors who are lackluster in their Islamic practices. Some donors, who sacrifice part of their wealth for Islamic projects, are not practicing Muslims. Money has become the driving force, while Islam has taken a back seat. We are in a *"catch-22"* situation. However, while some of these donors are not immersed in the tenets and doctrines of Islam, concerted efforts are being made by religious leaders to reach out to them. This is just one reason why it is important to support the Islamic institution in order to find a way to resolve this crucial issue. We want the community to enjoy the results of their donations while at the same time reaping in the benefits of Islam. That is why Islamic schools and mosques are needed, so as to provide our children with the development of an Islamic personality very early in their lives. That is why it is so important for the institution's leaders to fulfill their obligations by being focused and taking the time to strengthen relationships within the institution and the community.

Fulfillment of Trusts and Obligations

Allah gives everything man has in trust. In this way everyone is bound by certain promises and obligations. Some obligations are entered into by written or spoken agreement, while others are a matter of tacit understanding. Whatever the form of agreement, man has to fulfill all these trusts and obligations. If he fails to do so, he does not come up to the highest standards of humanity.

Man's body, heart and mind are all Trusts from Allah. It is, therefore, incumbent upon man to make the best use of these endowments within the limits decreed by Allah.

We have been created to fulfill the requirements of a test. That test is to obey Allah's Orders by holding our hearts firm, by restraining ourselves from committing evil, and by refraining from complaining about anything bad that happens to us even in times of adversity. In fulfilling our obligations in order to pass the test, we need to develop character. And character evolves into caring; honesty; accountability; respect; attitude; confidence; trust; etiquette and responsibility.

Let us look at the case example of Muslim marriages. Divorce and marital conflict are reaching endemic proportions in our Islamic community. Prospective marriage couples in our society devalue the advice of their elders. Instead, they seek their advice from peer groups. So what is the cause of this problem? The cause is that somewhere in their upbringing they have been devoid of receiving an Islamic education. They lack the true essence of spiritual development that cements one's Islamic personality.

Many Muslim couples enter into marriage each with their own set of luggage and their own individual conception of what marriage should be. There is no joint alliance in this contractual obligation. Mutual respect for one another in terms of Islamic behavior is weak. The marriage partners lack steadfastness and patience, as they demand their own private individuality. They do not have the faintest idea of what it means to share each other's garments. The end result is a marriage that collapses.

According to Islamic tradition, marriage is *ibada* (worship). Allah's Guidance should be sought on all matters, particularly the decision to marry and who to marry. Likewise, when we experience problems we must call on Allah to help us through difficult times. We find many couples spending months and months on preparation for their wedding. Yet, these same couples have not spent time preparing for their marriage. The end result is disaster.

A healthy marriage begins with a strong practice of Islam. Marriage partners must be pious as well as schooled and nurtured in the practices of Islam. Too often emphasis in marriage is placed on good looks and or social position in the society and less on whether or not they are practicing Muslims. In addition, problems such as religious incompatibility and domestic violence only further erode the marriage.

Constant remembrance of Allah is the key to a successful marriage. To remember Allah is to love Allah. The marriage couple keeps their obligations to Allah and remembers Him often, even in their most intimate affairs. Always they are guided by their intentions. As they strive in the way of Allah, they begin to understand the importance of mutual respect for one another. The spouses honor and ensure that each other's rights are fulfilled and they work together to develop a strong Islamic personality. Both engage in mutual consultation and exercise their obligations as they build upon their marriage.

Example of Obligations – Read and Understand the Qur'an

Muslims have an obligation to read and understand the Qur'an.[19] The first obligation is to have faith in the Qur'an, which is to avow that the Qur'an is the Revelation from Allah to Prophet Mohammad through the Angel Gabriel. This is a legal requirement for Muslims. The source of faith is the Qur'an, and the practice of pondering over the verses of the Qur'an heightens our awareness and consciousness.

The second obligation is to read the Qur'an slowly with correct pronunciation. The Qur'an needs to be read many times, and it must be read carefully in order to reflect on its messages. It must be read in a patient manner, pausing at proper places so as to enable one's heart to absorb its influence. Reciting from the Qur'an provides nourishment for our souls much the same as food nourishes our bodies and sustains our health.

The third obligation is to understand and comprehend the Qur'an according to one's level of intelligence and awareness. It does not matter if a person's intelligence is limited, or his knowledge of logic and philosophy is poor, or if he has no fine sense of language or literature, the Qur'an has been rendered very easy for the readers to gain guidance. Even here the reader can still understand the basic message of the Qur'an. Although the Qur'an can be read in different languages, it is required that the reader learns the Arabic language in order to fully understand the meaning of the Qur'an.

The fourth obligation is to act upon the teachings of the Qur'an, and to make it the guide for Muslims throughout their lives. Mus-

149

lims should pattern their lifestyle according to the teachings of the Qur'an.

The fifth obligation is to propagate the message of the Qur'an. This was the responsibility of Prophet Mohammad who fulfilled his obligation by conveying the Divine message to humanity. Likewise, we must carry the message forward.

Obligations and Unity

In short, we must fulfill all obligations whether divine, moral, mutual, complementary, voluntary or tacit. The fulfillment of these obligations provides us with the necessary growth in the development of our own Islamic personality. The foundation of fulfilling our obligations is unity. We must strive for unity in family, unity in congregation, unity in community and unity in diversity as we celebrate our differences as windows of opportunities. Any spiritual unity implies a certain degree of spiritual brotherhood. In Islam, the bond that unites Muslims is brotherly love. In Islam, the heart doesn't draw a line; that while we have differences among people and in our community, we are still one. Muslims owe an obligation to Allah – which is winning the unity! If we have good sense, if we have courage, if we have integrity, and if we work a little smarter, we will succeed in our quest for unity.

"And hold fast, all together, by the Rope which Allah stretches out for you, and be not divided among yourselves…." (Qur'an 3:103)

For in the end, it is to Allah that we all return.

Reconciliation
Definition of Reconciliation

The term reconciliation takes on many different meanings and interpretations. When the term reconciliation is mentioned, what does this really mean? Does reconciliation mean the same from a cultural perspective or a political perspective as it does from a religious perspective? What are the socio-psychological aspects of reconciliation? Who is accountable in bringing out reconciliation? How do different parties to a conflict respond to the concepts of justice and reconciliation? What are the major theoretical principles and lessons that can be drawn from different experiences in working on reconciliation? How do varying perceptions of justice contribute to or prevent reconciliation? How does Islam contribute to reconciliation?

Reconciliation may be defined as the act of bringing together persons for the purpose of settling their differences. Another aspect of reconciliation is the act of bringing people together in the direction of agreement, concord or harmony. Another definition looks at reconciliation as one of accountability, that is to render one account consistent with another by balancing apparent discrepancies. One can also reconcile different versions of the truth or different statements of fact. Even if it is not perfect, they are brought into some kind of accord.

We may look at the concept of reconciliation from a business standpoint. For example, balancing debits and credits in an account statement is the same as reconciling that account. Still another definition of reconciliation may be reuniting and inspiring a person back to his faith. This latter definition, of course, may take into account the act of purifying one's soul from the filth of contamination and corruption. In any of these definitions, truth, as painful as it may be, is essential to reconciliation. When we recognize concealed and agonizing truths, we take a major step towards the elimination of disagreements.

Building Cultures of Reconciliation

Recognizing the origins of conflicts is a major first step in the process of building cultures of reconciliation. This requires an understanding of the structure of conflicts and how to deal with them. These conflicts lie just beyond the horizon of our own interests. In order to attain mutual cooperation, we need to learn how to cope with practices and attitudes that contribute to conflicts. As social conflict is innate in human relations and internal to the involved parties, it is that which reveals difference. While the outcome of the parties in dispute can be destructive, all efforts should be made to achieve reconciliation and mutual happiness. This does not mean that the parties in dispute should forego their differences. Instead, these differences should lead to enrichment rather than provocation. Building cultures of reconciliation means developing proactive attitudes and practices that make cooperation possible.

Reconciliation advances as the parties in dispute begin to shape their lives in positive relation to one another. Reconciliation is a journey through conflict as well as an encounter. We need to have an understanding of the culture and emotions of the people who are in conflict. When they come to the realization and understanding as to what separates them, they will have made a major inroad into bridging the gap between their differences. As a result, this bridging the gap will enable them to live in peace with one another, not in isolation from one another.

While reconciliation is difficult to achieve, it can be attained. This, of course, will require moving into realms not yet considered or revealed, counting on the emergence of new possibilities. To reconcile necessitates an understanding that all parties in a conflict are hurt, and their wounds are deep. How we come about healing the wounds is to have a compassionate understanding about the conflict. This requires all parties to be non-judgmental and non-adversarial. Good listeners do not defend themselves in reconciliation but, rather, try to understand each other's perceptions. By listening they validate each other's right to those perceptions. This listening is not physical in nature but spiritual. The listener doesn't decide in advance who is right and who is wrong and then seeks to rectify it.

Criteria for Reconciliation

What leads to a genuine reconciliation is the sequence of specific facts, integrity and conflict resolution. These decisive factors are both ethical and moral. Promoting reconciliation is an arduous task, since we must be cautious about the pessimists and cynics who will say reconciliation is not possible. These skeptics believe that reconciliation is dreadfully culture bound, unattainable and unrealistic. The pessimists say it is better to strive for a practical compromise than for the perfect state or reconciliation.

Reconciliation signifies not merely a renewal of old relations, but moreover an intensification and reciprocal acknowledgment and admission of wrongdoings. In addition, there must be accountability, and for each party to continue to pursue the strengthening of the relation even far after reconciliation is done. The reason for this continuance of relationships is that even though parties are brought together and forgive one another, this may not be a genuine reconciliation. Rather, it is a step in the right direction. Reconciliation is desirable but not essential to forgiveness. For example, if an offender has serious character flaws, then the victim may feel that it is not in his best interest to reconcile. Reconciliation used in the sense that the offense is forgiven and forgotten, as if it never happened, is a theoretical concept and not practical. Forgiveness can be one-sided, while reconciliation must be reciprocal. We must unconditionally declare our willingness to forgive and reconcile.

We do not agree with skeptics who view forgiveness as ineffective. Rather, we must find the way to build the bridge of compassion between the dissenting parties. Anguish and pain are dealt with in different ways, and forgiveness requires emotional and moral resources many sufferers are unable to assemble. Reconciliation does not mean giving up of one's individuality or sacrificing one's principles, but it does mean doing whatever is reasonable to normalize relationships. Soothing relationships between parties occurs at any level of conflict, whether it is political, international, institutional, familial or communal.

If reconciliation is to benefit from significance and influence in the realm of conflict transformation, it must be positioned and encouraged, primarily within its innate environment. There needs to be education and discipline in order for reconciliation to be effective. This means we need to educate people about integrity and cooperation, whether it is at the political or cultural level, in order to achieve a lasting reconciliation. And that is the work that faith-based initiative groups have to be about first and foremost.

Reconciliation is very difficult because it necessitates the recommencement of relationships between those in conflict. It means the coming together in harmony of those who have been separated. To reconcile, attempts must be made to adjust to new responses and to new situations in a climate where aggression is fruitless and pointless.

In a given conflict, there are always issues of injustice. Justice is not the direct result of peace; rather, peace is based on justice. Peace is a vehicle whereby Muslims can work together for the sake of justice. Justice must be achieved while at the same time enhancing harmonious coexistence. Coexistence is the element that sustains peace. The role of Islam is essential to the process as well. Islam helps the reconciliation process. Ideally, in a reconciliation situation, the peace process must be inclusive, and that the ownership of each party be shared.

Relative to reconciliation, everyone has something to bring to the party, and all concerned must be willing to have an open mind and open heart, particularly with those with whom there is disagreement. To reconcile, we must realize that both sides to any hostility are hurt, and their injuries are in need of treatment. What goes a long way towards treatment is for all parties to be good listeners, which requires them to be non-critical and non-divergent in the exchange of discussion. By listening they corroborate with each other's insights. In effect, listening becomes a form of spirituality as the listener gives an open ear to all sides of the conflict. In order to resolve the conflict, effective listening requires that there is no predetermination as to who is right or wrong.

"If two parties among the believers fall in to a quarrel, you make peace between them: but if one of them transgresses beyond bounds against the other, then you (all) fight against the one that transgresses until it complies with the Command of Allah; but if it complies, then make peace between them with justice, and be fair: for Allah loves those who are fair (and just). The believers are but a single brotherhood: so make peace and reconciliation between your two contending brothers; and fear Allah, that ye may receive Mercy." (Qur'an 49:9-10)

When there is a quarrel between two parties, Muslims must act to resolve that quarrel. Muslims cannot be passive or silent, as they must find the solution for reconciliation. All efforts should be geared toward reconciliation between the parties rather than keeping the conflict raging.

Islam lays down a principle that makes it a duty to the Muslim community to try to bring about reconciliation between parties of believers who may be engaged in a quarrel. Sometimes this may mean that Muslims take the side of the aggressed and pursue the aggressor until he submits to peace with the other party. If one party is clearly the aggressor and continues to quarrel in spite of efforts at reconciliation, then the Muslim community at large should pressure those aggressors until they are willing to apply the rule of Islam. When the aggression has stopped, then a reconciliation that is fair to both sides should be brought about. As Muslims are required to help one another, then reconciliation between the quarrelling parties is not only a duty but also mandatory. What is essential is that there be fairness and respect for the highest principles. The enforcement of the Muslim brotherhood is the supreme social value of Islam. A united Islamic community must be supreme over everyone and seek peace as it resolves quarrels among individuals and groups.

"The recompense for an injury is an injury equal thereto in degree: but if a person forgives and makes reconciliation, his reward is due from Allah: for Allah loves not those who do wrong." (Qur'an 42:40)

The ideal approach is not to satisfy one's desire for revenge, but to follow improved ways leading to the improvement of the wrongdoer. The best means would be to transform enmity into amity. In this way, the Pleasure of Allah is achieved, for Allah does not accept those who tolerate or encourage wrong. When there is a conflict between two individuals or groups, they must seek reconciliation. According to the Qur'an, Allah has promised the highest reward for those who practice patience, which is the foundation for the establishment of reconciliation and peace. Patience is the price that has to be paid for the attainment of peace. It is not enough to just say we are Muslims. Rather we must be practicing Muslims and as such reconciliation is a major practice in the Islamic faith. Prophet Mohammad said:

"Reconciliation of your differences is more worthy than prayers in general and fasting in general."

Reconciling Differences

Bringing Muslims closer to each other in their beliefs, opinions and intentions is one of the utmost goals of Islam, and essential towards attaining Muslim unity. Disparities of views within the Islamic community have frequently been identified as one of the foremost reasons for disunity. Historical differences between the Islamic schools of thought have continued to permeate throughout Islamic communities, even though Islamic scholars from all sides have promoted the concept of unity.

While historical differences in jurisprudence and philosophy may differ, they should not be the basis for instilling in the minds of their followers hatred towards each other. True, Allah's Orders are evident. However, there are certain Commands that are interpreted differently. For example, inclusion or exclusion of certain words in the prayer, or as to which foods are fit to eat and which are not. Such interpretation requires reliance upon the adherence to a particular school of thought. Often, *ijtihad* (independent judgment regarding a legal or theological issue) is made to resolve contemporary issues, such as infertility, cloning or organ transplants.

There is a profound need to reconcile differences, particularly in today's society. Believers alike must rise above ignorance, find a common ground, and work together. It is not enough to live and let live; each of us must actively and constantly be part of the society by helping to reduce our differences. Harassment and hatred of Muslims continue to run rampant, and fragmentation of Islam only contributes to the problems. With this impending distressing state of affairs, are these differences between the Islamic schools of thought so divisive that unity cannot be achieved? We are not postulating that the schools of thought in Islam should be abolished; rather there should be a cohesive effort between them to coalesce together at the bedrock of Islam, which is winning the unity. There can be diversity of opinions and interpretations, as long as this diversity leads to and cements the unity.

Both Sunnis and Shi'as follow the *Sunnah*, which are the lifestyle, behavior and the traditions of the Prophet Mohammad. The Shi'as, however, carry this practice a step further to include the *Sunnah* within the Prophet's *Ahl al-Bayt*, that is, his Household. In addition, the Shi'as claim that the Prophet and his progeny are what constitute the *Sunnah* and *Ahl al-Bayt*. When a Muslim begins to emphasize that he is either a Sunni or Shi'a as a separate sect, then he is contributing to fragmentation. Rather, it is best for a Muslim to say that he belongs to a particular school of thought. Therefore, the concepts of Sunni and Shi'a should never lead to fragmentation, and should not be confused with the objectives and interpretations of the various schools of thought. From an historical perspective and evidence, it was the Sixth Imam, Ja'far as-Sadiq, who taught Abu Hanifah and Malik Ibn Anas, two of the renowned scholars of the major Sunni schools of thought. Both *Ahl al-Bayt* and *Sunnah* are sacred windows through which shines Allah's Blessings, and they constitute the strength of the *Rope of Allah*, which is the Qur'an.

In today's society, those who want to destroy Islam constantly face us with challenges and threats. With unity in diversity, we can utilize the shield of *sabr* (patience) to thwart off any temptation, threat, weakness or fear:

"So have sabr! Verily your sabr is from Allah, and do not let yourself be grieved or distressed because of their deceptions." (Qur'an 16:127)

Sabr strengthens the unity and binds the Muslims together as one:

"And hold fast, all together, by the Rope which Allah stretches out for you, and be not divided among yourselves...." (Qur'an 3:103)

Here the Qur'an declares the command of being united together with the prescription for attaining it. This bind or tie manifests itself in *sabr*. Muslims unify for the common goal of serving Allah. Muslims believe in the unity of mankind in all forms and aspects. With *sabr*, unity will be achieved.

We note that the word *sabr* usually precedes the pillars of Islam as well as concepts that form our Islamic foundation. For example, we note the terms *sabr* and prayer, *sabr* and struggle, *sabr* and faith, and *sabr* and comfort. The importance of *sabr* is emphasized by its position at the beginning of the phrase. In each situation, *sabr* strengthens and reinforces the other concept. For example, what good is *salwan* (comfort) in times of bereavement if the comforter has no *sabr* (patience)? Likewise, how can one truly defend the religion of Islam against evil if the spirit of *jihad* (struggle) does not translate into *sabr* (endurance and constancy)? Total obedience to each verse of the Qur'an and each command will create unity and harmony among its believers. Understanding of these commands may have to be based on interpretations from the Islamic schools of thought.

True unity can only be achieved by way of the Qur'an, which is the *Rope of Allah*. It is the Qur'an that is the certainty in Islam, for it is the knowledge of certainty, the perception of certainty, and the truth of certainty.

Competition Versus Cooperation

As a society, we have developed many illusions about competition. Some of these illusions are that competition is human nature; it is unavoidable; and it shapes and strengthens our character and self-esteem. As an example, competition has its winners and losers. If one loses, it does not build his self-esteem; rather, at times, it makes him frustrated and demoralized.

Living in a purely competitive society without any cooperation is not only unreasonable but chaotic as well. With no cooperation, there is no law enforcement, no order in the household, and no accountability for one's actions. All of these attributes are forms of cooperation. In a society where everyone competes against everyone else, only the strong will prevail. In a perfectly competitive world, the weak have no chance to survive. Competition becomes more severe as resources become scarcer. Even among the strongest that do survive, the competitive drive for power would be so intense that hostilities and confrontation would take place to see who is even stronger. For those who emerge as survivors, the rewards are minimal, for how prosperous and content can they be if they are isolated?

Looking at the Muslim society we find a great deal of competition taking place. The suspicions and fears that exist between Muslims still remain. In fact, there are places and cultures where the suspicions and fears have actually become enmity and resentment. We even find vast evidence of this type of competitiveness in a society wherein Muslims adhere to the same Islamic school of thought. For example, while these Muslims may belong to different Islamic organizations in the same community, they are competing with each other for the same projects. As there is virtually no consolidation of economic resources, the issue of capitalization and financing of these projects becomes severely impacted. Cooperation among these organizations is minimal at best. What happens is that there are no economies of scale from which to benefit. Had there been cooperation, the leaders could have saved enormous sums of monies by purchasing products and services together. This competitive attitude has led to division within the community and has imprisoned the present day consciousness that impedes all leaders of Islamic institutions from embarking into new relationships of trust and friendship.

With cooperation, Muslim leaders can begin to learn how to reconcile their differences and understand each other. This understanding would pave the way for future generations of Muslims to be able to better cope with their own attitudes and cultural outlooks. Cooperation breeds trust, mutual respect and tolerance.

Each Muslim within a community needs to understand the significance of peace, reconciliation, advancement and contemplation. They need to open their hearts and minds to each other in the direction of a more unified community. Every attempt must be made so that unity wins over division. This can only be accomplished by having a full understanding of each other's point of view and showing respect for one another's beliefs and feelings.

Empathy
Definition of Empathy

What goes on in the daily lives of people can be illustrated by the following:

· Kids care about computer games, television programs, and movies like Harry Potter.

· College students care about getting their degree while still enjoying life, the clothes they wear, and dating.

· Parents care about being able to keep up with mortgage payments, saving enough money to put their children through college, the ups and downs of the stock market, and whether or not they can afford to take a vacation.

In a nutshell, people care about big things, including their education, their careers, their money, and their entertainment. Have we ever had time to care about the feelings of others when they have lost their jobs, or had a divorce, or became disabled, or had death in the family, or have been orphaned, or have become hungry, or have lost their faith? Have we ever had time to think of the elderly, who have difficulty in moving about, or parents who have grown old and need help, or friends who have become depressed and lonely? In this age of information technology and fast life, we rush to develop our minds and chase our success. There is no time left to be aware of troubled waters, no time to be sensitive to others experiencing unhappiness, and no time to help others solve their problems. Oftentimes we neglect to develop our empathy.

Empathy is identification with and understanding of another's situation, feelings and motives. Empathy is being aware of, sensitive to, and experiencing the emotions and thoughts of others. Empathy may be tacit in that one feels what others feel without oral communication. Empathy is synonymous with compassion, compatibility, congeniality, responsiveness, warmth and understanding.

"(Charity is) for those in need, who, in Allah's Cause are restricted (from travel), and cannot move about in the land, seeking (for trade or work): the ignorant man thinks, because of their modesty, they are free from want. You shall know them by their (unfailing) mark: they do not beg importunately from all and sundry. And whatever of good you give, be assured Allah knows it well." (Qur'an 2:273)

Here is an example of how tacit empathy unfolds. For example, it is the duty of the rich or well to do to seek out and help the poor or those in dire need. This help is done quietly and without the notion of thanks from the needy. Tacit empathy becomes profound when a rich person gives without the poor person asking or begging for help. Random acts of charity are discouraged, as they may do more harm than good. The real beneficiaries of charity must be in need of help. Those who deserve the first consideration for charity are those who are confined in service to the cause of truth and in the way of Allah. This verse excludes the professional beggars from being entitled to charity.

Development of Empathy

The challenge is how to develop empathy. There are many aspects of the word empathy. For example, empathy is the emotional response of shared understanding in which each person assumes the other's perspective and cultural values as much as possible. Here, empathy requires mutual respect and goodwill between people, to have an understanding for another person's beliefs and values. Preconceived ideas, stereotyped notions, and personal biases and prejudices are factors that make it difficult to achieve a shared understanding of another person's feelings or emotions. For example, if we hold the stereotype of a particular ethnic group as "lazy," it will be difficult to empathize with a group of homeless people from that ethnic group.

Let us reflect on how we might practice empathy in a given situation. Following are examples of responses to another person's feeling, attitude, or emotion by labeling our own feeling, attitude, or emotion:

· *"When you are yelling and arguing, I feel intimidated."*
· *"You look upset. Did the discussion with your boss bother you?"*
· *"It's normal to feel angry and disappointed when you were not picked for the team. You worked really hard."*
· *"I would feel really proud too if I had received a perfect score on the exam. Great job!"*
· *"I know you are pleased with your work in this course. Do you plan to enter the degree program next semester?"*
· *"Maybe you could ask your advisor to change you to another section. Another teacher might give you the motivation you need right now."*

While sympathy means acknowledging the feelings of someone else as in *"I sympathize with you,"* empathy is a term for a deeper feeling. It means, *"I feel what you feel. I can put myself in your dilemma."* Sympathy results in kindness and sometimes pity. Empathy results in actually feeling the pain, or the joy, of the other person. Empathy is more than just awareness. We may be aware that our friend is feeling lonely; however, we are too busy to spend an afternoon with our lonely friend listening to that friend's marriage troubles. We don't lack awareness; rather, we are well informed about our lonely friend's problems. However, if we don't share our friend's feelings, don't feel our friend's predicament, don't even show how much we care about our friend's troubles, then we lack empathy. Tenderness and comfort are hallmarks of empathy.

People without any empathy always put themselves first. For example, take the situation where a husband puts his work and himself above everything else, doesn't remember his wife's or child's birthday, doesn't help his wife with her own emotional problems, and doesn't take an interest in his child's educational development. He seriously lacks empathy. How miserable for one to spend her life with an insensitive person who doesn't care about the emotions and problems of others in the same family. Similarly, a wife, who may not help her husband in operating the household and rearing the children, also lacks empathy. She has neglected her duties as a wife and parent. Another example is when a husband tries very hard to find work but is unsuccessful. Rather than his wife consoling and encouraging him to keep on trying, she opts to criticize and demean him and to call him a failure. This is a very serious case of a person who lacks empathy. Insensitivity and indifference to the agony and suffering of others is no less than someone living in a world filled with robots, a world without any feeling.

We regard empathy as a value the family engenders and strength to be cultivated at home. Yet, we see vast evidence of its absence in children and adults. Ironically enough there are a number of parents without much empathy for their children and vice-versa. What really matters is that empathy can be taught, and it should be taught very early in the life of a child, at home and at school. It is not a matter of family values; it is a matter of society and civilization. There needs to be connectivity in the family, the school, and the society. Empathy can save a family; it can save lives. We all need empathy, at home, in school, at work, and in our daily activities.

We can see how the willingness to be flexible comes more easily when we put ourselves in the other person's dilemma. Every human being has a deep need for his or her feelings to be recognized. Look at the example of an employee approaching his or her boss saying, *"I just found out that Ahmad makes two thousand dollars more a year than I do for the same job."* Trying to explain why Ahmad makes more money, even if the reason is a good one, only makes the employee angrier. Instead, we must acknowledge the fact and the feeling first by stating, *"You think we're taking advantage of you and you're angry. I can understand that, I'd probably feel the same way."* That isn't what an angry person expects. By acknowledging the employee's feelings, we've helped the person calm down. The next statement might be: *"Well, why shouldn't I make as much as Ahmad does?"* That shows he or she is ready to hear the explanation from the boss. The feeling of empathy is much easier to come by when we care about the other person and take the time to feel what they're feeling.

However, empathy should be controlled by wisdom. For example, parents should not just give in to their children's request for the sake of empathy. Wisdom should be exercised with caution as to whether or not to submit to their children's requests. Wisdom is incomplete without action and action is unfounded without compassion and connection to that which is discerned. The connection between wisdom and empathy is that of caring; however, caring must be tempered with judgment and justice. The components of wisdom are discernment, empathy and engagement, and strength of character. A wise person knows how to fit all the parts of the human persona together, which makes empathy a reality. Wisdom requires understanding, compassion and commitment. The key to wisdom is to know when to empathize. People heal when they make their wisdom and empathy work together.

Intrapersonal and Interpersonal Aspects of Empathy

Empathy for others starts with the same point: We cannot truly feel the pain or the joy or the emotion of another (interpersonal) until we are able to feel the same thing in ourselves (intrapersonal). Do we acknowledge our own pain? Can we feel our own joy? Real empathy lies in simply finding the same place within us that the other person is experiencing. We might not have had exactly the same experience but we've known the sadness of loss or the anger of feeling cheated, or the sense of righteousness at injustice. Some of us don't take the time to feel our own feelings, so when someone else expresses a feeling, we don't have much to refer to. We might be concerned that expressing a caring approach toward another person will result in the other person manipulating us. This isn't about abdicating our own needs or point of view. It simply means that we are able to enter into the mind of another and acknowledge that person's feelings. Having that ability is an asset.

We value what we feel strongly about. We value what is important to us. We value what we believe will make us happy. Our values come from our parents, our relatives, neighbors, friends, teachers but most of all from our Islamic faith. When we value something we will strive to get more of it. If we are hindered in pursuit of something we value we feel frustrated, unfulfilled. Oftentimes, people fall into despair and unhappiness, and their sense of values is severely impaired. Empathy can be the solution to restore that person's sense of worth, of belongingness. We need to empathize with others to restore their self-dignity, their self-confidence.

Simply said, empathy is the capacity to put oneself inside the soul of another person and to see the world through that person's eyes. Empathy implies that we have trained ourselves to consider how other people perceive situations, how they perceive us, and how they would describe us. If a person is lacking in empathy, he or she is likely to misread what is transpiring in a situation and misunderstand the intentions of others. Achieving empathy requires a great deal of diligence and thoughtfulness. It is difficult to have empathy when we are upset, angry, disappointed, or frustrated with another person. In such situations, our negative feelings will often serve as a roadblock, not permitting us to see the world through the eyes of the person with whom we are upset. We must learn to replace judgment with empathy, and ignorance with understanding. A vision of a good and sustainable society can be shared with those who are willing to take on this challenge.

Parents want the best for their children. Parents want their children to excel in school. Parents want their children to have friends. Suppose the parents have a bashful and timid child. In this situation, the parents can talk with their child privately by saying, *"I know that it isn't easy for you to speak in front of people. A lot of other children have the same difficulty. Maybe together we can figure out what will begin to help."* This action contains a heavy dose of empathy, compassion and hope to establish the foundation for a child to feel increasingly accepted. Regarding empathy, a golden rule for us to follow is, *"Never say or do to another person what we would not want said or done to us."*

Many parents confuse empathy with giving in to their children or not holding them accountable for their actions. However, empathy has nothing to do with giving in or making excuses for our children's unacceptable behaviors. Rather, empathy involves seeing the world through our children's eyes and asking such questions as: *"How can I speak with my children so that they will be most responsive to hearing what I have to say?"* and *"Would I want anyone to speak to me the way I am speaking with my child?"*

We are all born with the capacity of empathy. Empathy is like a muscle; if it is used it develops. We mirror what we see in life; empathy expands or contracts in response to our encounters. Empathy means we have the capacity to enter into someone else's dilemma, not necessarily having experienced it. Empathy is an active process; it must be put into action. Asking open questions, and slowing down our manner of responding are the first two steps. We can help enlist empathy from others by being open to others.

Empathy means reading people and situations correctly. Empathy does not mean that we automatically accept a situation without reacting. It allows us to set realistic limits by seeing the truth. It protects us, and it is really a guardian in that it allows us to move to a wider lens rather than a narrow vision. It means that we see into the minds and hearts of others. It is not enough to just listen with empathy; it has to be put into words or gestures and shared with another. We must also be careful regarding empathy. Empathy is accurately reading another, so it can be both a sword and a shield; it is a paradox. Sometimes people can read others accurately and then use that information to hurt or to help others.

Our ability to create pathways to relationships comes from within our minds and our hearts. Our minds take the empathy we have for others and construct a willful ability to feel the other's inner life, to identify, to empathize. A lack of empathy is a sign of moral failure. To empathize is to find the way to cross the bridge into another's mind. Crossing the bridge to reach connectivity is a path to healing. We must cross over and enter the perspective of the other person, in order to apprehend and appreciate what it is that can be seen from there. Understanding requires a conscious attempt to identify with the thought patterns and emotional tone of another person's convictions. In a sense, it is like crossing the threshold and experiencing the feelings in another's mind. Not only does one cross the threshold, but also experiences the threshold effect in his or her imagination.

Empathy - An Attribute of Fasting

During the month of Ramadan, fasting imparts empathy for the poor, strengthens the power of mind over body, and allows one to experience self-renewal and introspection. Fasting helps us get closer to those who have a limited means of subsistence or none at all. Ramadan serves as a training period as Muslims endeavor to practice self-restraint, good moral character, and an increased level of spirituality and empathy with those all over the world who are regularly hungry and thirsty. It is a time for self-improvement and recommitment to the basic principles of Islam. Muslims are reminded of the extra blessings they receive during the month of Ramadan for the good deeds they engage in. The rewards for doing good work such as giving charity, practicing empathy, and assisting those in need are multiplied during Ramadan.

Fasting strengthens one's self-discipline and increases that person's patience and endurance. Fasting accustoms Muslims to hunger and creates empathy with the poor and homeless who are often in a continual state of hunger and thirst. Man's sense of compassion springs from his feelings of pain.

Imam Ja'far as Sadiq said:
"Allah made fasting obligatory to make equity between the rich and the poor. A rich man does not feel the pains of hunger to have mercy for the poor, since he is able to obtain whatever he likes. By enjoining fasting, Allah wanted to put His creatures on an equal footing by making the rich taste the pain of hunger, so that he may pity and have mercy on the hungry…"

Feelings of empathy, not just sympathy, for the poor come about. While sympathy is when we feel for someone else, empathy is when we feel with someone else. Fasting is a way where a person shares the pain of the poor by temporarily living as they do – that is truly empathizing. How useful can food be if we are forever feeding our misguided self into action? By gaining greater empathy for Allah's nature, empathy with all of His Creation becomes more evident within one's self.

Empathy is born of character through its development. Fasting heightens our senses as we focus on our state of mind and body. The ritual of fasting evokes within people empathy for those less fortunate. It creates bonds of humanity and brotherhood as people come to realize they are not invincible, that they have the same basic needs for survival as the next person, especially the poor. Just as fasting teaches us to empathize with the poor and the needy, it also teaches us to be grateful for all the blessings we enjoy. Food and drink are Blessings from Allah. Because we have them every day, we do not realize their importance. But when we are required to restrain ourselves while fasting, we understand the importance of having enough to eat to satisfy the pangs of hunger.

Creation of empathy among Muslims, feeling for the poor and destitute, and participation in prescribed and voluntary charity are imbued in the ritual of fasting. As we reflect on our inner self during the month of Ramadan, let it be our hopes that we can all make a contribution towards alleviating the hunger and thirst of so many. With empathy, we can reach out to the homeless in their time of need. When fasting we should think about our obligations in Islam, for example, *zakat* (alms). Fulfilling some of our obligations and responsibilities with *zakat* can go a long way in alleviating the pain and suffering of the needy. Let empathy be our guide, as we strive for excellence in character, faith and unity.

Another evidence of how empathy unfolds is when we reflect on the martyrdom of Imam Hussein and the tragedy at Karbala, Iraq in the seventh century. All through the year, particularly during the month of Ramadan and the first ten days (*Ashura*) of the month of Muharram, we commemorate the tragedy with deep reflection and emotion. We begin to empathize, to envision ourselves in the tragedy, and to feel the pain, suffering and oppression of the Muslim world at that time. Tears are shed, as we begin to recount the tragedy. We cannot help but to act out the tragedy in our own minds and hearts. We truly live the tragedy, as if we were there.

Leadership
Aspects of Leadership

Leadership is a word on everyone's lips. Discussions on leadership are often as majestically useless as they are pretentious. Leadership is like the abominable snowman, whose footprint is everywhere but who is nowhere to be seen. Leadership is the process of moving a group in some direction through mostly noncoercive means. Effective leadership is that which produces movement in the long-term best interests of the group. While this definition of leadership is appropriate for those who manage companies or businesses, we as Muslims need to link ourselves to another kind of leadership: spiritual or Islamic leadership. Here leadership demands results and provides the courage to overcome ignorance, fear and denial. Ignorance holds back far more leaders than does either a lack of talent or skill.

Ethics of Leadership

Ethical practices have always been a crucial factor, particularly, when integrity is compromised. Ethical standards are a direct reflection of one's values. Questions dealing with trust, care and excellence are ethical characteristics of sound leadership. When these core values are instilled in leadership, it is more likely that consistent ethical decisions will be made.

Priority decisions made by leaders are often based on whether there is personal benefit and satisfaction for the leader. The leader's approach to being a successful leader is predicated on his ability to becoming efficient and effective. The bottom line for a leader is to succeed in his endeavors by getting the job done.

An ethical dilemma may occur when the leader become over-zealous and achieves his priority by suspicious and unprincipled means. If a leader's personal priority is one of power or wealth, then decisions will be based on that priority that will interfere with completion of a task. A leader seeking power or wealth wants to make it known that he is in charge. In addition, he wants to be viewed and respected by everyone, even to the point where it is felt that his very presence is needed for the viability and sustainability of an organization. This gives the leader a sense of supremacy.

A leader that wants to control everything just does not have the time, for example, to address minor problems. By not delegating authority to his subordinates, a leader is placed in a problematic state whereby overlooked minor problems can catapult into uncontrollable major problems in the future. Leaders in control want to deal with high visibility problems only, and they will not give authority to subordinates to deal with minor issues. The reason is that by giving authority, leaders lose control. When money controls decisions of leaders, morale is severely impacted and the organization suffers immensely. An effective leader is one that focuses on the organization by delegating authority to his subordinates.

Islam teaches us a code of ethics. Muslim leaders as well as Muslims in general must espouse admirable traits in life, by being friendly, sociable and kind. Another important trait is that of justice and the capacity to defend their own rights. As they must exhibit qualities of respect, equality, self-restraint, self-sacrifice and self-denial, they must not misbehave nor infringe upon other people's rights.

Leadership and Motivation

The style of leadership stimulates the intensity of motivation. Nonetheless, during one's lifetime, his motivation is intensified by transformation of aspirations and a style of leadership that he develops. The aspect of empowerment augments these aspirations. As he strives for empowerment leadership, the leadership of domination and authority wear off. Empowerment is team motivated.

With empowerment, motivation is based on creativity. The qualities of this type of leader are one of achievement and change. Conversely, domination and authority leadership is the principal style in our society, because the majority of people resists and dislikes change. For example, the affairs of a mosque are run by tradition, and the members of the congregation prefer the status quo as opposed to change. This is a reason why many Islamic institutions are finding it difficult to cope with contemporary societies. True, many mosques are being built with beautiful and remarkable architecture. However, it is neither the beauty nor the architecture of the mosque that brings out the good in Muslims but, rather, the Muslims themselves. What is needed is a change in the minds of the Muslims so as to become self-motivated and to take on Islamic responsibilities for the betterment of the individual, family and community. With empowerment leadership, seeking out opportunities, challenges and efficient and effective ways of building a more productive Islamic society motivates Muslims.

The world is rapidly changing due in large measure to the myriads of advances in technology. Because of this, Muslims must be willing to learn and apply new skills, and they must work together to resolve problems. The self-actualized Muslim will adapt to this change within the context of Islamic ethics, morals, rules and regulations. Muslims who want to advance the goals and objectives of a mosque are inspired in a team-motivated environment whereby each person becomes a leader of their input. In this way, recognition builds self-esteem in the individual, because he feels that his input, although one of many inputs, was so important that the project could not have been completed without him.

How to promote leadership unity in a mosque is a challenge. Muslim goals should be one of becoming proactive in the treatment of potential conflict as well as to understand the inclinations of other fellow Muslims. By working in faith groups at the mosque towards common principles, conflict becomes avoidable. Rather than being competitive, it is better to be complementary and cooperative with each other. This requires a commitment to develop more profound friendships and respect with other leaders in the mosque. Encouragement of a fellow leader can go a long way in building sound relationships.

Another issue is that family leadership is on the continual decline. Parents no longer enjoy the respect of their children that at one time was traditional and automatic. Yet, parents demand respect from their children. Respect can be achieved if it is a mutual respect between parents and children. Furthermore, parents must be pious, understanding and righteous in order to set the example for their children. Oftentimes, parents demand respect, even though their own lifestyles are highly questionable. In Islam, cultural values must be in synchronization with religious values. Leadership should begin in the home, with parents acting as role models for their children. Proper planning between parents can help attain harmony and respect within the family.

If we look at the successes of healthy families, we find common characteristics. To begin with, rules are implemented by which each family member must abide. There are no shortcuts, and mutual respect is the order of the day. High standards relative to attitude and behavior are established and implemented. When these standards are met, the children progressively instill powers of judgment and ethics. Rather than each family member taking on the authoritarian role of *me,* or the dictatorial role of *you,* it is more productive to function as *we.* This in turn reflects unity in the family. As a result, the healthy family grows in character and faith.

Just as a business has a set of standards and rules, so must the family also have a set of standards and rules? For example, a business operates within the framework of a mission statement, organizational structure, chain of command, budget requirements, and a set of performance objectives. Likewise, a family operates much the same way. If there is no chain of command in the family, then everyone is free to do as they wish. This presents a problem, as there is no accountability by anyone. The children, for example, could be encountering serious problems in their lives. If there is no one to counsel or direct them, then the end result is chaos.

Working together in the arena of *we* brings out a healthier framework and one that fosters structure within the family unit. By praying together as a family brings out the best in *we,* as Allah orders us to honor each other. In this way, leadership is built, nurtured and promoted as each member of the family unit is reared in the direction of a vision, a purpose and a design. Leadership in the family is one of shared views, priorities, communication, collaboration and mutual respect.

How this leadership unfolds within a family unit is as follows. Family leaders must demonstrate a genuine passion for each other in order to elicit acceptability by others in the same family. One of the main attributes of good leaders is that they have vision and can see even beyond the big picture. Effective communication is vital in order to have family members embrace religious and cultural values that drive the family's daily life. Creating an atmosphere of trust and truth are also vital to a family's healthy success. From another vantage point, leaders are like a rope for it can pull us up or drag us down. Prophet Mohammad and his progeny are like ropes that pull us up.

Leadership and Character

Character has a great deal to do with leadership. In building character, one needs to strengthen relationships and associations. Conversely, leadership leads to power, and power leads to relationships. Therefore, character and leadership are complementary. One cannot be an effective leader without genuine character. Throughout life we deal with both significant and insignificant situations. It doesn't matter how large or small an item is or how wealthy or poor a person is, but how we conduct ourselves with each item or each person. This conduct brings out the best in character and shapes us into effective leaders. Prophet Mohammad and his progeny taught us about character, and the best of character is when we fully submit our will to the Will of Allah and obey His Commandments and the teachings of His Messengers. We strive to become like the best of role models, that is, the Prophets and Imams. We try to imitate these role models and pattern our attitudes, behaviors and lifestyles after them.

What is necessary to build excellent character are integrity, accountability, ethics, humility, patience and courage. And it is this latter trait of courage that equips the leader to be confident as he moves towards drastically altering the course of events. As courage builds character, it at the same time gives the person enough stamina to lead the way. If one doesn't stand up for his own convictions or tries to hide his faith, then that person is not a leader and severely tarnishes his character.

In American society, Muslims who do not stand up for their faith when religious and political antagonists are attacking it, then these Muslims demean their character and leadership considerably. Courageous Muslim leaders stand up for justice and truth, even if they stand-alone. They uphold their Islamic values at all costs. Then there are those who do not take a stand at all; they remain neutral. These people are opportunists who wait until the final outcome to see who they side with, even at the expense of their own faith and morality.

Leadership must be earned. The character of the leader is vital, as he must possess certain characteristics to be successful. Some of these characteristics are courage, a great deal of energy, ethics, patience, being goal oriented, cool under pressure, setting and working priorities, being enthusiastic, helping others, and commitment. Leadership is both an art and a science. On the one hand, a leader must be adroit and understanding, while on the other hand he must be skillful in strategic thinking and organizational wisdom.

Where leaders fail is when they drastically make a shift in their focus and lose sight of what is important. They become deterred by affluence and fame. Rather than delegate responsibility and authority, they micro manage and pay too much attention to trivial matters and details. Where leaders succeed is when they instill character into leadership, establish open channels of communication, take risks, and stay the course with ethics.

Character like personality is comprised of different qualities. Strengths are elements of a person's basic personality and portray themselves across circumstances and occasions. These individual strengths are also compliant and they cultivate with the person through various occurrences and over time. The environment plays a major part in defining character. At the core of defining character are a number of qualities. For example, wisdom, courage, compassion, justice, self-control and spirituality are just a few of these qualities. Across this gamut of qualities and virtues, we begin with wisdom that deals with creativity and social intelligence, and we end with spirituality that deals with forgiveness and gratitude.

Leadership Traits

Forthrightly, no one can tell us how to lead or how to be a good leader. However, there are certain principles or maxims one should follow in order to establish good leadership traits. To be a good leader requires more than just being a good listener and empathetic; or more than just being accommodating and allowing others to perform their duties; or more than just being a team player and task oriented; or more than just inspiring others to be self-motivated and courageous. These characteristics of leadership do not assure effective leadership. Rather, leaders must develop their own persona or character so when others look at them they will surely differentiate them as true leaders. Following are selected maxims that the author has devised that should help shape the character of a leader:

Maxim I:	Be humble.
Maxim II:	Be accountable.
Maxim III:	Be judicial.
Maxim IV:	Be mature.
Maxim V:	Be determined.
Maxim VI:	Be prudent.
Maxim VII:	Be patient.
Maxim VIII:	Be dependable.
Maxim IX:	Be comforting.
Maxim X:	Be civil.

Humbleness requires a leader to come down to earth and think small, rather than always seeking to be *"Mr. Big."* Take responsibility by being accountable for one's actions and by not making excuses. By being judicial, one exercises caution when making decisions. Maturity is the capacity to restrain emotions and resolve discrepancies by peaceful means. Determination breeds persistency and persistency breeds power. By being prudent one displays wisdom in both ethics and philosophy. Patience is taking the initiative towards a goal or objective when dealing with others. By being dependable, leadership is about who we are as individuals. A pat on the shoulder or words of encouragement to a subordinate goes a long way in comforting the emotions of a subordinate. To be civil is to be honest and a good citizen and to respect authority.

Case Example of Leadership - Imam Hussein

Leadership was put to the test during the period of Yazid's illegal rule. Imam Hussein, the grandson of Prophet Mohammad and son of Imam Ali and Fatima, fought and died for the protection of Islam. To him, Islam was not only threatened but on the verge of collapse and destruction. But threatened by whom? Many scholars believe it was a fight against the tyrant and corrupt Caliph, Yazid, and his followers. A more in-depth analysis reveals that Imam Hussein's underlying mission was to put an end to those who compromised their Islamic values and ideals. What was compromised was the very essence of Islam, for Muslims had fallen back into the depths of ignorance.

Imam Hussein was born in Medina in the year 626 A.D. and

martyred in Karbala (Iraq) on Saturday, the tenth of the month of Muharram at the age of 58, after the time for the noon prayer. What led up to the martyrdom of Imam Hussein is the focus of our discussion. What led up to Imam Hussein's martyrdom is a tragedy, the story that has been repeatedly recounted over the centuries. For Imam Hussein, he had lived under the most difficult external circumstances of oppression and persecution. From the time of the death of Prophet Mohammad, Mu'awiyah (father of Yazid) and his followers made use of every possible scheme to destroy and dispose of the Household of the Prophet Mohammad, *Ahl al-Bayt*, and thus obliterate the name of Imam Ali and his family.

Imam Hussein took over the leadership of Islam, following the martyrdom of his brother, Imam Hassan. When Mu'awiyah died, the period of truce came to an end. This was the time for Imam Hussein to make public his authority and to fulfill his *jihad* (struggle). Mu'awiyah had taken severe measures to implement his plan, that of strengthening the basis of the Caliphate for his son, Yazid. During that time, Imam Hussein had to endure every kind of mental and spiritual anguish and suffering from Mu'awiyah and his followers.

With deception and fraudulent means, Mu'awiyah gained the support of Muslims who pledged their allegiance to Yazid. Mu'awiyah, who did not impose this requirement upon Imam Hussein, had advised his son, Yazid, not to force the issue. But Yazid did not listen as he continued to pursue Imam Hussein with impudence and treachery. Yazid's character was tantamount to that of the devil himself. Unrelenting, Yazid caused all kinds of disruption and interference in the precepts of Islam, as he practiced every malevolence and evil with the highest degree of impudence.

With determination and the zeal for justice, Imam Hussein would not give his allegiance to Yazid's injustice and tyranny. For Imam Hussein, he had to confront oppression and despotism by spreading the message of truth and justice to the Muslim community (*Ummah*). In order to safeguard the sanctuary of the holy place of Mecca from war, Imam Hussein decided to leave Mecca and proceed to Iraq. In Kufa, Iraq the people pledged their allegiance to Imam Hussein by promising and guaranteeing him their trust and contract. However, the people of Kufa later broke their pledge and deserted him.

Karbala was a town located in a desert about fifty miles from

Kufa. Here is where the battle for truth and justice took place. The army of Yazid numbered in the thousands, and they surrounded Imam Hussein and his followers. The event at Karbala lasted ten days. For the first eight days, Imam Hussein and his followers remained steadfast while the enemy's army continued to increase. On the seventh day the water supply was cut off from Imam Hussein's camp. Now began the torture of thirst and hunger. The Imam strengthened his resolve as he informed his companions that martyrdom was inevitable. Many of his companions dispersed, and what was left was a small contingent of about seventy devout Muslims that remained loyal. On the ninth day, the last challenge was made by the enemy to Imam Hussein to choose between allegiance and war. Imam Hussein refused allegiance and became determined to enter battle on the next day, the tenth day of Muharram.

At Karbala, Imam Hussein fought and died for the sanctity of Islam. On the tenth day of Muharram, he addressed his companions with the following speech:

"Allah has, this day, permitted us to be engaged in a Holy War and He shall reward us for our martyrdom. So prepare yourselves to fight against the enemies of Islam with patience and resistance. O sons of the noble and self-respecting persons, be patient! Death is nothing but a bridge that you must cross after facing trials and tribulations so as to reach Heaven and its joys. Which of you does not like to go from this prison (world) to the lofty palaces (Paradise)?"

To this, his companions replied:

"O our Master! We are all ready to defend you and your Ahl al-Bayt, and to sacrifice our lives for the cause of Islam."

When Imam Hussein raised his sword for the first time on the battlefield, it was against the tyranny, oppression, and false leadership of Yazid and his followers.

When he raised his lance for the second time, it was a symbolic gesture against those so-called allies who broke their treaty with Imam Hussein and would not support his mission at Karbala, because they compromised their Islamic values and ideals.

When Imam Hussein raised his lance for the third time, it was a message to those so-called Muslim friends and relatives who stayed home and awaited the outcome of the battle before declaring their allegiance to support Imam Hussein or the enemy. And this Imam Hussein saw as a compromise.

When he raised his sword for the fourth time, it was the most horrible moment in his life. In his vision, Imam Hussein saw the danger when Muslims in the centuries to follow would, likewise, compromise their Islamic values and ideals. Imam Hussein had to do something about it. He gave his life so that we can reflect on those horrid days at Karbala and, more importantly, upon our own situation in contemporary times to understand that we, too, have compromised our own Islamic values and ideals, perhaps, even as bad as those Muslims did during Imam Hussein's time.

The Imam and his companions fought until they were all martyred. Among those killed were two children of Imam Hassan, who were only eleven and thirteen years old; and a five-year old child and baby of Imam Hussein. The bodies of the martyrs were decapitated and denied burial.

For Imam Hussein, he was the essence of patience, because he was firm in his purpose, maintained his consciousness of Allah, and was guided by Allah to the straight path leading to his ultimate sacrifice to save Islam. What he left at Karbala was the example. And the very essence of that example was prayer. His perseverance in prayer at Karbala was the light that drew even some of the enemies to his side at that time. While Imam Hussein and his tiny contingent were in prayer, some of the opposition such as the well-known soldier, Hurr, was so drawn to the true believers that they crossed over and joined them.

It is important to understand that it was the prayer that Imam Hussein was safeguarding. He saw that Muslims were compromising their prayer. Make no mistake about this, the enemies at Karbala also prayed. But the prayers by the enemies were null and void. Can one pray and then proceed to murder the grandson of the Prophet Mohammad? No! So you see even prayer was distorted, and the reason was that the enemies lacked endurance in their prayer, and they had fallen from the straight path.

Imam Hussein's message is for people not to compromise Islam, and to realize that one's salvation is through the practice of endurance and prayer. The symbol of prayer was so dynamic and powerful that it was the means by which the continuation of the root of Imam Hussein followed. And that continuation was Imam Hussein's son, Imam Ali Zein al-Abideen. Seeking knowledge, understanding and wisdom, or striving towards prosperity and tranquility, cannot be meaningful without the security of the foundation of faith. That foundation is the prayer.

While it is important to seek knowledge and understanding, for example, these needs in Islam are nurtured in self-awareness once prayer is solidified. Imam Ali Zein al-Abideen was the leader of prayer, prostration and supplication, and he restored Islam by these means. It was Imam Ali Zein al-Abideen who continued the cause of Islam that his father had courageously died for. The Muslim world had to be reawakened to Islam, and it was Imam Ali Zein al-Abideen who successfully restored the Muslims back to the straight path. How he did this was by his example, and his example was prayer, the root essence of Islam. His numerous prayers and supplications are recorded in volumes of books, and they are the standard for all Muslims to follow.

The centuries following Imam Hussein's martyrdom saw Muslims time and time again compromising their Islamic values and ideals. Whether with the Umayyads, the Abbasids, or in contemporary times, we note that Islam for Muslims is being threatened throughout the world. Many Muslim countries, for example, grant fewer religious freedoms to their subjects than do leaders of Western nations. The problem here is deep-rooted; it is a problem of the Muslims themselves. In order to assimilate into the mainstream of a non-Islamic society, Muslims often feel it necessary to forego their Islamic traditions, lifestyles and behavior in order to be accepted by that society. These Muslims have fallen to the lowest form of degradation for they have substituted Islam for convenience and social compatibility.

Let us reflect on the martyrdom of Imam Hussein and learn from his example. What we learn is that Imam Hussein carried out the legacy of his grandfather, Prophet Mohammad. That legacy was that truth must prevail over evil, injustice, tyranny and deviation. That legacy was that faith must overcome disbelief. That legacy was that Muslims must fulfill all obligations.

Remember that Islam cannot be compromised. To know whether or not we have compromised Islam requires that we have knowledge of at least the basic fundamentals of Islam. This requires an understanding of what Islam is and what it is not. We must submit our will to Allah, become certain of our faith, believe in Imam Hussein's message, and accept the challenge that we will strive in the way of Allah to better ourselves as Muslims. We must be steadfast and actionable in our obligations to Islam. We must display the right attitude so that our faith can endure. We must let our behavior be one for others to follow, and above all we must be patient!

We should fulfill all obligations in order to strengthen our Islamic personality. Whether they are divine obligations in pleasing Allah as we pray and fast; or whether they are moral obligations such as avoiding backbiting and suspicion; or whether they are mutual obligations such as keeping the promise relative to a marriage contract; or whether they are tacit obligations such as empathy, gestures, intuitions, attitude and behavior; we should fulfill them by our remembrance of Allah and by our actions.

Developing a strong Islamic personality that is nurtured in the ideals of outer and inner cleanliness helps fulfill these obligations. It is not enough to just pray and fast. We have to make our prayers and fasting actionable by fulfilling all obligations. Each of us is responsible for fulfilling our own individual obligations by purifying ourselves and by creating a healthy body and mind so that the soul may return to Allah.

Trials of wealth; trials of power and authority; and trials of courage test our resolve. Whether they are the trials of ease or of hardship, only those who have understanding and whose hearts are filled with faith can remain steadfast. And the foundation for fulfilling our obligations is unity, and that is the message of Imam Hussein.

"And hold fast, altogether, by the Rope which Allah stretches out for you, and be not divided among yourselves...." (Qur'an 3:103)

CHAPTER 10: CONVERGENCE

"Ignorance is a disease and knowledge its cure."
(Tallal Turfe)

Leadership is much in need today in order for our Muslim community to flourish. For leadership there must be effective dialogue. The reality is that some of our Islamic societies are out of balance, as they are absorbed with the past and lack creative thinking on the issues we face today. To be sure there is dialogue between Islamic governments, between Muslim groups, and within the Muslim family. But we cannot have effective dialogue, unless we can identify our common goals and values. Here knowledge and education must triumph over ignorance. Much of the Islamic world has lost its way and became rigid, focusing on set patterns of thought that do not adequately address the problems of today.

Our energies are being engrossed in the confrontation of hostilities within the Muslim ranks. Muslims must start to unravel themselves from all types of inflexible spirituality whose features include intolerance and suspicion. Muslims must be conscious of the dangers of oversimplification that lead to complacency and impertinence for others. We must create collaboration between spiritual leaders and scholars. Islam is that which is in agreement with reality. Islam personifies purity and flexibility, responsibility and humility, justice and mercy. The problems we are confronted with cannot be resolved by anything less than a transformation in consciousness akin to the transformation that took place during the time of Prophet Mohammad. Perhaps this transformation of consciousness, this universality of courage and spirit, will be the consequence of the convergence of all Shi'as and Sunnis.

Muslim Identity
Broadened Understanding of Muslim Identity

This transformation of consciousness can be illustrated by delving into the Muslim identity. Seemingly, the traditional understanding of Muslim identity is limited to and measured by the frequency of attendance at religious functions, religious seminars, and fund-raising activities. Identity is heightened if one attends the congregational Friday Prayer, or if one fasts and prays, or if one performs a pilgrimage to Mecca, or if one contributes to charity. Too often we identify a Muslim because he says he is a Muslim.

There are many reasons why this is not enough. If the Muslim identity is to survive in the future, this traditional understanding has to be broadened. It is not enough for Muslim students to just be taught about Islam; they really need to catch the faith. What is needed is a reawakening of our school philosophy, to make it more profound, much deeper than the norm we witness today. The Muslim identity needs to permeate through every facet of a school's daily operations. Most importantly, the school's administration, faculty and staff must ardently and fervently accept their essential role as active teachers of the Qur'an and the *Sunnah* of Prophet Mohammad and his *Ahl al-Bayt*.

Our Muslim schools must infuse Islamic values into the content of all curriculum areas. A coordinated process is needed to implement these values. The end result is a genuine Muslim school with a genuine curriculum for its students.

Muslim Values in Action

There is unity of values in Islam. If the values are possessed in isolation, they are not really values any longer. For example, kindness without justice is softness. Justice without kindness is harsh. Honesty without kindness is insensitivity. Independence without kindness, justice and honesty is stagnant.

To begin with, let us choose a particular Muslim value to be taught at the school, for example, self-restraint. There is a common link between fasting and self-restraint. For example, fasting without self-restraint is weak. Self-restraint is heightened during the month of Ramadan, in which Muslims fast. Now how to relate this value of self-restraint during the month of Ramadan becomes a challenge. For instance, a school project would be to find ways to stimulate the value of self-restraint within the community so more Muslims would not only fast but be able to exercise self-restraint as well. Teachers find themselves unified toward a common goal of getting the community's acceptance, involvement, and support in this project. Some of the values that emanate from self-restraint are: courage; patience; faith; justice; and reconciliation.

Once the value of self-restraint is reviewed and studied, the teachers then put together resource materials. Quran'ic verses and supplications that relate to self-restraint are gathered and prepared for review. Stories, readings and articles relating to the value are gathered for assimilation into the teacher's course portfolio.

The next step in the process of infusing values is a faculty in-service. Each faculty member is given a reflection and prayer page with one or two Quran'ic passages that relate to the value of self-restraint and a few reflective questions seeking to evoke the teacher's thought about the value. From this, questions are developed as follows:

· What does the Qur'an and the supplications tell us about the particular Islamic value of self-restraint we are focusing upon? How is the Quran'ic understanding of this value different from the cultural perspective of this value?

· What does this value look like, sound like, and feel like when it is lived out?

· Relative to this value, what are the particular areas of strengths and weaknesses in our Islamic community? What are the underlying causes of these strengths and weaknesses?

· What can we do to foster or teach this value during the learning period in the school as well as within the family and community?

· How can the teacher infuse the value within the subject matter taught?

· What is our personal assessment of how we live this Islamic value?

Once the in-service processing is completed, the faculty now has the packet of resource materials that has been prepared. The faculty then integrates the value into their curriculum, with the purpose of teaching it to their students. For example, academic study takes deep thought and concentration on the part of the students. Here they can practice self-restraint in their study habits much like they practice self-restraint while fasting. Students who already perform the ritual of fasting have the rigor of concentration already infused within their persona. So the teacher plans the lesson on self-restraint and draws upon the fasting experience of the students to understand and absorb the value. Similarly, values such as courage, love and hope can also be taught and experienced.

The next step is to create reinforcements of the value. Visuals and computers can help highlight the value in focus. It is the responsibility of the school's administrators and faculty to make sure that the value is included in their activities, such as prayer. Reinforcement can also take place during parent-teacher conferences, by getting the parents to participate in enhancing the practice of the value at home. The final step is one of evaluation. Changes may need to be made for improving the approach and implementing the value.

Still other values can be infused within the student's persona. For example, during the first ten days (Ashura) of the month of Muharram, students can work together in unity by role-playing what took place at that time. They can work together on portraying the event and the importance of the value of justice. By working together they learn a great deal about many virtues, for example, justice, freedom and responsibility. Still another student project could be to take verses from the Qur'an relative to the creation, and then to explore together the marvels of nature. For example, the following verse from the Qur'an could be the basis for such a student project:

"Do they not observe the birds above them, spreading their wings and folding them in? None can uphold them except Allah Most Gracious: truly it is He that watches over all things." (Qur'an 67:19)

Students can take a field trip to the zoo and observe the activities of birds. Or they can go on a camping trip and spend several days in a forest studying the habitat of birds. While there, the students can pray together and work together and receive mutual gratification for their efforts. This rich and rewarding experience heightens the importance of unity.

Empowerment

The amazing feats of empowerment performed by Prophet Mohammad are the greatest manifestation of Divine Power, because Prophet Mohammad was the highest and most complete example that Allah sent. Today, we are striving to integrate Islam and Muslims in the society through community empowerment and outreach. The focus has been on the development of the Muslim character, and the top priority is to work with the youth, for example, activities such as camps, conferences, workshops and publications.

The Muslim identity is heightened when community empowerment is achieved. Action empowers Muslims to act for the welfare of the Muslim society. By empowerment, Islam does not mean to do one's own thing. Such action will not be effective if done without organized effort. The youth are given opportunities to develop mastery of skills, competency, and purpose in their lives to positively impact environments. Adults join together to support the youth during emotional moments. Boundaries and expectations are achieved when the youth have opportunities to engage in meaningful dialogue with adults to establish clear understanding. For example, the concept of unity is empowered by enforcing shared values and a common language between the adults and youth during the turbulent times of adolescence. The youth are then able to empower their own guidelines to work together for the common good of all.

Shared Values

The pillars of Islam define the basic identity of the Muslims – their faith, beliefs and practices – and bind together a worldwide community of believers into a fellowship of shared values and concerns. Frequently parents are worried about their children as to whether they are in some kind of trouble or are concealing their problems. Parents are usually kept in the dark as to how their children truly feel about themselves. Does their children seem lethargic, discourteous or lackadaisical? What have parents done to help their children's feelings grow and mature? To begin with, there needs to be family support. Work is cut out for parents, as they need to make sure that all is well at home, at school, in religious and social activities, and even in the children's minds. It is exhausting, yet necessary, for parents to ascertain how their children feel about themselves and how they treat others. Equally important is what their children expect out of life.

With shared values, both parents and children have a clearer understanding of what is expected on both sides. Shared values give rise to a unified family structure. Both parents and children make a list of the values that are most important to them. Both lists are shared with each other, and the criteria are established by which reward and punishment is enforced. Parents need to model their values for their children. If parents want their children to get involved, then parents must also get involved. For example, if parents are requiring their children to be honest, kind and understanding, then the parents must also be honest, kind and under-standing. Parents also need to share their family history with their children so as to embrace family traditions. In addition, parents need to exchange dialogue with their children on religious matters, and to underscore the importance of teaching Islamic ethics and morality.

There is a link rooted in Islam that unites the Muslim community, and this link is formed through shared values, beliefs and principles. It is based on integration and assimilation that should reduce the distance between Muslim communities. It will pave the way for understanding and empathy among the many diverse cultures and ethnic groups in Islam. This is why shared values should be incorporated very early in the school curriculum. In addition, the religious institutions should become the champions of shared values, and their leaders need to talk with passion about shared values embodied in Islam.

Ethics and Morality

Shared values require that we deal with each other at the highest level of ethics and morality. Ethics is the science that explains the process of values and why conduct is considered either good or bad, right or wrong. With ethics, we are better able to explain why we make the choices we do. The basis of unity in the Muslim community is to be cemented in ethics, as we strive towards fulfilling our moral obligations. We must learn to trust one another, if unity of the Muslim community is to be achieved. And that attainment can only come about if we practice ethics and sustain high moral standards.

Eternal moral values and principles are applicable everywhere, such as the *Ten Commandments* or the natural law of the Universe. Good consequences flow from good actions and bad consequences flow from bad actions. The judgment of good or bad is based upon the result or consequence of the act rather than the act itself. These acts are performed by man under the impact of certain sentiments and not necessarily with the intention of benefit. Acts performed at the instance of moral conscience are called acts of moral goodness.

Brotherhood and Solidarity

Unity in diversity is the cornerstone of brotherhood and solidarity, which are very important attributes in Islam. There are verses in the Qur'an that underscore the importance of brotherhood and solidarity, conveying the message that all believers are brothers. *Aqidah* is a term in Islam that relates to the firm creed that one's heart is fixed upon without any wavering or doubt. *Aqidah* excludes any supposition, doubt or suspicion. *Aqidah* is derived from the term *aqada*. We hear often one say "*aqada the rope*," which means the rope is tied firmly. In the concept of the *Rope of Allah*, we tie ourselves firmly to its strands in order to achieve ultimate unity within ourselves. *Aqidah* is a basic ingredient of brotherhood, for Muslims strive in the way of Islam with similar struggles and goals. Extending this thought on the macro community level, *aqidah* translates into solidarity.[20]

Holding firmly to the *Rope of Allah* takes a great deal of concentration and effort. Prophet Mohammad spent a great deal of time in Mecca transforming the community from one of ignorance to one of education and enlightenment. He taught his companions about faith (*iman*) first and then the Qur'an. The Prophet had to educate his companions on the principle of faith in order to change their beliefs to the straight path. So the companions of the Prophet first learned faith, then the Qur'an, and then their faith was increased manifold. In brotherhood and solidarity, the hearts of the believers must be firm by submitting and implementing the pillars of the Islamic faith. With the first obligation being faith, the path towards attainment of faith is knowledge. The Qur'an is the revelation and the source of faith and knowledge.

We witness communities being infected by ignorance, envy, egotism and ambition. These aspects are threats to achieving unity among the believers. In striving for unity in the community, we must be cautious and cognizant of these threats. We must stand on firm ground in thwarting off these threats and making the community a safe haven. Believers must address each other in the best possible manner in order to cement the solidarity. In many societies, we find people who want to obtain supremacy over others and establish themselves as leaders with a higher status. These people try to use coercive means by which to attain their supremacy, and as a result weaken their faith and trust in that community. Believers must guard themselves against such aggressive ambition and strive for reassurance within themselves as true believers unaffected by irrational behavior.

We find in Muslim societies believers promoting competitive tactics in order to achieve supremacy of their Islamic institution over other Islamic institutions in the same community. Competition breeds distrust, suspicion and disunity. Competition severely harms brotherhood. Competition damages the soul and leads to moral decay. Rather than competition in a community over the same Islamic objectives, believers should seek complementation and cooperation with one another. Believers must be compassionate toward one another. The bond of brotherhood and solidarity is built on *aqidah*, the principle that enlightens the soul.

"The believers are but a single brotherhood: so make peace and reconciliation between your two contending brothers; and fear Allah, that ye may receive Mercy." (Qur'an 49:10)

The enforcement of Muslim brotherhood is the greatest social ideal of Islam. And it is Islam that is the link that connects all creatures into a single unit. We must search within ourselves to discover our creative intelligence and rid ourselves of indifference and ignorance, as we strive for brotherhood and solidarity. Islam is the perfection and completion of all Abrahamic faiths. Islam asserts the Unity and Universal Divinity of Allah and seeks to bring together people of all races and creeds into a single unit of brotherhood. The Islamic belief in the unity of mankind is the consequence of the doctrine of the Unity of Allah.

Intrafaith Dialogue

Following the death of Prophet Mohammad, disputes took place as to who would be his successor as Caliph. The aim of the author is not to examine the myriads of disputes over this issue and others that emerged over time between the two main philosophies: (a) Sunni and (b) Shi'a. The many sects or factions that surfaced from these philosophies were not the result of differences of opinion relative to the issue of succession to the Caliphate but, rather, theoretical and theological differences as well as jurisdictional and practical disagreements. Over the centuries these disputes became greater and greater in magnitude to the point where division within the Muslim community has become widespread and endemic. In addition, Muslims today say they adhere to a particular school of thought, but in a number of instances they are following the interpretations of other schools of thought without even knowing it. It is not the intent of the author to give a detailed accounting of the philosophies of these schools of thought or to dwell on their differences. Rather, we will explore that which leads us towards unity based on common ground and common principles.

Common Ground – Common Principle

It is accepted that in contemporary times there are among the Shi'a scholars and Sunni scholars highly intellectual personalities. It is also known that in the 21st Century there is great enmity towards Islam and opposition to it by many forces. The influence of Western society has already infiltrated into the communities of the fragmented Islamic world. Those who wish to see Islam tarnished are hostile and belligerent towards Muslims throughout the world. Therefore, it is essential that Muslim scholars and leaders come together and stop quarrelling over disputes. Muslims must come together much the same way as Christians and Jews have come together in each of their respective faiths. Christians, who once fought and killed each other, are now standing together under the Assembly of World Churches. Jews, with their numerous disagreements amongst themselves, have come together when danger faces them. Likewise, Muslims must find the common link to unity by keeping the doors open between the different schools of thought.

While there will be differences in opinion and interpretations of Islam, we need to avoid discord within the Muslim community. While there is diversity in various Islamic schools of thought, there can be convergence towards common agreement on many issues. When dialogue on Islamic issues takes place, all parties in the discussion should proceed from the point of harmony. There is commonality among issues with the Muslim world, and we should build our alliance upon these agreements. We are all part and parcel of the great Islamic culture and civilization, and we should strive to keep ourselves within the circle of Islam. Only by achieving unity within the Muslim world can we thwart off the evils of oppression and colonialism.

Manifestations of Unity

There have been strides made to bring about that common link. Currently there are organizations that have been established for the purpose of bringing about unity between Sunnis and Shi'as. Some of these organizations are listed below:

· *Islamic Conference on Islamic Unity*: This organization is holding its 16th Conference in Tehran, Iran in the year 2003.[21] It consists of scholars and researchers interested in *"Islamic Unity"* and *"Proximity of Islamic Schools of Thought"* to participate in scientific and cultural dialogue by contributing papers on a number of topics, some of which are:

§ Universality of Islam, which includes a common Islamic identity, solidarity and brotherhood, and cultural diversity among Islamic nations.

§ Globalization, which includes a united and stable stance, and the duty of Muslim thinkers and intellectuals of Islamic sects in tackling issues.

The objective of the Islamic Conference on Islamic Unity is to unify Muslims, irrespective of their school of thought. In addition, the goal of the Conference is to underline the importance of unity between Muslims and to strengthen solidarity among the Islamic states in order to withstand the challenges the Islamic world faces. Furthermore, the Conference will deal with Islamic issues in various parts of the world. Its purpose is to bring together Islamic sects to engage in effective dialogue to find the means to eliminate certain differences for the interests of the Islamic states and their causes, and to be able to take their due position in the world.

The participants are trying to jointly find shared solutions on much needed projects dealing with the social, cultural and intellectual problems that the Islamic community is faced with. One such project is to work together to effectively utilize the tool of Islamic Shari'a towards addressing today's critical requirements of Muslims throughout the world. For example, the threat and invasion of Western powers on Islamic communities globally has put a strain on Muslims to find the means to protect themselves and to maintain their identity.

By working together, these Islamic intellectuals can communicate more effectively to the West and the rest of the world what

Islam is and what it is not. That Islam is a religion of peace and tolerance and respect for other faiths, and that Islam is against violence and aggression. As hostility against the Muslim community continues at an accelerated pace, Muslim societies have turned to Islam as a final answer to their dilemma and needs. For this reason, the Conference participants believe that they have no alternative but to be unified on all fronts in order to survive.

Additionally, scholars and intellectuals also address the root of the social and cultural problems of the Islamic communities in order to formulate strategies that would lead to strengthening the Islamic values and principles. Their goal is to convince these communities that unity among Muslims is the only salvation from the onslaught of hostility and aggression perpetrated against Islam. These scholars and intellectuals are truly committed to eliminating many of the obstacles in the way of achieving a united Muslim community, while at the same strengthening their shared ethical, religious and cultural beliefs.[22]

· _The Organization of the Islamic Conference (OIC)_: The OIC is an international group of 57 states that have pooled their resources together, combined their efforts, and speak with one voice to safeguard the interests and secure the progress and well being of their peoples and of all Muslims in the world. The OIC was established in Rabat, Morocco in the year 1969, as a result of the burning of al-Aqsa Mosque in Jerusalem.

Among its purposes are to strengthen the Islamic solidarity among Muslim states and to cooperate in the political, economic, social, cultural and scientific fields. The objective of the OIC is to embrace openness, progress and dialogue in order to revitalize the Islamic _Ummah_. In addition, there is the need for Muslims to emphasize the civilized and tolerant message of Islam, which has been tarnished around the world by an unfortunate fear of Islam.[23] The member nations of the OIC needs to strengthen their commitment to their own objectives and charters. There must be follow up, consensus and spirit in order to implement the goals of the OIC. Mutual cooperation and collaboration among the member nations of the OIC must be profound and unified.

For all Muslims, successful dialogue will create value. The failure of dialogue will, without exception, hasten the downfall or collapse of all concerned. In a Muslim society, the absence of dialogue implies the absence of value creation. Obviously, one party alone cannot establish dialogue. It comes about when parties who have differing standpoints, who are each characterized by self-awareness and autonomy, and who each understand the significance and value of dialogue itself, engage in trusting disclosure and exchange of the values of information that they possess.

Such is the case with the Shi'a and Sunni communities. If both parties share an active desire for the creation of value, even greater results can be expected. Dialogue pulls together all sorts of issues and problems having a human theme, and provides effective starting points or scenarios at radically altered levels for the solution of major difficulties. For unity to be achieved, this phenomenon is literally an historic inevitability, and cannot be circumvented by the Muslim community.

Effective dialogue must focus on the unity of the *Ummah* (Muslim Community), not simply a segment of it. Dialogue must be pursued through intellectual discussion and action programs that bring adherents of Islamic sects together for the purpose of facing those things that socially, educationally, morally and culturally challenge their beliefs and principles. What brings these adherents together is establishing a foundation whereby they can coexist for the purpose of engendering mutual concerns and endeavors irrespective of their religious differences. Dialogue is aimed at recognizing the social and developmental problems that confront all Muslims in the society. Muslims must get to know one another by fostering mutual respect, building strong relationships, and rectifying the stereotypes that give escalate widespread hostility and suspicion.

Dialogue avoids provocative discussion by stimulating intellectual and ethical integrity, which requires a prudent assessment of the indistinct images each side has drawn from the other. Rather than attempting to unify the religious sects into a singular sect, dialogue endeavors to strengthen the *Ummah* by bringing about respect for each other. Dialogue does not call for resolving which sect is better nor does it presume that one sect must yield on any point of belief or principle. Dialogue is an opportunity for Muslims to focus on common issues and challenges, as they unite in an awareness of mutual solidarity and shared destiny.

In order for effective dialogue to work, we must understand that the current atmosphere of conflict and discord between various Islamic sects is unproductive. Each Islamic sect has built its beliefs and principles that date back more than a thousand years. Neither sect can dominate the other. Sunnis and Shi'as cannot impose their doctrines upon each other. It is neither possible nor practical to ignore the different sects in Islam or to attempt to eliminate their long-standing disagreements.

Muslims need to be supportive and cooperative in order for a singular and absolute intellectual condition to succeed. The model of an ideal integrated Muslim community is analogous to the recognition of the perfect union of the Universe. This will allow them to overcome differences of opinions, to share goals, to overcome conflicts of interest, to realize mutual cooperation, and to engage in the creation of value. Muslims must realize that unity requires establishing trust with others Muslims, irrespective of which school of thought they adhere to. Once this is understood and trust pervades in the hearts and minds of Muslims, they are much more likely to strive for unity, overcoming all social barriers and constraints.

At the root of this brotherhood is Islam. Islam forms the basis of society and it must remain under the banner of Allah, to be ruled by His Commandments. It must enjoin to righteousness and prohibit evil. Its edict is *jihad* (struggle); its path is the call to Allah; and the Qur'an and the *Sunnah* of Prophet Mohammad and his *Ahl al-Bayt* guide its life. The strong among the Muslims are mild until their right is denied them, and the meek among them are mighty once they are wronged. They are allied to Allah, to His Messenger and to the believers. Their anger and indignation are for those who pursue disintegration, animosity and discord. They struggle to win over the faith. Islam is based on concord and unity and scowls upon division among Muslims. Those who engage in mutual love, mercy and affection are good examples of unified Muslims. Allah wishes for us to unite on the basis of truth and justice. While Islam is the vehicle to unite the people, the Muslim leadership today must do more to bind that unity.

Agreement Among Muslims

Jurisprudence (*fiqh*) is the science of the branches of religion. The majority of Sunnis follow any one of four major schools of thought on jurisprudence: Abu Hanifah, Malek Ibn Anas, al-Shafei, or Ahmad Ibn Mohammad Hanbal. The majority of Shi'as follow the school of thought of Imam Ja'far as-Sadiq. It was Imam Ja'far as-Sadiq, the Sixth Imam of the Twelve Imams espoused by Shi'as, who was the most celebrated of all scholars. Each of these renowned scholars gained many students who continued their work in Islamic law. They taught their students who in turn taught other students. Two of the most celebrated Sunni scholars, Abu Hanifah and Malek Ibn Anas, who each founded a school of thought, were in fact students of Imam Ja'far as-Sadiq. Moreover, al-Shafei was a student of Malik Ibn Anas and Ahmad Ibn Mohammad Hanbal was a student of al-Shafei. While there are differences of opinion between the five major schools of thought on some issues, however, they agree on many other issues.

To achieve a just and lasting unity does not mean that all schools of thought should adhere to just one school. It does not mean that unity should be based only on similarities and not differences. To pursue such a course of action is neither logical nor practical. For the sake of unity, there is no need for Muslims to make any compromise on the primary or secondary principles of their school of thought. By Islamic unity, we mean that Muslims should unite, if for anything else, to safeguard themselves against a common foe – those who wish to tarnish and destroy Islam. To bring about unity Muslims must be committed in spirit and mind and heart to succeed. There is a common denominator between Sunnis and Shi'as. Just to mention a few beliefs and practices, Sunnis and Shi'as agree on the following:

· The belief in the *tawhid* (Oneness of Allah) and Prophet Mohammad as the Final Messenger.

· The belief in the Angels, Prophets, Books of Allah, and the Hereafter.

· The core fundamentals of Islam, such as the declaration of faith, prayer, fasting, pilgrimage, and charity. However, within each of these fundamentals the scholar may exercise his interpretation according to the methodology of the school of thought being followed.

· The Ka'bah is their *qiblah* (direction of prayer).

· They read the same Qur'an, and they basically worship the same.

· They have similar ways of rearing their children and burying their dead.

In addition, Sunnis and Shi'as agree on the following:

·   The *Ummah* (Muslim Community) is a single nation of many countries with diverse cultures and different languages.

·   The *Ummah* is of numerous nationalities and tribes that share the same kind of civilization and follow the one faith of Islam.

·   The *Ummah* adheres to the *shari'ah* (Divine law) that does not change over time, although jurisprudence within that structure is subject to interpretation by the various schools of thought.

What Muslims need to do is to avoid insulting and accusing one another. In addition, they need to forego ridiculing the logic of one another, and they should abstain from hurting each other. Furthermore, saying repulsive things about the Prophet's companions should cease and desist.

In 1959, Sheikh Mahmoud Shaltout, Head of the School of Theology at al-Azhar University in Cairo, Egypt, issued a verdict recognizing the legitimacy of the Imam Ja'far as-Sadiq school of thought. In addition, Sheikh Shaltout stated that there are eight schools of Islamic thought. In addition to the five already mentioned above, he added three more: Abadi, Zaydi, and Dhahiri.[24] What is interesting is that this declaration by Sheikh Shaltout has remained unchanged, as it is still in effect today.

Beacon of Unity – Imam Ali

Another major agreement among the schools of thought is the leadership of Imam Ali. Imam Ali was born in the Sacred House (*Ka'bah*) in Mecca in the year 600 A.D. No one before or after him has ever been born in the House of Allah. He was the son of Abi Talib and Fatima. Both Imam Ali and Prophet Mohammad belonged to the same clan, Bani Hashim, and they were first cousins. Their fathers were brothers. As a child, Prophet Mohammad raised Imam Ali. Under the delicate care and education of Prophet Mohammad, Imam Ali attained nobility and respect. Imam Ali was the first male whom the Prophet summoned to Islam and who answered positively. He married Fatima, the daughter of Prophet Mohammad, and they had children two of who were Imam Hassan and Imam Hussein. He was martyred at the age of 63 during the month of Ramadan.

Sunni and Shi'a scholars agree completely on the following: (a) no one can match the loyalty to Prophet Mohammad as Imam Ali displayed; (b) he shared with the Prophet the persecutions, abuse and adversities; (c) he protected and safeguarded the Prophet against the polytheists and struggled with him against the unbelievers; and (d) he defended and shielded the Prophet with his own life from the enemies of Islam. Further, it is the consensus of the scholars that the following verse is attributed to Imam Ali:

"And there is the type of man who gives his life to earn the Pleasure of Allah; and Allah is full of Kindness to (His) devotees." (Qur'an 2:207)

This verse relates to the time when Imam Ali slept in the bed of Prophet Mohammad when the Prophet had to migrate from Mecca to Medina. Imam Ali offered himself to take the place of the Prophet by sleeping in his bed, even though the enemies of Islam came to kill the Prophet thinking he was in the bed. Imam Ali was ready to give his own life in order to safeguard the life of the Prophet. Here was a man who was willing to risk his own life to save Islam. His will and courage to sleep under the swords of the enemies further illustrates the courage and nobility of this great Imam. He never hesitated to give his life for the promotion of Islam.

We find yet another verse, of many verses, in the Qur'an that is attributed to Imam Ali, as confirmed by Sunni and Shi'a scholars:

"He grants wisdom to whom He pleases; and he to whom wisdom is granted receives indeed a benefit overflowing; but none will grasp the Message but men of understanding." (Qur'an 2:269)

In this verse the word *"wisdom"* implies the best knowledge seeking to act with fullness and soundness of one's own conscience. Imam Ali derived his vast knowledge and eloquence by virtue of his long and close relationship with Prophet Mohammad. With Divine inspiration, the Prophet was the source of all such knowledge and wisdom, and he taught Imam Ali these virtues. These gifts of wisdom and knowledge were bestowed upon the divinely chosen and purified ones, as revealed in the following verse:

"...And Allah only wishes to remove all abomination from you, ye Members of the Family, and to make you pure and spotless." (Qur'an 33:33)

Sunni and Shi'a scholars are in agreement that this verse was dedicated to Prophet Mohammad and his *Ahl al-Bayt* (Household), which include Imam Ali, Fatima, Imam Hassan and Imam Hussein. Yet, another verse was descended about Imam Ali, and it is these scholars that are unanimous in agreement:

"Your (real) friends are (no less than) Allah, His Messenger, and the (Fellowship of) Believers, - those who establish regular prayers and regular charity, and they bow down humbly (in worship). As to those who turn (for friendship) to Allah, His Messenger, and the (Fellowship of) Believers, - it is the Fellowship of Allah that must certainly triumph." (Qur'an 5:55-56)

The Sunni and Shi'a scholars agree that Imam Ali gave away in charity his ring while he was in a state of kneeling in his prayer. It was Imam Ali who more than anyone else resembled the Prophet with respect to his spiritual qualities, knowledge, devotion and insight.

Authority of Imam Ali

How we reconnect to the ideal Islamic community is to follow the example of Imam Ali. We need to cling to the attitude and behavior of Imam Ali, who sacrificed a great deal for the sanctity and unity of the Islamic community.

At Ghadir Khumm, Prophet Mohammad recited the following verse from the Qur'an:

"...This day have I perfected your religion for you, completed My Favor upon you, and have chosen for you Islam as your religion...." (Qur'an 5:3)

Allah perfected and completed Islam by revealing this verse towards the conclusion of the ministry of Prophet Mohammad. Sunni and Shi'a authorities are unanimous that this verse was revealed at Ghadir Khumm when the Prophet declared Imam Ali as his immediate successor and *wilayat* (authority):

"For whomever I am the authority and guide Ali is also his guide and authority. O Allah! Be friendly with the friends of Ali and the enemy of his enemies. Whoever helps, help him, and whoever leaves him, leave him."

The *wilayat* of Imam Ali is well accepted by all Islamic schools of thought but with different interpretations as to the declaration made by Prophet Mohammad at Ghadir Khumm. *Wilayat* means power, authority, or a right of a certain kind. It is authority invested in Prophet Mohammad and the *Ahl al-Bayt* as Allah's representatives. This authority is irrevocable and universal in nature, and it covers all aspects of spiritual and socio-political guidance.

Rather than cause division among the Muslims during his time, Imam Ali supported the leadership in the name of unity. Imam

Ali knew that the higher cause was to breed accord and not discord. He knew that by taking the position of the rightful leadership of the Muslim world by waging war, after the death of Prophet Mohammad, would have destroyed Islam. Since Imam Ali married from among the companions of Prophet Mohammad, he set the example of brotherhood. Even some of Imam Ali's children bear the names of Prophet Mohammad's companions. We should follow his example. Muslims agree more on Islamic ideals than they disagree. In fact, disagreement is so miniscule in terms of the number of Islamic principles and rulings that it is a wonder why unity in diversity has not yet been achieved. Vision without action is a dream. Action without vision is tedious and wasteful. Vision with action can transform the world. Both vision and action were manifested in Imam Ali.

All over the world, societies are undergoing transformation more rapidly than ever before. In the process, the role of Islam in public and private life is being questioned. Some Muslims promote the secularization of society. Others, alarmed at the pace and scope of change, are reemphasizing basic Islamic values and practices. The common linkage for Sunnis and Shi'as is Imam Ali, who was not only the symbol of truth but the manifestation of it as well.

Interfaith Dialogue
Faith-Based Initiatives

All faiths have instilled in their religious creed the concept of reconciliation. In their mutual social idyllic of peace, the Abrahamic faiths propose a peace that is one of justice, tolerance and respect for one another. Each adheres to the concept of the One Benevolent and Merciful God.

Faith-based initiatives are moving towards a better understanding among the Abrahamic faiths by exchanging ideas and focusing on similarities. These initiatives have made strides towards reconciliation by way of interfaith dialogue. In America and Europe, for example, there are a number of interfaith organizations, each with the mission of building bridges between religious groups. Their focus is one of conflict resolution, education and advocacy. Their focus is further heightened when they collectively address the bigger issues of mankind, for example, wars and natural disasters.

Wars and Natural Disasters

Today, the world is on the brink of nuclear obliteration. Several nations of the world possess weapons of mass destruction that can turn the Earth into a burned-out cinder. Wars are products of human failure and a violation of human and social nature. If it involves weapons of mass destruction, such as nuclear, biological or chemical, global wars present a serious threat to human survival. Human survival depends on increasing the effectiveness of peace groups, for example those funded by governments such as the United Nations and those driven by grassroots organizations.

Back in 1945, the United States detonated atomic bombs over Hiroshima and Nagasaki, Japan. The impact of these detonations was too horrible to fathom. For the first time in the history of our world, we witnessed the frightening potential to destroy all human life. Weapons have grown far more powerful and threatening since World War II. Besides the United States and Russia, at least five other nations have nuclear weapons: Britain, France, China, India and Pakistan. Other nations are actively pursuing nuclear warheads and delivery systems. The nuclear menace remains the most obvious threat to human survival.

While the nuclear threat is real, there are threats such as natural disasters. In addition to chemical, biological and conventional weapons, there is the threat of environmental destruction. Environmental conditions are rapidly worsening, for example, air, soil and water pollution are major threats to human health and even life. Diseases, such as AIDS (Acquired Immune Deficiency Syndrome) and Elboa, are endemic. Increasing soil depletion, water shortages, drought and social unrest raise the phantom of dreadful famines that could be imminent. Earthquakes, hurricanes, typhoons, floods and tornadoes take thousands of lives every year. Even the threat of asteroids and meteors presents a grave and deleterious situation.

The world is divided between the rich and the poor, and throughout history this divide caused great social upheavals. Poverty is already claiming many victims, as millions are starving daily. The irony is that while there is currently enough food to feed over six billion people daily, food supplies are scarcely reaching the poor and afflicted. This situation is further exacerbated by the fact that millions of people do not even have clean water for drinking.

Faith-based communities have stepped up to the challenge of counteracting poverty, for example, by providing services in health care and education. Today, faith-based communities must do even more. We need leaders from all religions to coalesce together to find the means to counteract not only poverty but war as well. There must be unification between the religious leaders and the political leaders of the world to effectively implement peace and stability.

While we can most assuredly learn from the past, however, the requirements and conditions of former periods have changed. That which was pertinent to human needs during the early history of mankind could neither meet nor fulfill the requirements of this day and age of modernization and consumption. Man must now become instilled with innovative qualities and powers, ethics and capabilities. To be sure, humanity is witnessing a reformation and a restructuring of the world order. For example, the laws of former governments and civilizations are in process of revision. In addition, advancement in technology and scientific breakthroughs are encountering a new scope of phenomena. Furthermore, we are unraveling the mysteries of the Universe with new inventions and discoveries.

In developing strategies for confronting and replacing political and social upheavals and wars, it is not sufficient to stipulate only what should be done. Without question, it is comparatively simple to identify preferred objectives and developments. For example, it would be wonderful to have effective disarmament treaties, improved procedures for preventing the propagation of weapons of mass destruction capabilities, more peace initiatives and education about the dangers of violence, terrorism and aggression, and more progress towards economic justice and political freedom. Unless a radical change in how institutions address the evils of wars is effectuated, there can only be a glimmer of hope in achieving these goals. A solution may be for political and social institutions to build upon the concept of nonviolence. Nonviolent action is a tool that can be practiced by all members of a society. Educating our communities about the effect of nonviolence is a movement in the right direction for both peace and stability. Effective leaders will gather and build upon the differences of their constituents, while ineffective leaders will utilize the differences to make division among their constituents.

We must find ways to penetrate the societies of these super-powers and nations with weapons of mass destruction in order to educate the masses about the importance of human survival. Religious and political leaders as well as scholars must be willing to work together for the sake of humanity and survival. Education and intellectual discourse as well as nonviolence are the vehicles for open and candid discussion. In fact, it was the *jihad* (struggle) of the intellect that Prophet Mohammad employed as a mechanism to bring the people of Mecca together to exchange in dialogue. Instead of war, Prophet Mohammad opted for dialogue to bring about peace. Today, we also need to implement the *jihad* of the intellect, as we seek the means for effective dialogue among the leaders of the nations of the world. It is no longer a matter of which religion is better or which political system is more practical but, rather, a question of mere survival. One such organization that has taken the initiative towards finding the means for peace and stability is The Millennium World Peace Summit.

The Millennium World Peace Summit

In August 2000, the United Nations hosted a one-week Millennium World Peace Summit of Religious and Spiritual Leaders from around the world. This event took place in New York, and United Nations Secretary-General Kofi Annan chaired it. The Honorary Chair was Ted Turner, a philanthropist who donated $1 billion dollars to a new foundation established to help support the United Nations. This was the first time in the history of the United Nations that such an event took place. I was selected among the world's 200 recognized religious and spiritual leaders from over 50 countries. The United Nations hosted the political leaders of the world the following week. All participants in both groups signed a Declaration of World Peace.

According to Bawa Jain, Secretary-General of the Millennium World Peace Summit, *"…we will be exploring how our religious and political institutions can work in partnership to secure greater peace, restore the integrity of the environment and end the desperation of poverty. In our coming together, let us offer our religious and spiritual resources in a spirit of cooperation and harmony, believing that our combined voices will have greater impact than our voices individually. Let us come committed to helping our communities break down barriers and build bonds of trust and goodwill. Let us come committed to action and to devoting our prayer energy to the success of these actions. Let this Summit be the beginning of our efforts to strengthen the work of the United Nations across the globe and to bring greater spiritual leadership to its endeavors."*

Spiritual leaders of every faith group in the world were present at the Summit. The participants made presentations, and the global media conducted interviews. The format for the Summit was as follows:

· A Call to Dialogue
· The Role of Religion in Conflict Transformation
· Towards Forgiveness and Reconciliation
· Ending the Violence of Poverty and Environmental Degradation

Advances in communications technology offer an opportunity for religions to work together across national and geographical boundaries. Unity in diversity was the underlying theme of the Summit, and global religious factions celebrated their differences as windows of opportunities to work together in peace and harmony. In many regions of the world, there is increased dialogue among leaders of different faiths. Finding solutions to global problems as well as regional conflicts is falling to the United Nations, which has had since its inception strong spiritual underpinnings. At the Summit, the religious leaders discussed how to harness the power of religious tolerance and spiritual faith to educate and mobilize their communities to focus on reducing divisions and ancient antipathies. Expected outcomes of the Summit were:

· Identifying early warning signs where conflict could erupt; alerting local, national and regional authorities; and suggesting actions that might prevent potential conflicts.
· Working to resolve conflicts after they have erupted by consulting with United Nations' officials, regional religious and spiritual leaders, political leaders and local grassroots organizations.
· Providing advice on the healing process after conflict has been halted and recommending steps to ensure that peace is sustained.

There were a number of criteria that governed the selection of participants:

· Persons who occupy the highest position in major religious institutions.

· Leaders who are acknowledged by the religious community concerned.

· Preeminent religious thinker, theologian, philosopher or scholar; leader of an important grassroots movement; person advanced in contemplative practices, an illuminated mystic; remarkable charismatic personality; and Nobel Peace Laureates.

The Summit was a great success and a necessary step towards cooperation and collaboration among the global religious and spiritual groups. My participation played an important role at the Summit, as I was able to articulate the numerous interfaith achievements by the Islamic institutions in our community during my one-hour interview and presentation remarks. My wife, Hajjah Neemat Turfe, made a major impact on the floor of the Summit as she reminded a dissident that the Summit was a forum for peace and reconciliation and not for argument and dissention. She received a resounding applause, and her effort was aired on CNN television.

World Council of Religious Leaders

In May 2003, the World Council of Religious Leaders in co-sponsorship with the Global Ethics Resource Center, Touro College Law School, and Fordham University Law School held a global conference at the United Nations headquarters in New York. The purpose of the conference was to review and analyze the use of religion to incite for violence within the context of contemporary human rights and humanitarian laws. In addition, the aim of the conference was to fill the gap in international law by pointing out the need for a resolution to be passed to include the use of religion to incite for violence and terrorism as a *crime against humanity.* The topics covered were:

· Religious perspectives on violence and terrorism.

· The impact of religion on populations and its tremendous potential to shape attitudes and human behavior.

· Historical and contemporary review of the use of religion for the incitement to violence and terrorism.

· Review and analysis of contemporary conflicts in Europe, the Middle East, Africa, and Asia and the threat to peace that results from the use of religion to incite for violence and terrorism.

· Identification of the human rights and humanitarian laws violated by those who use religion to incite for violence and terrorism.

· Categorization of the use of religion to incite for terrorism, as a form of terrorism, constituting a *"crime against humanity"* under international law.

· Explore ways for the adoption of a draft resolution to present to the United Nations.

The conference was open to United Nations diplomats and staff as well as invited distinguished international jurists and public figures. The conference was apolitical as it aimed to take a major and essential step in filling the gap in international law and to restore peace, security, understanding and prosperity among the peoples of different faiths and cultures around the world. I made a presentation (see Appendix), and it was said *"his participation as a guest speaker was crucial to the success of the conference and its ultimate goal in achieving lasting peace and security in the world."*

Global Ethics Initiative

In August 2003, I became a member of the International Council of the Millennium World Peace Summit Global Ethics Initiative. The Global Ethics Initiative has been created to facilitate the implementation of the goals envisaged in the Millennium World Peace Summit of Religious and Spiritual Leaders *Commitment to Global Peace*. The Global Ethics Initiative will advance and promote the achievement of peace, the protection of children and the environment, and the promotion of ethics in all walks of life. The Council is comprised of a small number of global humanitarian leaders some of whom are Nobel Peace Prize winners, former Presidents of countries, educators, entertainers, religious clerics and business entrepreneurs.

The Global Ethics Initiative was created to facilitate the implementation of the goals envisaged in the Millennium World Peace Summit of Religious and Spiritual Leaders *Commitment to Global Peace*. The Global Ethics Initiative will harness the extraordinary force and diversity of world religions to address the growing body of universally shared norms and values within the context of *global ethics* and provide the resources required to implement the goals set forth in the *Commitment to Global Peace*. Topics that will be addressed on the global agenda are: (a) sustainable development; (b) eradication of poverty; (c) global peace and security; (d) respect for minorities and vulnerable groups (children, women, and refugees); (e) protection of animal, human rights, bioethics, development ethics, business ethics, and legislative ethics, to mention a few. The goal is to address these issues within the context of the participation of world religions as major players in the effort to achieve a more just and ethical world.

Muslim and Christian Dialogue

While similar in their belief in the One God, Muslims and Christians have different thoughts and perceptions about the Omniscient, Omnipresent, and Omnipotent God. As a result, they have treated each other with suspicion and distrust. Over the centuries, they have engaged in wars relative to their differences in theology. Recently, much has been done to cement the relationships between Muslims and Christians, particularly, in America and Europe. Interfaith dialogue is increasingly becoming important, as understanding and cooperation have become vital. Christians and Muslims are making strides in getting to know each other better.

We now find many Muslim and Christian clerics visiting each other's house of worship, and giving presentations in the way of better understanding each other's faith. The tragedy of September 11, 2001 has necessitated and mandated that there be interfaith dialogue on an increasing scale. Many misconceptions about Islam have resulted in Muslims being harassed and mistreated. In America, for example, Muslims are being unjustly singled out and punished all in the name of fear and misunderstanding.

Many Christian clerics are beginning to understand Islam; however, there are still those clerics who are trying to mislead their constituents by breeding discord and hatred against Muslims. These clerics are purposely trying to demean and denigrate Islam with their lies and misinterpretations of passages from the Qur'an. In short, they need to be educated about Islam

Islam is not new, as it was the religion that was revealed to the Prophets before Prophet Mohammad. More so than just a religion, Islam is a complete way of life. Everything a Muslim does in his daily activities is part of his faith. Islam is more than just praying and fasting; it involves every fiber of our internal self. Peace and forgiveness are hallmarks of that internal self. Muslims believe in the One God, a God Who is Benevolent and Merciful and Just. Muslims believe in the Prophets and Imams, Angels, Books of God, Resurrection, the Day of Judgment, and the Here-after. There are thousands of Prophets in Islam, and twenty-five of them are mentioned by name in the Qur'an. These Prophets begin with Adam and include the Major Prophets: Noah; Abraham; Moses; Jesus; and Mohammad. Muslims believe that the Angel Gabriel delivered God's Revelation to Prophet Mohammad. The Qur'an reveals the importance of dialogue:

"And you do not dispute with the People of the Book, except with means better (than mere disputation), unless it be with those of them who inflict wrong (and injury): but say, 'We believe in the Revelation which has come down to us and in that which came down to you; our God (Allah) and your God (Allah) is One; and it is to Him we bow (in Islam).'" (Qur'an 29:46)

Here Muslims are reminded of the importance of dialogue among the People of the Book, for example, Jews and Christians. That it is best to find the common ground and common principle on which constructive dialogue can be established. For the God of Islam is also the God of Judaism and Christianity.

Simply said, Islam means the complete submission of one's will to the Will of Allah. Allah is the Islamic name for God. Allah is the Almighty Creator and Sustainer of the Universe, who is similar to nothing, and nothing is comparable to Him. The nature of Islam is that we have been created to pass a test. And that test is one of patience in order to remember Allah and to love Allah in every aspect of our lives, to refrain from committing evil, and never to complain when something bad happens to us such as adversity or hardship. We strive to be patient as we fulfill our obligation of happiness. It is the same test that Prophet Job had passed.

We can illustrate the relationship between Muslims and Chris-tians by the concept of happiness. Why did God create us? According to Islam, one of the main reasons for our creation is to strive for happiness. To worship Allah is complete happiness. To worship Allah is to have all the good things and joy in life. While we may not achieve complete happiness in this life, however, we must make great efforts in this direction. Why people have difficulty in achieving complete happiness is because they are beset with many problems both individually and in groups. Here their problems may be physical or spiritual or both. Some of these problems are: envy, jealousy, anger, pessimism, suspicion and arrogance. Those who enter Paradise will achieve complete happiness.

"Behold! Verily on the friends of Allah there is no fear, nor shall they grieve: Those who believe and (constantly) guard against evil; for them are glad tidings, in the life of the present and in the Hereafter: no change can there be in the Words of Allah. This is indeed the supreme felicity." (Qur'an 10:62-64)

Those whose records and deeds in this life are good will attain real and eternal happiness in Paradise, the abode of perfect bliss. Eternal life in the abode of happiness is the biggest challenge that man seeks to attain. In Islam, the spiritual life, material life, and rational life are vital elements of happiness provided they are governed by Islamic beliefs, practices and values. Man is a combination of body, mind and spirit. Happiness is an exclusive quality of the soul, and it depends totally on the degree of growth and development attained by the soul.

A fundamental purpose in Islam is for us to pursue and attain happiness in this worldly life in order to achieve ultimate happiness in the Hereafter. There is a very strong connection between happiness in this world and happiness in the Hereafter. It is the self that governs whether our character is good or bad. It is the self that makes the choice between happiness and misery. The self makes the determination as to whether or not its actions are in conformity with the certainty (*yakine*) of knowledge, perception and truth. Happiness in this life is not an end in itself. Rather, this life prepares us for the ultimate happiness, which is the love of Allah. As our priority is to fulfill our obligations in life, we must live a life that pleases Allah. We must have pure intentions as we carry out Allah's Commandments.

One way of attaining happiness is through good manners, which along with emotional balance have their effects on man's development and happiness. How we relate our affections and good manners will have a major impact on the level of our happiness. Real happiness does not lie in power or wealth. History is replete with examples of leaders who were unhappy, even though they had power and wealth, for example, the Caesars of the Roman Empire. The secret of happiness is manifested in righteousness. To be righteous one must develop a sense of optimism and trust as well as a positive outlook on creation. To be righteous is to be content, and to be content is to be happy. How to develop contentment is to be grateful for what we have because others may have less.

Gratitude goes hand in hand with patience. We need to endure hardships, and even poverty, with patience so that we may acquire the happiness in Paradise. Contentment also derives from empathy, as we feel for the poor and reflect on their needs. But above all we should be content at what we already have and be thankful to Allah.

From the Christian perspective, happiness comes from a proper relationship with God:

"For what shall it profit a man, if he shall gain the whole world, and lose his own soul?" (Mark 8:36)

True happiness and joy come from the relationship with God. For Christians, while happiness is from within, it is not from within them but, rather, it comes from God. They believe that happiness is not so much a reward as it is a result. Furthermore, that God does not just arbitrarily dole out happiness and joy. It is a result of faith in God and obedience to His Word.

For Christians, the concept of happiness is getting what they want. For them, God's concept of happiness is summed up in the simple proverb: *"Happy is the man who wants what he has."* As long as they are focusing on what they do not have, they will be unhappy. But when they begin to appreciate what they already have, they will begin to experience the joys of life. To be really happy is to learn to be thankful for what they have and not covet what they do not have. The New Testament reveals that happiness does not come from self-centeredness but, rather, from obedience, and that God rewards those who seek him. In addition, that happiness is temporal (living a good life on Earth) and supernatural (eternal happiness with God in Paradise). However, while the goal of happiness is both temporal and supernatural, it is the supernatural happiness that is of much importance.

The monotheistic faiths of Judaism, Christianity, and Islam go back to Prophet Abraham, and each of these faiths taught the importance of happiness. Their Prophets are directly descended from Abraham's sons. Prophet Moses and Prophet Jesus are descended from Prophet Isaac, and Prophet Mohammad from Prophet Ishmael. The Qur'an contains a number of chapters that illustrate the lives of these Prophets. The Qur'an deals with everything that concerns us, whether it is knowledge, wisdom, laws, piety, or justice. The Qur'an is our guide, as it is the basis for our complete way of life and conduct and ultimate happiness.

Prophet Jesus holds the highest respect in Islam, as does his mother, Mary. The Muslims of the Shi'a branch of Islam believe that Prophet Jesus will return, along with the Twelfth Imam, Mohammad al-Mahdi. When they return, both of them together will bring truth and justice to mankind. The Qur'an authenticates the miraculous birth of Prophet Jesus. In addition, the Qur'an contains a chapter in the name of Mary, the only woman mentioned by name in the Qur'an. In Islam, Mary is considered pure and perfect:

"Behold! The angels said: 'O Mary! God hath chosen thee and purified thee – chosen thee above the women of all nations.'" (Qur'an 3:42)

As with the miraculous birth of Prophet Adam, who had no father or mother, so too was Prophet Jesus who was born without a father.

"The similitude of Jesus before God is as that of Adam; He created him from dust, then said to him: 'Be' and he was." (Qur'an 3:59)

One of the characteristics of Prophets is that they perform miracles. And Prophet Jesus performed many miracles:

"...I have come to you, with a Sign from your Lord, in that I make for you out of clay, as it were, the figure of a bird, and breathe into it, and it becomes a bird by God's leave: And I heal those born blind, and the lepers, and I quicken the dead, by God's leave...." (Qur'an 3:49)

"So peace is on me the day I was born, the day that I die, and the day that I shall be raised up to life again!" (Qur'an 19:33)

Both Prophet Jesus and Prophet Mohammad validated the fundamental tenet of the belief in the One God. A significant difference between Christianity and Islam is the understanding of the term *paraclete*. For Christians, the term evolved into the Holy Trinity. For Muslims, the term refers to Prophet Jesus proclaiming the coming of Prophet Mohammad. The term itself means *yet another*. How the *yet another* unfolded over the centuries has caused a major difference between the two religions.

Understanding Islam goes beyond the traditional definition of peace and submission of one's will to the Will of Allah. Islam is the attitude, the zenith of which is endurance; endurance is submission; submission is certainty; certainty is believing; believing is acceptance; acceptance is adherence; adherence is behavior; behavior is action the essence of which is patience, and the Patient is Allah, the Beneficent, the Merciful.

How to fulfill Islam within this broader definition is to practice *jihad* (struggle). There are two segments of *jihad*. We have the minor *jihad*, which is to defend Islam by performing good deeds and prohibiting evil. One must be tolerant and understanding and seek unity in brotherhood. Good deeds lead to faith, and faith leads to good deeds. The major *jihad* is to contain one's inner ego, to suppress it, in order to strengthen the personality.

There are four Books in Islam: Torah; Psalms of David; Gospel; and the Qur'an. As Muslims, we accept all these Books in their original forms, without editing or changes. The only Book in existence today that meets these criteria is the Qur'an.

"Those who believe in the Qur'an, and those who follow the Jewish scriptures, and the Christians and the Sabians, and who believe in God and the Last Day, and work righteousness, shall have their reward with their Lord: on them shall be no fear, nor shall they grieve." (Qur'an 2:62)

Christians and Muslims do agree on a number of tenets. They both believe in the One God. They both affirm the miraculous birth of Prophet Jesus as well as his infallibility and return to mankind. Christians hold to the belief that God revealed Himself to Prophets, and that He later revealed Himself in the person of Jesus. Therefore, for Christians, the point of contact with the Almighty is Jesus. For Muslims, their point of contact with God is the Qur'an. Muslims believe that the Qur'an is not man-made but divine and everlasting. Thus, while the Christians look to a person, to Jesus, as their contact point with God, the Muslims look to the Qur'an as their contact point with God. Although the principle in both is the same, namely that God revealed Himself, the contact point with the Divine has caused much consternation and misunderstanding.

There are other similarities between Muslims and Christians. For example, let's look at just a few. The Opening Chapter of the Qur'an (*Surah al-Fatiha*) for Muslims and the *Lord's Prayer* for Christians are both universal prayers. Both prayers emphasize adoration, submission and supplication. Both Bibles also reveal God's Creation and Commandments as well as a set of moral guidelines and practices. Where they differ is in the concept of the Trinity and the status of Jesus. In addition, other differences occur relative to the Names and Attributes of God. Muslims believe in the 99 Beautiful Names of God. Christians believe in only the Beautiful Aspects of God such as Love. Muslims believe mankind is born pure and is only responsible for their own sins. Christians, however, cling tenaciously to the *Original Sin* wherein all of mankind is held responsible for the sins of Adam and Eve, and that baptism is atonement. While Prophets are considered infallible in Islam, they are not in Christianity. Muslims do not believe in the separation of church and state, while Christians hold to a secular form of government.

As humans, we exist only for God Who is the Center of everything. Muslims and Christians must learn to live together and understand one another. Bigger problems, such as atheism and agnosticism, run rampant in today's society. Both Muslims and Christians must instill faith within their communities.

National Conference for Community and Justice

An organization that helps build bridges between various ethnic, racial and religious groups in America is the National Conference for Community and Justice (NCCJ).

"The National Conference for Community and Justice (NCCJ) is a human relations organization dedicated to fighting bias, bigotry and racism in America. NCCJ promotes understanding and respect among all races, religions and cultures through advocacy, conflict resolution and education."

NCCJ transforms communities to be inclusive and just, through institutional change, by empowering leaders. NCCJ facilitates community and interfaith dialogues, provides workplace consultations, youth leadership development, seminarian and educator training. The role of NCCJ is to advocate, educate and resolve conflict – relative to issues of discrimination and oppression of individuals and groups.

NCCJ has more than sixty regional offices in the United States. One such region is the Michigan Region of the United States. The author was the former Chairman and President of that Region. Some of the successes of that Region are:

·   Leadership in the New Century (LINC) programs, which offer learning experiences to develop and expand young leaders' understanding of religious, ethnic and cultural diversity.

·   Interfaith Round Table (IRT) uses trialogue programs with Muslims, Christians and Jews to provide an opportunity for clergy and lay leaders to gain a greater awareness of and respect for different religious traditions.

·   Different People-Common Ground is a series of small group dialogues about the human relations barriers that sometimes confound our best efforts to understand one another and live and work better together. This awareness can be a first step in the process of building a more inclusive and respectful community.

· Advocates and Leaders for Police and Community and Trust (ALPACT) builds trust among community stakeholders, federal and local law enforcement to combat illegal police profiling.

NCCJ has its historical roots in engaging diverse faith communities in purposeful, goal-directed dialogue to learn more about one another and begin to reduce the stereotypes and myths that support injustice. Faith leadership is uniquely positioned to play a major role in the reconciliation, healing and building of communities as they address discrimination, bias, bigotry, stereotyping and racism across the divides of race, ethnicity, culture and faith within our society. Faith communities set a tone and spirit for attitudinal change and establish action programs and initiatives that result in behavioral change.

CHAPTER 11: PROMOTING THE UNITY

"The good of knowledge prevails over the evil of ignorance."
(Tallal Turfe)

While convergence of brotherhood has met with some success, much more still needs to be done. To be sure, Muslims have made inroads into cooperation and collaboration with one another. Muslims have also been engaged in faith-based initiatives and dialogue with non-Muslims. More and more non-Muslims are beginning to understand Islam and its contributions to the world. Yet, winning the unity among Muslims has been met with obstacles. Some of these obstacles have severely impacted the true nature of Islam, as rogues have distorted the faith with their blatant and dastardly objectives. These rogues have succeeded at the expense of a fragmented and ignorant Muslim society.

What is needed is a mechanism to effectively promote the unity. That mechanism is knowledge. To promote unity is to promote knowledge, which is an inescapable duty imposed on every Muslim. Knowledge and ignorance are always at war with each other. To oppose knowledge is ignorant. Knowledge is the light and the means of reaching the threshold of unity. Knowledge is parallel with guidance, while ignorance is akin to torment. Knowledge gives rise to wisdom.

Wisdom consists of judgment, perception, insight, and all the branches of mind that come under the area of knowing. The knowing capacity transcends intellectual knowledge. Spiritual judgment constantly positions wisdom above the other faculties of mind and reveals that knowledge and intelligence are supplementary to understanding. As experience results in knowledge, knowledge results in change. Knowledge being the forerunner of wisdom, the more we know, the more we become. Where there is wisdom, there is neither fear nor ignorance. To dispel fear is to lift the veil of uncertainty to help advance unity. Not essentially unity of accord, but of mutual respect and understanding. For example, to promote the unity means that we must overcome our prejudices. Prejudice is a sign of ignorance and the lack of ethical sensitivity. We promote the unity by rebelling against the ignorance of intolerance and fanaticism. It is through the spirit of detachment that we experience the meaning of freedom to help influence change for the sake of unity.

Winning the Unity

The catastrophe of September 11, 2001 taught the Muslims worldwide an unfortunate but grave lesson, which is winning the unity among them. Distrust and hatred that has rankled the lives of Muslims over the centuries has caused much confusion and discord within the Muslim communities. Islamic schools of thought have evolved, over the centuries, to the point that a clear and distinct fragmentation among Muslims does in fact exist.

While the schools of thought started out as interpretations of Islamic jurisprudence, Muslim followers of these ideologies began to drift into ignorance, darkness and despair. While Muslims speak of unity, and they make attempts to unify, the end result has been dismal. The reason is that over the centuries this enmity and hatred among each other has been inculcated and imbedded within the minds of Muslims. Their offspring carry on the dissention and, at times, even magnify the fragmentation to even greater heights of animosity. We must bear in mind that the Sixth Imam, Ja'far as-Sadiq, was the teacher of some of those who decided to launch their own interpretations; therefore, the formation of various schools of thought.

We are guided by the Quran'ic verse:
"As for those who divide their religion and break up into sects, Thou Hast no part in them in the least: their affair is with Allah: He will in the end tell them the truth of all that they did." (Qur'an 6:159)

When Muslims break up into sects and espouse views that cause disunity, then they have erred and will have to answer to Allah. Prophet Mohammad had said that Islam would divide into seventy-three sects, all which are condemned except one. Here the Prophet was conveying to the Muslims to take a unified position in Islam as an undivided single brotherhood. The concept of unity is at three levels: (a) unity of humanity, (b) unity of the society, and (c) unity of the Muslim nation.

Differences in jurisprudence should not deter Muslim unity, since all schools of thought have agreement, for the most part, on similar historical facts. Jurisprudence is a major criterion in Islam and is the means by which those scholars who are qualified are able to interpret and apply Islamic laws. Nonetheless, jurisprudence interpretation must not be infected by individual aspirations and arrogance. Muslim unity is one of the goals of the Muslim society and is an obligation on all Muslims.

To hold fast onto the *Rope of Allah* means to uphold and comply with Allah's Commands. We need to hold fast so as not to deviate from the straight path. While it is one's right to believe that the Islamic school of thought he follows is the best school of thought, it is not right to admonish the followers of other schools of thought. Here we should not put a wedge or barrier between the followers of different schools of thought. Rather, we should meet with each other to find the solution of how to work with each other.

Having pride in one's own family is encouraged; however, that sense of pride should not translate into belittling other families who may be experiencing hardships in life. This latter type of pride destroys the Islamic personality and further drifts Muslims away from each other. This drifting away erodes into the community. Those who want to destroy Islam feed upon this erosion, as they insidiously plot their evil doings. As this erosion widens, the Islamic community weakens, and its members may become victimized and oppressed by wicked leaders who usurp their rights. Instead of coming together in unity to receive Allah's Blessings, this erosion leads the community into the realm of darkness and ignorance.

What is needed to resolve this erosion is for Muslims to come together and work together in the direction of complementation and cooperation. Rather than compete against each other for the purpose of supremacy, power, prestige or monetary gain, we should work together by intensifying our efforts towards Islamic endeavors, for example, a school project.

Islamic Values

To bring about the unity, we must immerse ourselves in the Islamic values, which are many. These values can help us towards a solution relative to unity. Three very important values are tolerance, mercy and flexibility.

Tolerance

"Let there be no compulsion in religion…." (Qur'an 2:256)

"If it had been your Lord's Will, they would all have believed, - all who are on Earth! Will you then compel mankind, against their will, to believe?" (Qur'an 10:99)

Compulsion or force is unacceptable in Islam. Religion is built upon faith and will, which would be pointless if provoked by force. In Islam, people are not compelled to change their faith. Forced faith is no faith. Faith is a moral achievement and as such mandates us to thwart off evil. As such, we must not be impatient or angry; rather, we should exercise tolerance. Tolerance is one of the greatest strengths of Islam, because it is the attitude of truth. In Islam, tolerance is a religious moral duty. Tolerance means to bear or put up with the convictions of other people and not to impose one's will upon the will of others.

In Islam, tolerance acknowledges self-respect, equality, and freedom of all people. The world is made up of many cultures, and these cultures are diverse in nature. Tolerance is to have respect and understanding of these diverse cultures. Each culture has their distinct form of expression, and we need to find ways to communicate and be open and compassionate.

Tolerance is a key to resolving disputes between parties. For example, tolerance can be very effective in driving home the unity among Muslims. In this regard, Muslims would be willing to listen to those with whom they have differences in the hope of coming to an amicable understanding and resolution of their differences. This does not mean the abandonment or weakening of one's convictions. But recognizing diversity of opinions and convictions is a step in the right direction, and that direction is unity. This recognition is fostered by knowledge and freedom of thought. Tolerance is harmony in diversity, and tolerance is our Islamic legacy. To be tolerant, we must see beyond what is in front of us.

Mercy, Flexibility and Ease

Prophet Mohammad's mission was one of a great number of duties and responsibilities. One of these was the aspect of mercy:

"We sent you not, but as a Mercy for all creatures." (Qur'an 21:107)

Here the Mercy (*Al-Rahim*) of Allah is for all mankind. Likewise, Prophet Mohammad was neither for any particular race, color or creed nor for any nation or geographical boundary. Rather, he was for all mankind in its totality. The concept of mercy transcends all boundaries of race, age, color, and regional features. As such, Allah sent Prophet Mohammad to be the best example of mercy. The word mercy pertains to every facet of life and embodies comprehension that links all activities of awareness and form together. Such an easy and frequently used word that so often gets abandoned as we go about our daily lives; but what vast wisdom it represents. The very basic nature of mercy is that without this energy there is a void in linking the soul with man. In this regard, mercy strengthens the soul and is the governing criterion for fulfilling the unity within man's life. We need to fill our hearts with mercy, and to render mercy to others when needed.

When we recite a *surah* (chapter) from the Qur'an, we start by describing Allah as the Beneficent (*Al-Rahman*) the Merciful (*Al-Rahim*). Allah's Mercy descended upon Prophet Mohammad who in turn taught mercy to others. Even when his enemies were persecuting him, Prophet Mohammad displayed mercy. For example, the people of al-Taif (a city located in Saudi Arabia) hurt the Prophet by hitting him and calling him bad names. Yet, the Prophet extended to them his mercy, for he did not will them to be destroyed. Another example took place during the Battle of Uhud in which many of the Prophet's companions were killed and the Prophet was wounded. Yet, the Prophet displayed mercy rather than cruelty towards his enemies. Other examples of mercy are to lower our wing of humility to our parents, to tend to the needs of the orphans, and to maintain relations with our relatives. Even when we slaughter an animal for food, we apply mercy in that act by mentioning the name of Allah as well as sharpening the knife so as to alleviate the suffering of that animal. As we these examples, it is also incumbent upon us to render mercy to the entire brotherhood of the Islamic community. Since the source of Mercy is Allah, we should try to be merciful towards one another, as well as towards non-Muslims and all living creatures.

The concept of brotherhood is mandated in the Qur'an (49:10), as it is the cornerstone of Islamic unity. Brotherhood originates from mutual respect and emotional feelings for one another, whether it is a family or community. The enforcement of brotherhood is the greatest social ideal of Islam. Brotherhood is a notion based on faith and equality. It unites mankind on the basis of beliefs and principles. Brotherhood and mercy are inseparable. If we hold fast to the *Rope of Allah*, then we will attain brotherhood.

Islam teaches that the human family is one, that there is no superiority of white over black or black over white. Islam rejects all notions of racial prejudice and teaches that the only basis of distinction between human beings is their individual moral qualities. To complete one's faith in Islam necessitates that one is imbued with mercy for others. We should also know that it is our duty to be merciful to each other. Hatred and enmity is the work of Satan. Disputes are a sign of missing the Mercy of Allah. Allah might shield His Mercy from people when they do not deserve it. Those who do not deserve the Mercy of Allah are people who do not protect one another and who do not enjoin good and prohibit evil. In addition, those who do not establish regular prayers and give charity do not deserve the Mercy of Allah. We should remember Allah and His Mercy. We should never despair in the Mercy of Allah. Our faith and mercy are strengthened, as we put our trust and reliance on Allah and His Mercy:

"Mohammad is the Messenger of Allah; and those who are with him are strong against unbelievers, (but) compassionate amongst each other...Allah has promised those among them who believe and do righteous deeds forgiveness and a great reward." (Qur'an 48:29).

This verse means that those who are devout Muslims are in a perpetual struggle against evil for themselves as well as for others. They are compassionate towards their brethren in faith, as they strive to help each other. They are humble with each other and unified against evil. For example Mohammad, they defended Islam with their hearts and souls in support of Prophet during the battles against the enemy in the early years of Islam. These are the characteristics of the people who deserve the Mercy of Allah. These are the people who will join their hearts in love. Allah will always rise up the people who will follow the true spirit of Islam:

"O you who believe! If any from among you turn back from his faith, soon will Allah produce a people whom He will love as they will love Him...." (Qur'an 5:54)

The spirit is manifested in two ways. First, the believers will love Allah and Allah will love them. Second, the attitude of the believers will be one of mercy and humility as they strive for truth and justice. Their faith is strong and together they are committed to the cause of Islam, as they move forward undaunted by any outside influences.

This type of spirit even extends to the family. For example, let us look at the sacrifice and attention that a mother provides for her child. During months of pregnancy, the mother is filled with anxiety, stress and worry regarding the safety of the child while still in her womb. The mother puts her trust and reliance on Allah, as she knows her child is safe. After birth, the mother rears her child with love and gratitude. As our parents have shown us mercy in their care and sacrifice, we should likewise provide the same kind of mercy for our parents. We should always be grateful to our parents.

In our remembrance and love of Allah, we must be grateful for His Benevolence and Mercy. Allah's Benevolence and Mercy are manifested in His Creation and Revelations. Here mercy comes full circle, as it is a universal mercy that embraces everything. And Allah chose Prophet Mohammad to spread the message of universal mercy among all people and creatures. And it is the Qur'an, the *Rope of Allah*, which explains what this universal mercy is. This mercy is heightened when people live in harmony with one another and unify in the common cause of brotherhood and solidarity. So it is with the Muslim *Ummah* (community), as they must find the means to cooperate and complement one another in the spirit of mercy and mutual respect.

One of the main reasons why Islam as a faith survives to this day is because of the flexibility in Islam. The nature of Islam is such that it has a great deal of flexibility and practicability and can cope with any arising situation. Muslims are encouraged to think about the laws of Islam and try to deduce laws for things that have no clear-cut evidence. We see many scholars dedicating their lives towards understanding these laws and making use of the great flexibility in Islam. Islam does not prevent the human mind from thinking, but instead it gives our mind guidance and assistance. However, within this flexibility, we must use our minds to think within the guidance of the Qur'an. We should not be thinking about the areas that the mind could not reach like unseen words and divine rules, as the source of all of these is the Revelation from Allah.

Islam encourages reasoning, thought and personal opinion. It is this flexibility in having differences of opinion among the scholars that underscores the meaning of Allah's Mercy. As

Muslims, we seek to understand and explore the secrets of nature and of the creation. As such, we deepen our faith. We increase our awareness and knowledge of creation. We explore nature's beauty and symmetry as well as harmony. Islam is universal and comprehensive. It promotes human dignity, equality and honor. Its basic principles are permanent and it has flexibility according to the conditions of the people and their needs.

The beauty of the *shari'a* (law) of Islam is its flexibility, as it is a framework appropriate for all times, all places and all peoples. To ensure the eternal relevance of His Revelation, Allah provided for inherent mobility and flexibility. By providing us with the *shari'a*, He established the legal boundaries within which the community can develop and flourish in concord with the requirements of the changing times. As it is the Divine Law, the *shari'a* cannot be changed. However, because there are so many facets and contingencies of life, and because the *shari'a* does not cover all these details in minuscule form, there is room for interpretation. In other words, there is room for flexibility. This flexibility transforms into *ijtihad* or independent reasoning. With each new era comes a new set of laws. Islam is a faith that endures over time, and a faith that meets the requirements of any new era. As such, flexibility and adjustability to these requirements are in compliance with the teachings of Islam. It is *ijtihad* that copes with the ever-changing pattern of the requirements of life.

We should note that the *shari'a* does not change nor can it be revised. However, the application of *shari'a* may change over time. For example, the issues of organ transplants and surrogate mothers did not arise were non-existent at the time of Prophet Mohammad. Today, these issues are very much in the news and are real. The flexibility in the *shari'a* allows Islamic scholars to rule on these issues. Another example has to do with consumer products that did not exist at the time of Prophet Mohammad. A consumer product, such as cigarettes, has taken many modifications over the centuries. Currently, the smoking of cigarettes is considered dangerous to one's health, as it can cause lung cancer. According to Islam, a product that adversely impacts one's health is taboo. The flexibility in Islam allows Islamic scholars to rule on the issue of cigarette smoking, even though this was not an issue during the time of Prophet Mohammad.

One of the criteria of Islam is the concept of ease:

"…Allah intends every facility for you; He does not want to put you to difficulties…." (Qur'an 2:185)

"And We will make it easy for you (to follow) the simple (path)." (Qur'an 87:8)

Since Allah eases our difficulties, then why do we find Muslims lacking in the practice of Islam? Some of the reasons may be due to a weakness in their spirituality; laziness; inconvenience in the environment in which they live; or just plain ignorance. The reality is that Allah smoothes the path for us, as ease encompasses our entire life. Just as Allah created the Cosmos with ease, He grants us with ease in discovering the beauty and marvels of the Universe. Allah made Islam very easy, so that Muslims can live by it.

Allah does not make Islam more difficult than we are able to tolerate, nor does He make it entirely easy. As He provides us with ease and difficulty, He provides us more ease through this difficulty. While there are hardships in life, we persevere in overcoming these hardships within our capacity to do so. Ease is the sense of knowing how to overcome these hardships. The fundamental precept of Islam is that it never forgets the nature of man and the limits of his capacities. Yet, as man is immersed in the principles of Islam, he is able to self-actualize in his faith with ease, confidence and moderation. When the inner self is unified with nature and its needs are fulfilled, then the path towards harmony will be one of ease.

Just as tolerance, mercy, flexibility and ease are essential in Islam so must they be essential to achieving brotherhood and solidarity. Muslims from all sects must display tolerance and mercy for each other and at the same time exhibit ease and flexibility for the purpose of driving home the unity. Tolerance and mercy not only bring out forgiveness but also compassion as well. The ease and flexibility in Islam removes the difficulties for Muslims so that they can engage in constructive dialogue and seek windows of opportunities for more productive negotiations. However, if we continue on the path of discord, then we will have incurred the Wrath of Allah:

"O you who believe! Do not turn (for friendship) to people on who is the Wrath of Allah. Of the Hereafter they are already in despair, just as the unbelievers are in despair about those (buried) in graves." (Qur'an 60:13)

"And when there comes to them a Book from Allah, confirming what is with them, - although from of old they had prayed for victory against those

without faith, - when there comes to them that which they (should) have recognized, they refuse to believe in it but the curse of Allah is on those without faith. Miserable is the price for which they have sold their souls, in that they deny (the Revelation) which Allah has sent down, in insolent envy that Allah of His Grace should send it to any of His servants He pleases: thus have they drawn on themselves Wrath upon Wrath. And humiliating is the punishment of those who reject faith." (Qur'an 2-89-90)

These are just two of many verses in the Qur'an that reveal the Anger of Allah. When Allah is angry, He will punish. Allah will be angry against people who commit mischief and tyranny, such as was the behavior of Satan, Adolph Hitler, Abu Lahab, Abu Jahl (*Father of Ignorance*) and Genghis Khan. Allah commands us to forgive others, even when we are angry. We can lose our balance when angry. However, Allah never loses His Balance. Even when wrathful, Allah would not subject anyone to a punishment that is more than what he actually deserved. Allah imposes His Wrath on those who have closed all doors of Allah's Mercy upon themselves. Examples of Allah's Anger are when we humiliate and abuse the scholars of Islam, the pious and the virtuous. Allah becomes angered and declares war on those committing heinous crimes against His Authority, by insulting and harming His pious servants. The only way to avoid Allah's Wrath is to submit to Him while there is still time and to comply with His Commands. A major Command is that of unity and brotherhood.

Brotherhood in Islam derives from certain rights. According to Prophet Mohammad, some of the following rights are predicated on a strong foundation wherein each part of that foundation reinforces and strengthens the other part:

- Return a greeting when greeted.
- Visit those who are ill.
- Attend funerals.
- Accept invitations.
- Pray for your brethren.
- Feel earnestly for a Muslim brother.
- Defend the honor and dignity of a Muslim.
- Secretly inform Muslims of their faults or weaknesses.
- Do not be suspicious nor bear enmity against each other.
- Do not be jealous of each other nor indulge in backbiting.
- Help Muslims in time of need.
- Refrain from speaking about that which is disliked by your

brother.
- Overlook the mistakes of others.
- Protection of honor.
- Sanctity and security of private life.
- Security of personal freedom.
- Freedom of expression.
- Freedom of association.
- Freedom of conscience and conviction.
- Protection of religious sentiments.
- Right to basic necessities in life.
- Equality before law.

Channels of Communication

Promoting tolerance, mercy and flexibility among the various sects in Islam is our biggest challenge. This challenge is for the entire Muslim *Ummah*. In order for tolerance, mercy and flexibility to work, we must uproot intolerance, admonishment and inflexibility that have devastated the Muslim unity. How we overcome these weaknesses and ignorance is by educating Muslims on the values in Islam very early in childhood. Children must be schooled on Islamic values with unity in mind, as their attitudes and perceptions will be governed by their schooling and upbringing. These attitudes and perceptions will have a permanent and immense influence on their approach to life. Our challenge, therefore, is to bring about understanding and harmony with each other. Religious leaders and scholars have a responsibility to plant the seeds of religious tolerance, mercy and flexibility in the hearts and minds of their followers. These leaders and scholars must collaborate in the spirit of mutual understanding and patience that will enable them to work together for the advancement of unity.

By enriching our Islamic personality, we thwart off the malevolence of conceit. Achieving spiritual emancipation requires that we be rightly trained in the methods of detachment and discernment. Islam fosters the essential development of personality. Islam emphasizes unity in diversity, and it is the panacea for purification and self-actualization of mind and heart. There is commonality among the Islamic schools of thought, in that all stress human values and spirituality. In addition, all schools of thought promote righteous conduct and morality as well as tolerance, mercy and flexibility for one another.

We must recapture the legacy of the early years of Islam when Muslims were one *Ummah* (community). Their legacy was one of seeking knowledge and applying that knowledge. Their legacy was one of linking knowledge with ethics. Intellectual formation and establishment of priorities should be the platform for today's *Ummah*. The knowledge of ethics teaches us how to act and how to conduct ourselves relative to duties and behavior. Here we will understand and distinguish between good and evil, useful and harmful matters. By doing good deeds, such as restoring the unity, we will become self-actualized in our faith. There needs to be open discussions among the Islamic sects in order to promote the unity. In this way we can remove misunderstandings between the sects as well as confront our common enemy, which is ignorance. We need these open discussions in order to avoid making false allegations and accusations.

Essential Requirements in Pursuit of Unity

For constructive dialogue among the religious leaders and scholars of the Islamic schools of thought to be successful, essential requirements are necessary. First, in their quest for unity, they must place their reliance on Allah. They must surrender themselves to the Will of Allah. They must be committed towards laying aside their prejudices so as to achieve the unity. Reliance is the start of the journey, surrender is its end, and commitment is its result. This, of course, necessitates some of the following guidelines:

· Prepare for the dialogue by thinking ahead as to group dynamics and the directions in which the discussion might go.
· Establish an atmosphere of trust and relaxation by focusing differences on ideas rather than on personalities.
· Institute clear guidelines for discussion by encouraging openness and respect for honest opinions.
· Share concerns and beliefs by listening carefully to others and strive to understand the position of those who disagree.

The spirit of tolerance, mercy and flexibility, which was very much the custom of jurisprudence during the early years of Islam, must be revived among the Muslims of today. Religious leaders and scholars should awaken to the realization that Islam is much more than mere nit picking at minor judicial and theological disputes. Their objective should be one of unity, rather than the domination of one sect by another. There is mutual agreement among the sects that they all agree on obeying Allah and His Messenger, Prophet Mohammad. There is also mutual agreement that piety, adherence of the principles of the Qur'an, and striving for goodness in daily life are the greatest virtues. In addition, they agree on the need for a strong ethical and moral code to regulate human behavior in all its manifestations. Since these agreements among Shi'as and Sunnis are already in effect, this sets the stage for pursuing unity on other issues in Islam.

With the objective being unity within the Muslim *Ummah*, disagreements as to interpretations of Islamic Law can be harmonized. We must realize that the existing ambiance of conflict and discord pervasive among various Muslim sects is utterly ineffective and absurd. The Islamic civilization has now existed for over fourteen centuries, and each of these sects have been part and parcel of this great culture.

As it is futile, we need to cease and desist in spending enormous amounts of time, energies and resources in promoting the dominance of one sect over the other. It is nothing more than a delusion that one faction can somehow eliminate the other. It is neither feasible nor practical to either ignore the existence of different sects in Islam or to try and remove their long-standing differences. With tolerance, mercy and flexibility we can acknowledge the right of each sect to practice what it believes, while at the same time cooperate with each other towards the common goal of unity. This would be a more viable and workable alternative rather than trying to deal with the issue of Shi'a versus Sunni. This alternative can work and it has, for example, in the case of the Government of Iran. The Iranian Constitution states that while its law is based on the jurisprudence of Imam Ja'far as-Sadiq, all Islamic schools of thought are free to practice their own jurisprudence in that country. We should capitalize on the Iranian imperative as we seek unity within the broader Muslim *Ummah*.

Many other Islamic values, such as patience, forbearance, kindness, temperance and courage can help immensely in the way of unity. We need to instill within our minds and hearts these virtues, if we are going to be successful in our pursuit for unity. One of the causes of disunity is that many Muslims are ignorant about their obligation to strive for unity and to maintain it. This, of course, stems back to education and learning the important Islamic principles. We should consider the convergence of Muslim thoughts and discuss topics of interest in which there is common agreement. Accentuate the positive and eliminate the negative. Let us dwell on issues we can come to an agreement on, and forego those issues that cause heated discussions and disputes. We have many things in common, so why not build an alliance on these agreements. Some of our common agreements are:

· We have the same Declaration of Faith: that there is one God and Mohammad is His Prophet.

· We perform similar obligations, such as prayer, fasting, charity and pilgrimage.

· We are all part of the great Islamic culture and civilization.

What we need now is a strong sense of brotherhood, whereby Muslims tolerate and respect one another. It is important to familiarize and educate Muslims about holding dialogues in order to move forward and build a strong and cohesive Islamic society. To achieve this requires that we should no longer attack other Muslim sects publicly or verbally or by means of force. Otherwise, we open the door to the enemies of Islam who employ their vicious objectives to destroy Islam.

Unless we remove the aura of dominance of one sect over the other, it will be difficult to achieve the unity. Let us work for the future, even if unity is not in reach today. Like a cemented structure in battle array, let us confront the enemies of Islam who continue to promote despair so unity cannot be achieved. Only be achieving this united Islamic *Ummah* can we stop the oppression and the domination by the enemies of Islam. Henceforth, justice, security and peace will become dominant facts of life.

Whenever we discuss a disputed matter we must be civilized, open minded and kind to others. We should also acquire in-depth knowledge of the points of view of all parties. We should be positive and respectful towards other Muslims regardless of difference in opinions. We should not condemn each other. Rather we should promote empathy so that we can understand each other's point of view. The differences in the Shi'a and Sunni sects are quite basic and not trivial; yet, we must find the way to reconcile these differences. Despite disagreements among sects within the Islamic world, the unity and coordination of Islamic thought across various parts of the Islamic world has been phenomenal. Muslims possess the foundations for a solid unity that can create a powerful cultural movement in the future. We possess a common historical bond and system of values in Islam, and our Islamic civilization and heritage still represents the greatest source of shared experience among all Muslims. In addition, the increasing awareness of Muslims has instilled a sense of unity of purpose among Muslims, as we perceive ourselves as the victims of prejudice and exploitation in various forms.

To realize the unity, we must have a foundation in a system of values as follows:

· All Muslims are equivalent with equal rights and equal duties.
· Confrontation should be replaced by collaboration and mutual respect.
· Intrafaith dialogue leads to a mutually enriching union and in the long run will lead to a more universal homogeneity and a final global unity.

Dialogue is only possible when we respect each other's individuality. Thus, knowledge of others in their cultural setting is essential. By recognizing and accepting social, cultural, and religious diversity, an exchange of mutual values and a union in collaboration ultimately will lead to the unity of the Muslim *Ummah*.

Promoting the unity also entails the importance of understanding the Muslim community and the recognition that education is much more than just communication. Educating Muslims about the concept of unity entails the following:

· Understanding the needs and perceptions of the Shi'a and Sunni communities is a vital stage.
· Developing unity skills and capabilities.
· Implementing unified religious services and sound communication programs.
· Empowering partnerships between Shi'a and Sunni groups.

A useful starting point is to think about the importance of education and societal mobilization. Education is not simply about transferring facts; it is about cultivating self-assurance, capabilities and empowerment. The first step is to really exhibit humility and put forth the effort to comprehend the Muslim community's situations, needs and perceptions. This is a big obstacle for many Muslims. The goal is to aim for a strategic alliance among the Muslim groups, schools of thought and ideologies. This partnership building requires trust and maturity on all sides.

Partnerships take a great deal of time and energy in order to cement the relationship. The end result is a win-win for all parties. Community representatives get to exercise responsibility and accountability while at the same time benefit from a rich and rewarding learning experience. Religious leaders get infusions of energy, enthusiasm and credibility as well as great ideas. Imagination is a vital element in building a better future. The Muslim leadership must imagine and promote a more sustainable unity of Muslim brotherhood and solidarity, if they are going to enlist the Muslim community to join. But how to harness each other's imagination is key to attaining the unity, and Muslims achieve this by starting to liberate their own.

Some examples of unity are (a) when more than one Islamic school exists in the same community, then all schools should work together for the common good, for economies of scale, and for consolidation of economic resources; and (b) leaders of Islamic institutions within the same community should complement each other with shared programs; rotation of mosques and religious leaders for prayer and lectures; or an exchange program whereby board members of one mosque serve a short time on the board of another mosque. A simple format for getting started is the following:

·   Analyze and assess the needs of Muslims and the environment they live in.

·   Identify key opportunities to better and more efficiently meet the needs of the Muslim community.

·   Figure out how to act on those opportunities.

·   Implement the plan.

Plan of Action

Muslims who adhere to a specific sect can still hold to their principles, so long as it does not breed discord and ignorance. This means that Shi'as can uphold the concept of the *Imamah* (succession of Prophet Mohammad), while Sunnis can espouse the historical Islamic leadership based on *shura* or consultation. What is important here is that while they hold to their principles they must at the same time preserve the unity.

How we go about preserving the unity is by way of education.

We must work to educate Muslims about the importance of unity. We can conduct educational seminars and invite leading scholars to speak about unity. Academic sessions will attract prominent scholars to engage in conversations about a variety of topics relative to unity. We can write books on the subject of unity and give our readers a workable plan of action in attaining the unity. Whether we hold seminars or write books, the participants or readers will experience euphoria. They will be excited and jubilant about winning the unity. Since a great number of our youth access the Internet, then utilizing web-based videos relative to topics on unity can be very effective. Even the use of full-color video and audio streaming features can generate enthusiasm among the users. Other suggestions for complementation deal with cooperation in the areas of global economics, science, technology and culture.

In addition, discussions on unity can take place at the highest level of Islamic leadership, for example, between the Shi'a *maraja'a* and the Sunni heads of Islamic institutions. Or discussions on unity can take place with other Muslim religious leaders and scholars locally, nationally and globally. Even members of the Muslim community in general should be engaged in discussions on unity. Offering college scholarships to high-school senior students who compete by writing on the topic of unity can generate a great deal of enthusiasm. Shia and Sunni high-school senior students can be paired together to write the essay. In this way these students get to know one another and share in the other's point of view. Strategies for funding the scholarship program can come from local fund raising activities, corporate sponsorship and philanthropic sources.

To generate enthusiasm among Muslims for the purpose of unity, religious leaders must maintain a congenial relationship with their constituents. Religious leaders must be role models. Psychology teaches that people repeat the behaviors that leaders call attention to, whether good or bad. It is not enough to keep the community informed; keeping the community involved is critical. When a community takes responsibility for its future, things happen. The best way of building relationships and unity in the community is to offer opportunities to a wide range of people to get involved. Encouraging community involvement transcends beyond just involvement in education, business, government and religion. It is a total effort encompassing all aspects of life.

Shi'as and Sunnis can work together to address the myriad of social problems in the world today. For example, they can cooperate with each other to find ways of reducing poverty. They can find solutions to problems such as drug addiction and alcoholism as well as the devastating disease of Acquired Immune Deficiency Syndrome (AIDS). Yet, other major problems, particularly in Western nations, are that of suicide and prostitution as well as homosexuality. We need to educate Muslims about these social problems and the repercussions for being victimized by them.

Let us examine just one of these social problems, i.e., suicide. Educating Muslims that suicide is not only prohibited by Allah but the punishment for having committed this evil is beyond comprehension. For those who commit suicide their eternal abode is Hell. In Western nations, there is a growing number of Muslims who do not understand the issue of suicide, and they need to be educated as to Islam's stand on the issue. Many Muslims are caught up in the Western world of technology, fun and games, and as a result have not made time available to be educated about Islam. Shi'as and Sunnis can draw upon the *shari'a* (laws) for the solutions to suicide and other social problems. The Qur'an and the teachings of Prophet Mohammad provide us with the means by which to remedy these problems.

Unity should be on the lips of every Muslim, and each Muslim must do their best in fulfilling the obligation of a lasting and just unity. Unity must be pursued on all fronts, both with the highest level of religious leadership and equally with the entire Muslim community. The sum of the parts does equal the whole, and if each Muslim begins to preach unity, then it will help cement that unity. Unity leads to strength, and this strength is needed to address the ills of the society and those who wish to distort and destroy Islam. Some of the basic solutions for achieving unity are as follows:

· Steer on the straight path of Islam and avoid prejudice and suspicion between each other.

· Believe entirely in the faith of Islam and implement this belief into our daily lives.

· Avoid selfish transgression between each other and protect the rights of others.

· Earn the Mercy of Allah by being righteous.

· Unity can only be created through the message of the Qur'an.

· Recognize that as we belong to the same *Ummah* there must be tolerance, respect and merit for all Muslims.

- Recognize our responsibilities and duties towards all creation.
- Draw on ethical and moral principles of honesty and sincerity that emphasize the principle of brotherhood.
- Implement the concept of unity in diversity as a vehicle for effective dialogue.
- Spread the message of Islam that brings out the compassion and true understanding as a way of life.

By channeling efforts worldwide for cooperation and complementation, at least one organization has met with some success. The Organization of the Islamic Conference (OIC) is an international organization grouping of fifty seven countries that have decided to pool their resources together, combine their efforts, and speak with one voice to safeguard the interests and secure the progress and well-being of their peoples and of all Muslims in the world. Others must follow this example. In doing so, essential characteristics must be adhered to if the exchange relationship between parties is to succeed. These characteristics are: (a) honesty and fairness; (b) no hidden agenda; (c) open communication; (d) targeted approach; (e) value driven; and (f) goal oriented.

Effective and workable communication among Muslims is necessary. Both Shi'a and Sunni religious leaders must make a joint declaration of unity. The joint alliance must be implemented whereby both Shi'a and Sunni religious leaders issue joint declarations of unity to Muslims all over the world. The joint declaration must further stipulate that religious leaders should not engage in profane language directed at other Muslims, whether historical or current. While talking negatively about Abu Lahab and his wife is acceptable, swearing at the companions of Prophet Mohammad is unacceptable. Muslims who engage in vulgar and profane language should be held accountable for their actions. The religious leaders themselves would be responsible for carrying out the judgments against those who engage in such vile actions.

Joint declarations must be issued to reproach those Muslims who are deviating from and tarnishing Islam for their own personal benefit. There should be an exchange of students and teachers between the Islamic schools. Support organizations such as the OIC, which are channels whereby religious scholars meet and promote the concept of unity as well as discuss and agree on issues deemed necessary for all Muslims. The Muslim *Ummah* needs to meet the challenges of the mass media by becoming involved in enhancing the perception and image of Islam on a global basis.

Diversity

Diversity is an effective tool in bridging the gap between those in dispute. Diversity in Islam is the awareness that divergent issues do exist among the various schools of thought, and these issues are fomented by distinctly different and significant views. In Islam, diversity can pave the way for reconciliation among the various schools of thought. The first question that comes to mind is the nature of Islamic unity. Barriers towards achieving this unity have exacerbated meaningful dialogue. Muslim religious leaders and the community who intentionally propagate division on the basis of pride, suspicion, and self-interest are guilty.

Islam demands unity, and that an unwillingness to accept this is a sin against that unity. If our mission is to confront the moral, political and social influences of each of the Islamic schools of thought, then surely there is sufficient basis for common cause. Apparently, the Shi'a and Sunni communities have been marked more by discord than by collaboration, more by hostility than by mercy, more by doubt than by trust, more by misinformation and lack of knowledge than by respect for the truth.

Moreover we do not take the time to comprehend the issues, but are simply satisfied to rudely pass along unnecessary insults in the place of frank and insightful reflection. In many instances, we have been motivated by pride and prejudice. It is not that disparities between Shi'as and Sunnis do not or should not matter. The issue in the minds of the Muslim community is whether these disparities should be allowed to restrain both groups from dealing with a greater common enemy: disunity.

There must be mutual support, irrespective of how profound our differences are with one another. As Shi'as and Sunnis have shared Islam's great history during the last fourteen centuries, they have no reason not to develop mutual partnerships and work together for the betterment of the Muslim community. Unity necessitates awareness, patience and concentration in order to work.

Diversity must be respected; diversity must be valued; and diversity must be managed. How to respect diversity is to promote tolerance and mercy and flexibility among the Muslim community.

How to value diversity is to understand and appreciate our Islamic heritage. How to manage diversity is to be goal oriented in order to achieve that unity. To respect diversity we must be willing to listen to the points of view of others. To value diversity requires a qualitative sense of well being that is based on ethics and ideals. To manage diversity necessitates that we be strategically driven, pragmatic and synergistic.

Diversity must ensure peace and stability. However, there are difficulties in achieving diversity. For example, all parties must be convinced that unity is needed. If unity in diversity is going to be promoted, then the costs associated with it must be available. There will, of course, be bitterness and cynicism stemming from those who may feel they have been excluded.

By changing the current state of affairs, Muslim leaders may feel their leadership is threatened and thereby decide to polarize. The challenge for diversity is to convince all parties that mutual exchange is mandatory. For diversity to work, the process must be continuously evaluated for accountability and improvement. With diversity, perceptions and points of view change through recognizing individual prejudices and moral attitudes as well as confronting preconceptions and stereotypes.

The concept of pluralism has wide application in Islam. Pluralism is the doctrine that reality consists of several basic substances or elements. For example, in Islam we have a situation in which groups have separate identities, cultures and religious structures. Yet, in Islam, pluralism means the coexistence of schools of thought within a community even though they hold divergent and incompatible views with regard to religious ideology.

Diversity focuses on distinctions among people with respect to ethnicity, religion and other human differences. On the other hand, pluralism incorporates mutual respect, acceptance and teamwork among people who are diverse in the dimensions of human differences. Pluralism holds to one's school of thought, and at the same time, engages other schools of thought to learn more about their path and how they want to be understood. Pluralism and dialogue are the means for building bridges and relationships that create harmony and peace in the Muslim society. Pluralism does not mean just to tolerate religious differences but, rather, to accept the other's point of view albeit cultural, political, psychological, sociological or philosophical disparities. Having a broader perspective can mean tolerance, and it can also mean understanding a variety of meanings. Pluralism is unity plus diversity. Despite diversity of opinion between various Islamic sects, they need to come together on sacred occasions to revisit the past and reunite it with their daily lives.

Purpose

We must take charge of the future of the Islamic community. The role for the Muslim leadership is to accomplish the community's purpose with value and stability. This is done with the larger community or *Ummah* in mind. Our purpose is based on three criteria:

· What do we want to preserve?
· What do we want to change?
· What do we want to create?

Perhaps, reasons why unified efforts in the past have failed may be because the Muslim leadership did not have a clear and shared understanding of their purpose and the outcomes they wanted. In addition, political reasons could have been a deterrent to understanding each other. Or some Muslims may have put more emphasis on power and the necessity to be in control. Shared purpose, values and vision provide the critical guidelines for weighing options and opportunities. They also provide the basis for evaluating if community efforts are making a difference. Merely the process of developing these guidelines creates ownership, commitment and participation by all the parties. The Muslim leadership then evaluates how well they met these guidelines. Did they reach their goals? What has been left undone?

Vision

In order to succeed in our vision of unity, all participants must share in that vision. One person can make a difference; collectively we can transform the community. People are naturally good and are motivated by their capacity to genuinely serve. Human relationships are venerated and interactive in nature. Successful decision-making unites the efforts of both heart and mind. Each person is a unique and valued part of the whole. It is only through collaboration and teamwork that we can truly attain unity. We revere unity in all that we do. All our decisions and actions are as a result of our influence on the Muslim community. New ideas necessitate an atmosphere that cultivates diverse perspectives.

The Muslim leadership needs to develop a vision. A vision provides guidance and motivation for the community to think about the future it wants. The process for the Muslim community is as follows:

· Provides a comprehensible awareness of values.
· Identifies issues and trends that impact progress.
· Communicates an all-inclusive vision to direct short and long-term decision-making.
· Develops action plans and implementation tools to accomplish an ideal outlook.

A sustainable Muslim community can meet the future with self-assurance, because it has a reliable and renewable supply of resources, a resilient social fabric, and a healthy environment. This unites to sustain all varieties of life for the long term. Involvement, exchange of ideas, and coordination are essential facets of strategic planning. In addition, there needs to be a decision support system to adopt the vision. There needs to be the advancement of a monitoring and evaluation system to assess how the Muslim community is developing relative to the specific goals under the vision or strategic plan.

The strategic plan has a set of objectives, which are:

· Establish a solid plan that will guide subsequent strategies and plans.
· Differentiate a span of crucial issues and subsequent strategies.
· Help encourage participation in all sectors of the Muslim community.
· Recognize and promote values in the Muslim community.
· Establish mutual ownership of plans.
· Create and put into operation a decision support system.
· Develop measures to assess the progress.
· Build a reporting scheme that will flow back into the strategic plan.

Process

Once the purpose and vision have been established, we need to

understand the process of how our plan works:
- Where are we now?
- Where are we going?
- Where do we want to be?
- How did we get there?
- How are we going?

All of these questions engulf the central core, which is the Muslim community. These questions represent ideas and actions. For example, is there diversity? Does the Muslim community celebrate diversity? Diversity is a word of many different meanings. It is a word overused; yet, it is often a concept that is overlooked. In the Islamic community the theme of diversity has been woven throughout history. With the advent of the agricultural revolution, the technological revolution, the income revolution, and the Internet revolution, a disconnection has happened. Throughout the evolution of these revolutions, there has been a shift in power. In addition, with capitalism, there has been an increased focus on materialism and profit-oriented growth.

These power shifts and zeal toward wealth have led to a disconnected society. The Muslim community within the disconnected society has been adversely affected. Some Muslims have fallen into the spiral trap of materialism and capitalistic endeavors. Through a unified Muslim community, a reconnection is possible. To the degree that the community may become sustainable and healthy, Muslims within that community must respect and understand one another. This reconnection involves an effort towards self-reliance, decentralization, simplicity, and active participation in the activities of the community.

Mission Statement

Following is a mission statement that encompasses the spirit of unity:

"With tolerance, diversity and reconciliation, it is the mutual commitment of all Islamic schools of thought to form a cohesive coalition as they partner and demonstrate in harmony shared values of compassion, peace, justice and respect for one another so as to seek Allah's Benevolence and Mercy by affirming His Commands for strengthening the bonds of brotherhood and solidarity within an inclusive and unified Muslim community." (Tallal Turfe)

Emotional Intelligence

The mission statement requires a great deal of reflection and utilization of our emotional intelligence. Emotional intelligence is a type of social intelligence that involves the ability to monitor each other's emotions, to discriminate among them, and to use the information to guide our thinking and actions. Here the Muslim leadership can apply emotional intelligence towards bringing home the unity. Emotional intelligence is the ability of the Muslim leadership to acquire and apply knowledge from their emotions and the emotions of other Muslims in order to be more successful in becoming unified.

Developing emotional intelligence skills allows people to think more clearly under pressure, eliminating time wasted by feelings of anger, anxiety and fear. People with high emotional intelligence skills get along better and don't let anxieties and frustrations get in the way of efficiently solving problems. It increases the understanding between people, which minimizes time wasted arguing and being defensive. How this emotional intelligence unfolds is as follows: [25]

· Personal Competence:
o Self-Awareness
o Self-Regulation
o Self-Motivation

· Social Competence:
o Empathy
o Managing Relationships

Self-awareness, self-regulation and self-motivation are intrapersonal, i.e., within the individual, while empathy and managing relationships are interpersonal, between people. One must have good intrapersonal skills to develop good interpersonal skills. Intrapersonal skills derive from the ability to be aware of, make sense of, use and manage the information from one's own emotional states, for example, assertiveness, self-regard and independence. Interpersonal skills derive from the ability to perceive the moods, motivations and intentions of others, for example, social responsibility.

Self-awareness means having a profound understanding of one's emotions and how their feelings affect them and other people. Self-awareness is having an accurate understanding of how we interact and behave with each other, how sensitive we are to the emotional well being of others, and how we are able to convey this awareness to others. It is recognizing when we are becoming negative, angry and defensive. Self-awareness is recognizing our feelings as they occur, with a confident sense of integrity, openness and with a high level of self-esteem.

Through self-regulation, people are able to promote an atmosphere of trust and fairness. Time management is regulated by not engaging in negativism and redundancy. With self-regulation, we can get rid ourselves of anxiety and despair by maintaining an emotional perspective. We can relax in pressure situations and handle feelings and information in such a way that they are properly managed. By grasping the beliefs and values that lie behind our feelings, we can find productive ways to handle our anxiety, despair and fear.

Bringing the Muslim leadership together requires a great deal of self-motivation, and the leadership must be passionate about achieving the unity. Highly motivated people are driven by their desire to achieve rather than driven by external rewards. They do not admit defeat, as they are determined in achieving the goal of unity. They are able to channel emotions to achieve a goal, and they persevere in the face of frustration undaunted by external pressure. They are able to regroup quickly after a setback. Muslims should perpetuate in their endeavors to do good deeds in order to be rewarded by Allah and to gain Allah's Pleasure. For example, attending funerals and visiting the sick pleases Allah. Allah rewards all of these actions because they bring joy to the heart of the believers. We should educate ourselves as to how to win the Pleasure of Allah. Some of the other good deeds that win the Pleasure of Allah are: (a) *sadaqah* or giving of charity; (b) *ma'roof* or courtesy that includes all forms of righteous action, particularly when helping others; and (c) *sulha* or reconciliation that brings Muslims in dispute back to Islam to resolve their differences.

Empathy is the ability to exchange information on a meaningful level. With empathy, people become proficient in skills essential for organizing groups and building teams, negotiating solutions, reconciling conflict among others, developing consensus, and creating personal connections. Empathy is being compassionate to the feelings and concerns of others as well as respecting their viewpoints.

With managing relationships, people are more productive as they do not squander time arguing and second-guessing themselves. They are aware of the emotions and feelings of others, and they are good listeners. They are able to collaborate with others in order to bring about a solution. They recognize when others are distressed, and they manage emotions with social competence and skill.

Let's just reflect on one of the aspects of emotional intelligence, i.e., team capabilities or team building. Team building is a social competence skill, and the coalition unity can support, delineate and attain success through collaborative goal setting and utilizing their capacity to achieve them. Critical issues are defined and discussed. Team building provides a vehicle for winning the unity as the participants comprehend and grasp the know-how needed to be major contributors. Team building members will acquire the knowledge, skills and abilities to:

·   Define what is expected from the coalition unity and the expectations of its stakeholders as to goals and outcomes.

·   Develop rules of engagement for the team members.

·   Identify barriers and critical success factors that enable the team to complete its mission.

·   Define critical team responsibilities and accountabilities as well as measurements of progress and success.

·   Develop problem solving and problem prevention techniques as well as feedback.

The primary aspect of emotional intelligence for Muslims is to create good feelings in the people they lead. They do this by maintaining those same positive feelings in themselves. In addition, they have to create change, sustain change, and build an emotional intelligence component within themselves. Most effective leaders are value-driven, flexible and informal, and open and frank. They are more connected to people and to networks. More especially, they exude resonance. They have genuine passion for their mission, and that passion is contagious. Their enthusiasm and excitement spread spontaneously, invigorating those who lead. The stronger a person is in emotional intelligence the better leader he or she will become. Unless we are aware of our own emotions, we will not know how to control them. Understanding emotional intelligence can be very effective in winning the unity among Muslims. If we are to succeed in this endeavor, then we must be able to control our emotions and be empathetic towards others. We must be ready to submit our will to the Will of Allah, as we proceed towards a more unified Muslim society. We pray to Allah to continue to guide us in our quest for unity and a more peaceful and prosperous life.

Back to Basics

We must restore the ethics and morals of Islamic behavior that have fallen prey to ignorance, discord and strife. Allah had warned us, as stated in the Qur'an:

"And obey Allah and His Messenger; and fall into no disputes, lest you lose heart and your power depart; and be patient and persevering: for Allah is with those who patiently persevere." (Qur'an 8:46)

We have a beautiful and enriching history of Islam, and the Qur'an illustrates how earlier Prophets warned us about disunity. The Qur'an is replete with examples of the rise and fall of nations and civilizations and their impact on the society. How the decline of nations and civilizations came about was because of discord within their communities. Although the Prophets preached unity, the followers broke that covenant, as they opted to fragment into sects:

"You turn back in repentance to Him, and fear Him: establish regular prayers, and you be not among those who join gods with Allah, - those who split up their Religion, and become (mere) sects, - each party rejoicing in that which is with itself!" (Qur'an 30:31-32)

Religion stands for Islam, and to be steadfast is to submit our will to the Will of Allah. How we submit is to live according to the *Shari'a* (Law), which Allah has ordained for us. Disunity is a disease, as it violates the canons of *Shari'a* and abandons the guidance of Prophet Mohammad. Jealousy, suspicion and division are contributing factors towards the erosion of faith. The disease of disunity runs rampant in the Islamic society today. However, there is hope to restore the unity, provided we come back to the basics of Islam. Some of these basics are:

· Consciousness of Allah and His Oneness (*Tawhid*), which is to obey Him and acknowledge that He alone is worthy of worship.

· Adherence to the Articles of Faith and the Branches of Faith, the latter that has prayer as its pivotal point.

· Regular recitation of the Qur'an, the *Hadith* (Traditions) and supplication.

· Friends should be chosen with discretion, so as not to stagnate from the straight path of Islam.

· Avoidance of the evils of the society, such as intoxicants, adultery, pornography and slander.

We all subscribe to the basics in Islam. If we go back to the basics that we all accept, then it is possible for us to unite. More now than ever must the Muslim *Ummah* unite, as we have witnessed the desecration of our holy places, the oppression and tyranny in our Muslim societies, and the threats from outside the Muslim world. We need to restore the *Ummah* (community) back to a healthy and vital state of cohesiveness. While our responsibility is to adhere to the basics of Islam, we must also be willing to recognize the following:

· There are disparities in the perceptions of how people think and administer their affairs.

· Diversity is the mechanism by which the Islamic society can understand each other and flourish.

· Intellectual development and cross-fertilization of ideas can be the vehicle by which to better understand the perspectives of each other.

· Divergent issues should be approached in a more balanced and collaborative posture so as to encompass the magnitude of these issues.

· Knowledge and ethics must be linked and cemented with the aim of restoring the unity.

· The gap between the ideals of Islam and the realities of the Muslim *Ummah* must be bridged.

· Muslim scholars must address contemporary issues and challenges in the direction of overcoming them, as they teach their students the legacy of unity of the early followers of Islam.

· Brotherhood and solidarity must be preserved.

· We must maintain a deep consciousness of Allah, as we seek His Pleasure and Guidance to unify us.

When the Muslim community becomes aware of its Islamic responsibilities, it will win back the unity. Each Muslim must search his or her conscious and bring it into harmony with the consciousness of other Muslims. This will bring about the unity, and the *Ummah* will once again prosper and flourish as it did during the days of Prophet Mohammad.

EPILOGUE

"The balance that day will be true (to a nicety): Those whose scale (of good) will be heavy, will prosper: Those whose scale will be light, will find their souls in perdition, for that they wrongfully treated Our Signs." (Qur'an 7:8-9)

The scale of life is a weighing of our deeds and actions. As the scale teeters throughout our lives, it is our quest to balance it. In Islam, justice is established according to the balance. Islam warns against ignorance and extremism and mandates knowledge and moderation as the way of life. On the Day of Judgment, there will be a weighing scale to measure our good deeds and evil deeds. The scale of balance manifests itself in the concept of unity.

As Muslims we need to resolve our spiritual dilemma not just with ethical principles and moral guidelines, but also with the will to change. This change requires us to lay aside our prejudices and hatred, to have our insurgence turned into love, to transform our inner self to what is ethically and morally in line with Allah's Commands, and to make the reality of brotherhood and solidarity a workable fact of life. These are not mere rhetorical expressions; they do in fact refer to the realities of our predicament. Nothing less than this is required if we are to truly achieve unity and the ultimate fulfillment of the significance of our existence. Unity is the only way to bring us closer to Allah. As there is One Allah that manifests one creation, so there is One Allah that is the source of all conscious beings, whether on earth or elsewhere in the Cosmos. We must strive towards a change in our lives in order to truly love one another.

We have the means and strength by which to achieve this unity, that is, the *Rope of Allah*. Attainment of unity is not realized by just reading the Qur'an and the *hadiths* (traditions) of the Prophet Mohammad. It is realized when we truly live by Allah's Commandments and emulate the lifestyle of our Prophets and Imams. To hold fast to the *Rope of Allah* takes a great deal of concentration and concerted effort as well as a pure heart. Those who are sanctimonious and pretentious have a superfluous complacency, and it is difficult for them to see and think straight. We must overcome our inner desires; seek Allah's Forgiveness, and exercise humility and empathy.

Unity is the key to a better understanding of our roles as

Muslims. Unity shapes and molds the way we behave and act. Our very lifestyles must depend on unity if we are to truly cling to the *Rope of Allah* and achieve His Compassion and Mercy. We must tie down our uncontrolled fears, prejudices, egos, weaknesses and ignorance. We need unity to bear the assaults of evil and to persevere in our faith. Unity weeps tears of comfort and finds content in the midst of discontent. Unity turns hostility into kindness. The power of unity is more than just a miracle. Unity brings about the Pleasure of Allah.

Allah wishes that we developed this power of unity in order to defeat both internal and external forces hostile to truth. It is with the quality of unity that Muslims declare themselves satisfied with Allah's Pleasure. Unity is the armor by which one defends his soul. With unity we strive towards becoming closer to Allah. In unity, we seek out the pious and join with them in pleasing Allah. Diversity, distinction and differences must be met with mutual respect; acceptance and even celebration, while the deeper foundations of unity are held steadily in view.

The *Rope of Allah* establishes a strong connectivity between man and Allah and unites all believers together as one. Our deepest point of unity transcends race, culture, gender, and profession, even the level of intelligence or emotional make-up, since all these attributes vary widely among people. To take a strong and secure hold onto the *Rope of Allah* signifies that believers should seek knowledge and ascribe intense importance to their way of life. Only in this way can the believers hope to attain ultimate happiness and solidarity. With this frame of mind, the believers are in reach of Paradise, as they hold firm to the *Rope of Allah*. The *Rope of Allah* loops through time. With intensity and enlightenment, it demands from us endurance, submission, certainty, believing, acceptance, adherence, action and patience as well as a lasso-sense of obedience and gratitude. The *Rope of Allah* is straightforward and made up of tightly curled strands. We cannot separate them. We can only strengthen them. We are what we are as we cling steadfastly to each strand. We are what we have – the Qur'an and the *Sunnah* of Prophet Mohammad and his *Ahl al-Bayt*.

APPENDIX

Topic: Islam's Perspective on Violence and Terrorism

Professor Tallal Alie Turfe
At the United Nations
May 21, 2003

His Excellency the Secretary General...Honorable Ambassadors to the United Nations...distinguished international jurists and public figures...my fellow speakers...ladies and gentlemen...*Assalamu Alaikum – peace be with you.*

Overview

On the subject of violence and terrorism, Islam has been at the center stage of discussion for the past twenty-five years. To be sure, no religion is fundamentally violent, and Islam is no exception. The use of religion to justify and incite violence and terrorism has been the result of transgressions by individuals who render their own interpretation of what that religion is. Whether it is Islam or any other religion, we can cite many examples in each of these faiths where transgressions have occurred. As terrifying as it is, violence has become a way of life for these extremists who appeal to a religious ideology that is abhorred by the faith they follow. To be sure, terrorists have no religion, for no religion advocates hatred or endorses killing of innocent people.

There is a great misconception about Islam throughout the world. Islam is inaccurately viewed as a complex, inhumane and backward religion that promotes violence and terrorism. Islam is incorrectly perceived as one where suicide is the easiest way to Paradise, and where the concept of *jihad* is one of terror. Ironically, some of the terrorists, who profess to be Muslims, try to justify their violence in the name of Islam. Equally ironic is the fact that this numerically insignificant minority can exert considerable influence over the majority who tend to ignore these claims as silent spectators. A sad situation indeed!

Islam's Position on Violence and Terrorism

Islam means the submission of one's will to the Will of God. Islam is more than just a religion; it is a way of life. Its message is one of peace, tolerance and understanding. It abhors violence, killing, exploitation and injustice. Islam promotes human rights, service to humanity, and freedom of conscience, justice and equality. Violence and terrorism and outrageous attacks against humanity are blatant violations of the doctrines of Islam.

Islam not only considers acts of violence, terrorism, aggression and corruption as despicable, but also considers these acts tantamount to waging war against God. Consequently, Islam prohibits man's injustice to his fellow man, and condemns those who cause harm to people, not only in the Muslim world, but also anywhere in the world. Moreover, Islam orders its believers to keep away from anything that may cause turmoil, and warns against its evil consequences.

Islam demands the unconditional freedom of all religions, and it deplores the killing or even the persecution of people just because they embrace a different faith. Muslims are permitted to fight only for self-defense and to enforce peace. A basic requirement in Islam is that Muslims treat all people with compassion and fairness.

Unjust killings are categorically forbidden in Islam, as these evil acts amount to disbelief:

"...If any one slew a person – unless it be for murder or for spreading mischief in the land – it would be as if he slew the whole people; and if any one saved a life, it would be as if he saved the life of the whole people...." (Qur'an 5:32)

Sources of Violence and Terrorism

Just who are the sources of violence and terrorism? If one gave a seven-year old boy a loaded pistol, the youngster most likely would begin firing it as though it were a water pistol. So the major blame lies with the one who gave the boy the pistol. Likewise, giving terrorists the means for weapons of mass destruction can only lead to disaster. What we need is a resolution stating that at least two parties are held accountable – the one who supplied the means for weapons of mass destruction and the one who fired the weapons.

Terrorism feeds and propagates on discord within the global society. The world's major powers must be unified in their efforts for peace and security, with no exception. And the United Nations must be the vehicle to drive home these objectives. However, if the world's major powers continue to provide the means for weapons of mass destruction to well-established and known terrorist regimes, then the end result is chaos and havoc. For example, Saddam Hussein was in power for a long time in Iraq, and during his tenure it was the consensus of the world that he committed atrocities and crimes against humanity for more than a quarter of a century. Why, then, was he supplied with the means for weapons of mass destruction? It is a paradox indeed!

The question before us is how can the world's major powers combat violence and terrorism when there is so much distrust with and between them; they are simply not believable. Muslims believe that wars against their nations are for the purpose of oil and exploitation and not for self-determination or democracy or human rights. Muslims believe that the major world powers are supporting arrogant rogue states and other groups that do exactly as they please.

Yet, another source of violence and terrorism is that of the inner self. We see evidence of egocentric dictators with an insatiable craving for power and wealth. Despotic regimes have tried to control all aspects of religious and political life. They have even tried to co-opt Islamic movements, in part by implementing their rhetoric. They have even used their office to enrich themselves on a grand scale. Corruption is endemic.

Jihad's Impact on Attitudes and Human Behavior

In Islam, *jihad* opposes all forms of violence and terrorism, and it defends the homeland against occupation, plunder and colonialism. *Jihad* is waged against those who support others in driving people out of their homes, as well as against those who are in breach of their covenants. *Jihad* is a struggle against oppression, exploitation, tyranny, fear, corruption and denying the masses basic human rights (Qur'an 4:75-76). It is ordained to establish peace and justice, freedom of religion and security, compassion and equity (Qur'an 2:193).

245

Jihad is not meant for domination nor to achieve personal, territorial and economical gains nor to exercise power and control. Those who perform *jihad* must spiritually and morally reform themselves, as they struggle to overcome the self. (Qur'an 22:78).

However, some Muslims must bear responsibility for the bad name given to *jihad*. Some governments and groups in Muslim countries have made illicit use of *jihad* only to hide their moral, social and political bankruptcy. In the process they kill the innocent, cause only death and destruction, and do not advance the cause of peace and justice. But regrettably they are the ones who show up regularly in the media.

A great misconception that prevails is one that equates *jihad* with war. The word *jihad* sends shivers down the spines of many non-Muslims. *Jihad* is looked upon as one of holy war against non-Muslims, a kind of Crusade in reverse. This is contrary to the Islamic teachings. The true *jihad* is when one controls his own desires and self-actualizes himself in the virtues of tolerance, empathy, reconciliation and forgiveness.

It is the physical *jihad* that receives so much criticism and, as such, those who do not understand it equate it with terror. However, the very purpose of this physical *jihad* is to answer the call of those who cry out for freedom and yearn to be liberated from tyranny and bondage. It is a means of defense, but only for the cause of righteousness and justice. Other types of *jihad* are charity, empathy and scholarly works, and the self-sacrifice one makes may be in terms of wealth, property or forgiveness. For example, to reconcile differences with each other is at the pinnacle of *jihad*. Prophet Mohammad (pbuh) said:

"Reconciliation of your differences is more worthy than all prayers and all fasting."

Reality of Islam

So what is the reality of Islam? How does one dispel the myths that have been created and spread so viciously? The only way to examine Islam is to simply examine its teachings and beliefs. This is the way to find the truth about what Islam says about violence and terrorism. The very name Islam comes from the Arabic word *salama*, which means *peace*. Its followers do not get tired of greeting each other with *assalamu alaikum*, which means *peace be with you*. If such a religion is based on the notion of peace, then how is it that so many acts done by its adherents are contrary to peace? The answer is simple. Such actions, if not endorsed by the religion, have no place within it. Acts of terrorism and aggression are hated by God and as such are denounced in Islam:

"Call on your Lord with humility and in private: for God does not love those who trespass beyond bounds. Do no mischief on the earth, after it has been sent in order, but call on Him with fear and longing in your hearts: for the Mercy of God is always near to those who do good." (Qur'an 7:55-56)

Aggression against innocent people is strongly denounced by all religions including Islam. However, we must not confuse terrorism with freedom fighters. Islam condemns extremism and violence and stands firmly against terrorist practices. However, the fight against aggression and occupation is regarded as a legitimate right. While Muslims must defend themselves, they must not be antagonistic. While Islam requires its believers to be strong, it mandates that this strength be used to achieve peace and security for the society, and that aggression is not an option.

Many non-Muslims picture Islam as one of religious fanatics on camels with a sword in one hand and a Qur'an in the other hand. This myth, which was made popular in Europe during the Crusades, is totally baseless. The Qur'an clearly says:

"Let there be no compulsion in religion…."(Qur'an 2:256)

Compulsion or force is unacceptable in Islam. People are not compelled to change their faith. Tolerance is a religious moral duty in Islam, and it acknowledges the self-respect, equality and freedom of all people. Tolerance is to have respect and under-standing of diverse cultures and faiths. Islam teaches that a person's faith must be pure and sincere, so it is certainly not something that can be forced on someone. Tolerance leads to brotherly love (Qur'an 49:10), which is the cornerstone of Islam. Brotherly love originates from mutual respect and empathy for one another, whether it is a Muslim or non-Muslim. The enforcement of broth-erhood is the greatest social ideal of Islam.

Misrepresentation of Islam

Some Muslims groups, who are hoodwinked by their fraudulent leaders, continue their acts of aggression against innocent civilians. Let there be no misunderstanding, Islam condemns these acts.

Islam does not punish those that embrace a different faith, nor does it allow Muslims to fight against those who disagree with them on religious questions. Islam does not change, people do. Those who perpetrate such terrorist acts are not following Islam, even though they profess to do so.

Unfortunately, terrorist groups have gone to extremes by using the name of Islam to promote their cause, and this gave many non-Muslims a chance to denigrate Islam and classify the Muslims as terrorists. Prophet Mohammad (pbuh) said:

"Those who go to extremes are destroyed."

Suicide bombing is undoubtedly an extremity that has reached the ranks of the Muslims. In the rules of warfare, we find no sanction for such an act either in the Qur'an or from the behavior and words of Prophet Mohammad (pbuh). Unfortunately, some misguided Muslims believe that such acts are paving the way for an Islamic revival. The taking of innocent lives, which is so often the case with suicide bombing, is forbidden, as human life is indeed precious. All other types of extremities such as hostage taking, aerial hijacking and planting bombs in public places, are clearly forbidden in Islam.

The teachings of Islam have been distorted and misrepresented by terrorist regimes for their own benefit. Some rulers profess to be Muslims, but their concept of Islam is a version of their own invention and evil whims. Terrorists, who persecute and murder innocent people, do not represent Islam, which at its core is a religion of peace. Prophet Mohammad (pbuh) said:

"Whoever hurts a non-Muslim citizen of a Muslim state hurts me, and he who hurts me annoys God."

Quran'ic Verses Taken Out of Context

Often poor communication leads to animosity and distrust. Some non-Muslim clerics are well informed about Islam, but they continue to distort that faith by spreading lies in their sermons in order to delude their congregations. As a result, seeds of hatred and enmity are planted in the minds of their congregations, and when they air their sermons on television, the impact of this repugnance has a far-reaching audience. This type of falsification about Islam may lead non-Muslims to violence and terrorism.

Some non-Muslim clerics have taken Quran'ic verses out of

context. For example, let us examine a couple of these verses:

"Deaf, dumb and blind, they will not return (to the path)." (Qur'an 2:18)

This verse means that it is not the physical nature of deaf, dumb and blind but the spiritual nature. There are those who do not want to hear, speak or see relative to faith. Nor do they want to adhere to God's Commandments.

"On the Day when some faces will be lit up with white, and some faces will be in the gloom of black: to those, whose faces will be black, will be said: 'did you reject Faith after accepting it? Taste then the Penalty for rejecting Faith.' But those whose faces will be lit with white, - they will be in the light of God's Mercy: therein to dwell forever." (Qur'an 3:106-107)

This verse means that on the Day of Judgment white faces are distinguished from black faces, not in the physical sense, but in the spiritual sense. Those whose hearts are pure in faith are like the color of light, which is white. Those whose hearts are impure in faith are like the color of darkness, which is black.

Muslims Combating Violence and Terrorism

The great majority of Muslims have responded to despotism and corruption in peaceful ways, not through militancy. For example, one response has been to turn to personal piety, intensified religious adherence, and spiritual self-restraint. Another response has been to combine personal devotion with communal action to recast social, political and economic institutions as Islamic institutions. Their platform is one of cultural reform and social services, not militancy.

History is replete with examples of how pious and brave Muslims fought against tyranny and oppression. The greatest example was an event that took place in the latter part of the seventh century. At that time, Islam was under the corrupt rule of a tyrant, who committed virtually every vile act known to mankind. Something had to be done about it. So a champion emerges to save Islam. That champion was Imam Hussein (as), the grandson of Prophet Mohammad (pbuh), who fought and died for the protection of Islam. To him, Islam was not only threatened but on the verge of collapse and destruction. What led to Imam Hussein's (as) martyrdom is a tragedy, the story that has been repeatedly recounted over the centuries.

Imam Hussein (as) would not give his allegiance to the ruler's injustice and tyranny. For Imam Hussein he had to confront despotism and oppression by spreading the message of truth and justice to the Muslim community. As a result, a battle at Karbala, Iraq took place. The Muslim army of the tyrant numbered in the thousands, and they surrounded Imam Hussein (as) and his small contingent of seventy-two followers. While history reveals that other victims of terrorism opted for suicide, this was not the case with Imam Hussein (as). He and his companions fought with honor until they were all martyred. Even some of their bodies were decapitated. By military standards, the battle should have been over in a matter of minutes, but actually lasted for several hours. What Imam Hussein (as) left at Karbala was the example, which ultimately transcended into the Muslim community rising up to topple the tyrannical regime. Imam Hussein's (as) example was that criminal regimes should not be allowed to continue, for they must be overthrown at all costs.

Muslims Protecting Non-Muslims

History is filled with examples whereby Muslims have protected non-Muslims. While under Islamic rule for many centuries, non-Muslims had complete freedom to practice their faith, establish places of worship, and institute their own judicial system. For example, when Muslims ruled Spain, both the Jews and Christians were very secure and prosperous, as they enjoyed all the rights of freedom while living in harmony with their Muslim neighbors. Another example is when Constantinople was under Islamic rule; the seat of the Orthodox Church was highly esteemed and Christians were completely free to practice their faith. In addition, when Jews faced persecution in Europe in the fifteenth century, many of them fled for safety to North Africa to be under the security of Muslims. What is remarkable is that while Muslims ruled all the islands in the Mediterranean Sea for almost ten centuries, they were a minority.

During the reign of the Islamic Empire that lasted for many centuries, non-Muslims attained high positions within the Muslim society. This came about because of Islam's tolerance and respect for other faiths. During that time, Islam was spread from Spain and Morocco in the West to India and China in the East. How can a small contingent of Muslims compel these people to convert to a religion against their will? Moreover, when the Mongols conquered major segments of the Islamic Empire, they willingly adopted the faith of Islam rather than destroy it. Since the Mongols were the conquerors, they could not have been compelled to embrace the religion of the conquered.

Prophet Mohammad (pbuh) decreed that people of other faiths in an Islamic society were under his personal protection, forever. Prophet Mohammad (pbuh) called upon his followers to be friendly, considerate and benevolent to their neighbors, regardless of their beliefs, creed or race. He encouraged his followers to exchange gifts with their friends of different faiths.

Role of the Media

Before the dust of the World Trade Center and the Pentagon even began to settle from the horrific attacks of September 11, 2001, Muslims and Arabs were once again the leading suspects of terrorism from abroad. The media depicted the heinous crimes as that of Islam rather than that of individuals. Similarly, in the case of the Oklahoma City bombing in 1995, Islam was depicted as the culprit. In fact, a headline in a leading American newspaper read, *"In the Name of Islam."* Even a police artist sketch of the terrorist was shown for many days on television as that of an Arab man. Later, of course, it was proven that this bigoted assumption was incorrect. When it was revealed that a person of the Christian faith actually committed the Oklahoma City crime, Christianity was not the victim but, rather, the individual who just happens to be a Christian. The media has portrayed Islam to be something that it is not.

The media is painting a bleak picture of Islam, as it is inculcating in the minds of their audiences a misrepresentation of what Islam is. These audiences are being deceived, and they have a right to know what is really going on. Certainly, the misuse and abuse of *jihad* by terrorists and extremists leads to the negative portrayal of Islam by the media. However, the media should use caution and discretion when they make their reports, as these acts of terrorism are committed by a relatively small number of those who call themselves Muslims.

The media is awash with tales of terror and oppression. The

word *jihad* frightens a lot of people, and the media capitalizes on this fear. To them, this term means bloodshed and violence. Yet, to the overwhelming majority of Muslims, the word *jihad* means the struggle to be good. The public sees Osama bin Laden and his partners on television and believes them to be ambassadors of Islam. To the media, peace is not newsworthy, violence is!

The present manifestation of *jihad* by terrorists has great audience appeal. Action, suspense, exhilaration and damnation are what audiences appeal to. The media follows suit. In this way *jihad,* as it is presented, will always have a place in the media for as long as terrorists choose to represent it thus. In less than ten minutes after the Twin Towers collapsed, CNN had the phrase *"Holy War"* coined on the air. Perhaps the media had taken more liberties than it should in handling sensitive issues of religion, but that has not stopped them from doing it. What happens when negative images of Islam prevail in the audience's frame of mind? Acts of aggression are seen as religious acts. Aggression committed by terrorists is seen as acts sanctioned by their God.

Unfortunately, when an Arab commits a terrorist act, the media labels him as a *"Muslim terrorist,"* even though he may adhere to a faith other than Islam. However, when Serbs murdered and raped innocent women in Bosnia, they were not called *"Christian terrorists."* The media does not portray activities of the Ku Klux Klan or those of priests who have engaged in pedophilia as acts sanctioned by Christianity. One could certainly conclude that there is a double standard in the media. Saddam Hussein and Osama bin Laden had about as much to do with Islam, as Adolph Hitler and Slobodon Milosevic had to do with Christianity.

Crimes Against Humanity – Reflections

In our struggle against terrorism we need to understand why these perpetrators engage in such heinous acts of violence. We must arrive at a workable definition of just what terrorism is. We do not have a firm grip as to the causes and prevention of terrorism. To be sure our knowledge regarding terrorism is fragmentary and incomplete. We are still in the dark as to how to deal with this evil.

To combat terrorism we must understand it. To understand it we must study it. We must identify the real terrorists and bring them to justice, and those who protect and nurture them must be held accountable. Terrorism does negate our most basic and treasured principles and values. We need to address the evils of terrorism and dispense justice with impartiality. The real cure for terrorism consists in removing the conditions that have brought it about. We must deal with the circumstances and motives that bring about terrorism.

United we stand against all kinds of violence and terrorism, as only through unity can we bring about peace and justice. From its inception, Islam has been an upholder of peace and justice, not violence.

Terrorists belong to a variety of religions, each erroneously claiming exclusive rights to redemption. Sadly, for centuries, the world has allowed these terrorists to misuse religion for their own personal interests. It is time that the world wakes up to undo this exploitation of religions. It is also time that the world depicts these terrorists as rogues and not as Muslims or as those of any other faith.

Conclusion

We have a great challenge before us. And that challenge is to combat violence and terrorism. Our success can be achieved with patience, forbearance and diligence. Let us seek to convert, not towards each other's faith but, rather, towards tolerance and compassion and love. As we engage in dialogue, let us seek to understand before we seek to be understood. Let empathy be our beacon as we begin to feel for each other. Let us walk in each other's shoes and share our experiences for the noble cause of bringing about peace and justice in the world.

The hour of our generation may by the dusk and sunset of peace. As we close this day, let it be our prayer that through the cooperative efforts of all freedom-loving people our generation will see the dawn and sunrise of permanent peace. Today is a sunrise of hope, a unique and wonderful opportunity for us to work together toward a better and more peaceful world. As the bloody pages of violence and terrorism have unfolded in our presence, we can no longer shut our eyes to the tale of mankind's suffering; we can no longer close our ears to the call for peace and justice; we can no longer narrow our minds by being simple-minded; and we can no longer harden our hearts by selfishness. May God give us the strength and wisdom to see the light and to eliminate the destructive spiral of violence and terrorism?

Suggested Resolutions to the World Council of Religious Leaders
Proposal to the Secretary General of the United Nations

Professor Tallal Alie Turfe

· RESOLVED that the World Council of Religious Leaders reaffirms its support for all Security Council Resolutions related to the issue of combating terrorism.

· RESOLVED that the World Council of Religious Leaders strongly condemns violence, aggression and terrorism in all its forms and manifestations and further condemns the perpetrators of such heinous crimes who pretend to act in the name of religion or under any other pretext.

· RESOLVED that since the World Council of Religious Leaders is confident there is an international consensus on combating and eliminating the causes of terrorism in all its forms, which jeopardizes the rights and endangers the life and property of innocent people as well as violates the sovereignty of nations, it proposes a sustained strategy to eradicate terrorism be jointly made by both the political leaders and the religious leaders of all nations.

· RESOLVED that the World Council of Religious Leaders recommends that the international community agree on the criteria that define the many forms and manifestations of terrorism and how to differentiate between terrorism and the legitimate struggle of freedom fighters for self-determination and national liberation against occupation and aggression.

· RESOLVED that the World Council of Religious Leaders proposes that an international judicial system be established, with irrevocable powers not subject to veto by any nation, in order to identify, apprehend and prosecute terrorists.

· RESOLVED that the World Council of Religious Leaders recommends that a long-term strategy be crafted that addresses the root causes of extremism and terrorism, such as poverty, foreign occupation and injustice.

· RESOLVED that in order to achieve peace and global stability, the World Council of Religious Leaders are engaged in mutual exchange of dialogue for the purpose of establishing common ground and common principle in the direction of heightening the awareness of the international community to renounce violence and combat terrorism through the vehicles of conflict resolution, tolerance, education and advocacy.

· RESOLVED that the World Council of Religious Leaders strongly believes that moral and ethical values that govern human behavior will triumph, and the banners of peace and security should never be sullied by warfare for conquest save to bring freedom and justice to all beneath their folds.

· RESOLVED that the World Council of Religious Leaders believes that tolerance among all religions must be the vehicle to drive home the unity against violence and terrorism, as there must be respect and understanding of diverse cultures and faiths.

· RESOLVED that the World Council of Religious Leaders strongly believe that people of different faiths be allowed to practice their religion anywhere in the world, free of retaliation and without reprisals of any kind.

· RESOLVED that the World Council of Religious Leaders agrees that attacks on civilians are condemned by all religions, which denounce extremism and violence, and stand firmly against terrorist practices.

· RESOLVED that the World Council of Religious Leaders proclaims that the true *jihad* of Islam is one of an internal and external struggle for peace and justice that opposes all forms of violence, aggression and terrorism.

· RESOLVED that the World Council of Religious Leaders declares that Islam is innocent of all forms and manifestations of terrorism that involve the killing of innocent people, and it calls upon all nations not to grant asylum to terrorists but, rather, to bring them to justice.

· RESOLVED that the World Council of Religious Leaders declares that international terrorism is complex and multifaceted and can only be defeated by a sustained and comprehensive approach.

· RESOLVED that the World Council of Religious Leaders recommends that an international humanitarian order be estab-lished in partnership among the nations whereby justice and equality are derived from a genuine foundation of mutual coopera-tion, forgiveness, reconciliation and solidarity.

· RESOLVED that the World Council of Religious Leaders are jointly working together to find the common denominators in their faiths to craft a unified response to all forms of intolerance, aggression or acts that violate the rights of innocent people and their properties.

·　RESOLVED that the World Council of Religious Leaders believes that no distinction be made between individual terrorism and state-sponsored terrorism, and that not only the perpetrators of violence and terrorism be held accountable but also those who supply them with the means for weapons of mass destruction with the aim of destabilizing countries and communities.

·　RESOLVED that the World Council of Religious Leaders believes that non-proliferation measures in the biological, chemical and nuclear fields must be strengthened in order to deny terrorists access to weapons of mass destruction.

·　RESOLVED that the World Council of Religious Leaders recommends that research be undertaken to study historical reasons why individuals have used religion to justify violence and terrorism, and why violence has become a way of life for terrorists who render their own interpretation of religion and appeal to an ideology that is abhorred by the faith they follow.

·　RESOLVED that the World Council of Religious Leaders recommends that the services of the behavioral scientists be engaged to study and analyze the various forms of terrorism as to its definition, causes, similarities and dissimilarities among religions, and socio-psychological patterns over time.

·　RESOLVED that the World Council of Religious Leaders emphatically affirms that suicide bombing and other acts of extremism, such as hostage taking, aerial hijacking and planting bombs in public places, against innocent civilians are forbidden.

FOOTNOTES

1. G. F. Haddad, *Compound Ignorance (Jahl Murakkab)* (Living Islam: Islamic Tradition, 2000).

2. Ibn Qudaamah al Maqdisee, *Mukhtasar Minhaj al-Qaasideen.*

3. Sayyid Abul A'ala Mawdudi, *Towards Understanding Islam* (Leicester: Islamic Foundation, 1988).

4. Dr. Bhupendra Kumar Modi, *One God* (New Delhi: Modi Foundation, 2000).

5. Kevin MacDonald, *The Culture of Critique* (Westport: Praeger Publishers, 1998).

6. Modi, *One God.*

7. *Dreaming at Swoon: Your Everyday Oracle* (Internet).

8. *The Admiralty "Manual of Seamanship"* (Vol. 2, 1951).

9. Henderson Marine Supply, Inc. (2003).

10. Shaykh Ahmed Abdur Rashid, *The Oneness of Allah and The Oneness of His Community* (Internet).

11. Sadruddin Islahi, *The Obligation of Iqaamat-ul-Deen.*

12. Imam Abu Hamid al-Ghazali, *The Alchemy of Happiness* (Lahore: Sh. Muhammad Ashraf, 1954).

13. Ahmad Farid, *Purification of the Soul* (Dar al-Taqwa, 1993).

14. Khwaja Kamal-ul-Din, *Brief Notes on the Qur'an: The Last Seven Chapters* (Lahore: The Lahore Ahmadiyya Movement for the Propagation of Islam).

15. Mohamed Baianonie, *The Causes of Division and Disputes Among the Muslims* (Islamic Association of Raleigh, North Carolina, March

4, 1988).

16. Franz Rosenthal Khaldun, *Ibn Khaldun: The Muqaddimah* (Princeton: Bollingen Series, 1969).

17. Ayatollah Ja'far Sobhani, *Doctrines of Shi'i Islam: A Compendium of Imami Beliefs and Practices* (translated and edited by Reza Shah-Kazemi) (London: I. B. Tauris in association with The Institute of Ismaili Studies, 2001).

18. Sezai Ozcelik, *Nonviolent Action and Third Party Role in Islamic World* (George Mason University – Institute for Conflict Analysis and Resolution, 2000).

19. Dr. Israr Ahmad, *The Obligations the Muslims Owe to the Qur'an* (Pakistan: Institute Al-Islam, 1999).

20. Shaykh 'Abdul-'Azees Ibn Baz, *The Correct Islaamic 'Aqeedah & That Which Opposes It* (Houston: Darussalam, no date).

21. The World Forum for Proximity of Islamic Schools of Thought (Tehran: 2003).

22. *Tawhid Quarterly Journal* (Tehran: Vol. 15, No. 3, Autumn 1999).

23. The Organization of the Islamic Conference (Rabat, Morocco).

24. Shaykh Muhammad Hisham Kabbani, *Sunni and Shi'a Seek Reconciliation* (Washington, D.C.: The Islamic Supreme Council of America, October 1999).

25. Dr. Daniel Goleman, *Emotional Intelligence* (New York: Bantam Books, 1995).

SELECTED BIBLIOGRAPHY

Abu-Said, Mahmoud. *Concept of Islam*. Indianapolis: American Trust Publications, 1983.

Ahmad, Dr. Israr. *The Obligations the Muslims Owe to the Qur'an*. Pakistan: Institue Al-Islam, 1999.

Ahmad, Hazrat Mirza Ghulam. *Teachings of Islam*. Pakistan: Ahmadiyyah Anjuman Isha'at Islam, 1983.

Ahmad, K. J. *Hundred Great Muslims*. Chicago: Kazi Publications, Inc., 1987.

Al-Askari, Allalmah Murtaza. *A Probe into the History of Hadith*. Pakistan: Al-Khoei Foundation, 1991.

Al-Ghazali, Abu Hamid. *The Alchemy of Happiness*. Lahore: Sh. Muhammad Ashraf, 1954.

Ali, Abdullah Yusuf. *The Holy Qur'an: Text, Translation and Commentary*. Washington, D.C.: The Islamic Center, 1978.

Ali, S. V. Mir Ahmed. *The Holy Qur'an*. Elmhurst, New York: Tahrike Tarsile Qur'an, Inc., 1995.

Al-Majlisi, Muhammad Baqir. *Bihar al-Anwar (Ocean of Light)*. (Encyclopedia of Hadiths), 17th Century.

Al Maqdisee, Ibn Qudaamah. *Mukhtasar Minhaj al-Qaasideen*.

Al-Ma'soomi, Sheikh Muhammad Sultan. *Should A Muslim Follow a Particular Madhhab?* Houston: Darussalam, (no date).

Al-Mufid, Shaykh. Kitab Al-Irshad: *The Book of Guidance into the Lives of the Twelve Imams*. Tehran: Ansariyan Publication, (no date).

Al-Musawi, Hashim. *The Shia: Their Origin and Beliefs*. Beirut: Al-Ghadeer Center for Islamic Studies, 1996.

Amir-Moezzi, Mohammad Ali. *The Divine Guide in Early Shi'ism*. (translated by David Streight). Albany: State University of New York Press, 1994.

Arberry, A. J. *Revelation and Reason in Islam*. New York: The Macmillan Company, 1957.

Arjomand, Said Amir. *Authority and Political Culture in Shi'ism*. Albany: State University of New York Press, 1988.

Athar, Alia N. *Prophets: Models for Humanity*. Chicago: Kazi Publications, Inc., 1993.

Ayati, Dr. Ibrahim. *A Probe into the History of Ashura*. Pakistan: Al-Khoei Foundation, 1991.

Baianonie, Mohamed. *The Causes of Division and Disputes Among the Muslims*. North Carolina: Islamic Association of Raleigh, March 4, 1988.

Baz, Shaykh 'Abdul-'Azeez Ibn. *The Correct Islaamic 'Aqeedah & That Which Opposes It*. Houston: Darussalam (no date).

Benson, H. & M. Z. Klipper. *The Relaxation Response*. New York: Avon Books, 1975.

Dabashi, Hamid. *Authority in Islam*. London: Transaction Publishers, 1989.

Davis, W. Summer. Losing Faith: *A Quest for Truth and the Origins of Life*. Nebraska: iUniverse, 1901.

Dreaming at Swoon: Your Everyday Oracle (Internet).

El Zein, Samih Atef, et al. *Imam Ali Ibn Abi Taleb: Nahjul Balagah*. Beirut: Dar Al-Kitab Al-Lubnani, 1989.

Esposito, John L. *Islam: The Straight Path*. New York: Oxford University Press, 1991.

Farid, Ahmad. *Purification of the Soul.* Dar al-Taqwa, 1993.

Gardner, H. *Leading Minds: An Anatomy of Leadership.* New York: Basic Books, 1995.

Goleman, Dr. Daniel. *Emotional Intelligence.* New York: Bantam Books, 1995.

Haddad, G. F. *Compound Ignorance (Jahl Murakkab).* Living Islam: Islamic Tradition, 2000.

Hasan, Dr. Suhaib. *The Muslim Creed.* Houston: Darussalam, (no date).

Henderson Marine Supply, Inc., 2003.

Hunt, M. *The Story of Psychology.* New York: Anchor Books, 1993.

Ibrahim, I. A. *A Brief Illustrated Guide to Understanding Islam.* Houston: Darussalam, 1997.

International Council of the Millennium World Peace Summit Global Ethics Initiative. New York, New York: August 2003.

Islahi, Sadruddin. *The Obligation of Iqaamat-ul-Deen.*

Jafarzadeh, Mirghasem. *A Comparative Study Under English Law, the Convention on Contracts for the International Sale of Goods 1980, Iranian and Shi'ah Law.* Tehran: Shahid Beheshti University, 2001.

Jandt, F. E. *Win-Win Negotiating: Turning Conflict into Agreement.* New York: Wiley, 1985.

Kabbani, Shaykh Muhammad Hisham. *Sunni and Shi'a Seek Reconciliation.* Washington, D.C.: The Islamic Supreme Council of America, October 1999.

Kamal-ul-Din, Khwaja. *Brief Notes on the Qur'an: The Last Seven Chapters.* Lahore: The Lahore Ahmadiyya Movement for the Propagation of Islam.

Khaldun, Franz Rosenthal. *Ibn Khaldun: The Muqaddimah*. Princeton: Bollingen Series, 1969.

Khan, Muhammad Muhsin. *The Translation of the Meanings of Sahih Al-Bukhari: Arabic-English*. Riyadh, Saudi Arabia: Maktabat Al-Riyadh Al-Hadeethah, Vols. 1-9, 1982.

Kohn, A. *The Brighter Side of Human Nature: Altruism and Empathy in Everyday Life*. New York: Basic Books, 1990.

Kotler, Dr. Philip. *Marketing Management*. New Jersey: Prentice Hall, 2002.

Kotter, John P. *John P. Kotter on What Leaders Really Do*. Boston: Harvard Business School Press, 1999.

Lalani, Arzina R. *Early Shi'i Thought: The Teachings of Imam Muhammad al-Baqir*. London: I. B. Tauris (in association with the Institute of Ismaili Studies), 2000.

Lari, Sayyid Mujtaba Musavi. *Ethics and Spiritual Growth*. Tehran: Foundation of Islamic Cultural Propagation in the World, 1997.

Lari, Sayyid Mujtaba Musavi. *God and His Attributes*. Maryland: Islamic Education Center, 1989.

Lari, Sayyid Mujtaba Musavi. *Imamate and Leadership: Lessons on Islamic Doctrine (Book Four)*. Tehran: Foundation of Islamic Cultural Propagation in the World, 1996.

Lari, Sayyid Mujtaba Musavi. *The Seal of the Prophets and His Message*. Maryland: Islamic Education Center, (no date).

Lazarus, R. S. *Emotion and Adaptation*. New York: Oxford University Press, 1991.

Lewicki, Roy J., et al. *Essentials of Negotiation*. Columbus: McGraw-Hill, 2000.

Lewis, Bernard. *Islam in History*. Chicago: Open Court, 1993.

MacDonald, Kevin. *The Culture of Critique*. Westport: Praeger Publishers, 1998.

Madelung, Wilferd. *The Succession to Muhammad: A Study of the Early Caliphate*. Cambridge: Cambridge University Press, 1997.

Mawdudi, Sayyid Abul A'ala. *Towards Understanding Islam*. Leicester: Islamic Foundation, 1988.

Modi, Dr. Bhupendra Kumar. *One God*. New Delhi: Modi Foundation, 2000.

Mutahheri, Allamah Murtaza. *Man and Universe*. Pakistan: Al-Khoei Foundation, 1991.

Nasr, Seyyed Hossein, et al. *Shi'ism: Doctrines, Thought, and Spirituality*. Albany: State University of New York Press, 1988.

National Conference for Community and Justice. New York, New York.

Nelson, Thomas. *The Holy Bible, New King James Version*. Nashville, Tennessee: 1982.

Ornstein, R. *The Evolution of the Consciousness: The Origins of the Way We Think*. New York: Simon & Schuster, 1991.

Ozcelik, Sezai. *Nonviolent Action and Third Party Role in Islamic World*. George Mason University – Institute for Conflict Analysis and Resolution, 2000.

Qara'ati, Muhsin. *Lessons from Qur'an*. Pakistan: Al-Khoei Foundation, 1993.

Rabbani, Mohammad Ali. *Dialogue Among Islamic Schools of Thought*. Qum: Al-Tawhid Quarterly Journal, Vol. 15, No. 3, Autumn 1999.

Rahman, Afzahur. *The Essentials of Islam: Faith and Worship*. London: Kazi Publications, Inc., 1980.

Rashid, Shaykh Ahmed Abdur. *The Oneness of Allah and the Oneness of His Community* (Internet)

Siddiqui, Abdul Hamid. *Sahih Muslim: English Translation*. Lahore: Sh. Muhammad Ashraf, Vols. 1-4, 1973-1975.

Smith, Huston. *The World's Religions: Our Great Wisdom Traditions*. San Francisco: Harper, 1992.

Sobhani, Ayatollah Ja'far. *Doctrines of Shi'i Islam: A Compendium of Imami Beliefs and Practices*. (translated and edited by Reza Shah-Kazemi). London: I. B. Tauris (in association with The Institute of Ismaili Studies), 2001.

Tabataba'i, Ayatullah Sayyid Muhammad Husayn. *Islamic Teachings in Brief*. Tehran: Islamic Propagation Organization, 1991.

Tabatabai, Allamah. *Shiite Islam*. Albany: State University of New York Press, 1975.

Tawhid Quarterly Journal. Tehran, Iran: Vol. 15, No. 3, Autumn 1999.

The Admiralty "Manual of Seamanship." Vol. 2, 1951.

The Holy Bible: New Revised Standard Version. London: Oxford University Press, 1989.

The Millennium World Peace Summit of Religious and Spiritual Leaders (United Nations). New York, New York: August 2000.

The New England Bible. London: Oxford University Press, 1970.

The Organization of the Islamic Conference. Rabat, Morocco.

The Torah: A New Translation of the Holy Scriptures According to the Masoretic Text. Philadelphia: Jewish Publication Society, 1963.

The World Forum for Proximity of Islamic Schools of Thought. Tehran, Iran: 2003.

Turfe, Tallal Alie. *Patience in Islam: Sabr.* New York: Tahrike Tarsile Qur'an, Inc., 1996.

World Council of Religious Leaders (United Nations). New York, New York: May 2003.

GLOSSARY

'Adl	Justice
'Asr	Afternoon
'Isha	Night
'Umra	Informal Pilgrimage
A'mal	Actions
Ahl al-Bayt	Household of Prophet Mohammad
Al-'Afuw	The Restorer of Forgiveness
Al-Ghafoor	The Most Forgiving
Al-Haleem	The Clement
Al-Rahim	The Merciful
Al-Rahman	The Beneficent
Al-Tawwab	The Acceptor of Repentance
Aman an-Nafs	Self-Security
Aqidah	Creed and Beliefs
Asabiyyah	Tribalism or Social Structure
Asas an-Nafs	Self-Foundation
Asma al-Husna	Beautiful Names
Ayah	Verse
Azan	Call to Prayer
Bay'a	Pledge of Allegiance
Bid'ah	Innovation or Deviation
Du'a	Supplication
Envy	Hasad
Fajr	Dawn
Fardh 'Ain	Individual Obligation
Fardh al-Kifaya	General Obligation
Fatiha	Opening Chapter
Fiqh	Jurisprudence or Religious Laws
Ghusl	Bath
Hadith	Tradition
Hajj	Pilgrimage
Halal	Allowable
Haram	Forbidden
Hayya 'ala Khayril 'Amal	Hasten to the Best Act
I'atisaam	Hold Fast
Ibada	Worship
Idrak an-Nafs	Self-Realization
Ihsan	Kindness

Ijma'	Consensus
Ijtihad	Rules of Law via Juristic Reasoning
Ikhtilaf	Differences of Opinion
Ikhtilaf al-Fuqaha'	Differences in the Position of the Jurists
'Ilm	Knowledge
Imamah	Succession of Prophet Mohammad
Iman	Faith
Injeel	Gospel
Iqamat-ul-deen	Establishment of A Way of Life
Jahil	Ignorance
Jahil Basit	Simple Ignorance
Jahiliyah	Age of Ignorance
Jahil Murakkab	Compound Ignorance
Jihad	Struggle
Ka'bah	Holy Shrine in Mecca
Khums	One-Fifth
Khutbah	Sermon
Kitab as-Salaat	Discipline of Prayer
Kitab as-Sunnah	Traditions of the Prophet
Kiyas	Reasoning by Analogy
Kutub	Books
Libas	Garment
Ma'ad	Resurrection
Ma'roof	Courtesy
Maghrib	Evening
Maraja'a	Religious Hierarchy of Clerics
Mawla	Successor
Muhajirun	Quraysh
Muhasaba	Self-Criticism or Self-Evaluation
Mujtahid	Islamic Scholar
Musnad	Traditions
Mut'a	Temporary Marriage
Nass	Designation
Niyyah	Intention
Nubuwwa	Prophets
Qada' and Qadar	Divine Decree and Destiny
Qiblah	Direction of Prayer
Qur'an	Holy Book of Islam
Ra'y	Logic Deduction

Retha an-Nafs	Self-Satisfaction
Rikat	Part
Ritha-a-Nafs	Self-Complacency
Sabr	Patience and Endurance
Sadaqah	Charity
Sakina	Tranquility
Salwan	Comfort
Sayyid	Descendant of Prophet Mohammad
Shari'a	Law
Shura	Consultation
Sirat al-Mustakim	Straight Path
Siyam	Fasting
Sulha	Reconciliation
Sunnah	Lifestyle of Prophet Mohammad
Surah	Chapter
Tafsir	Commentary
Taharah	Purification
Tahkeek an-Nafs	Self-Achievement
Tahkim	Arbitration
Taqiya	Dissimulation
Taqlid	Guide or Reference
Taqwah	Piety
Taurat	Torah
Tawaf	Circumambulation
Tawhid	Oneness of Allah
Ulema	Religious Teachers
Umm	Mother
Ummah	Nation or Community
Ummah Wasat	Community of the Middle Way
Usul	Beliefs
Waee an-Nafs	Self-Awareness
Wasata	Mediation
Wilayat	Authority
Wudu'	Ablution
Yakine	Certainty
Zakat	Alms
Zuboor	Psalms
Zuhr	Noon
Zul-Hajj	Last Month of Islamic Calendar

LIST OF QUR'ANS:

Holy Qur'an by Abdullah YusufAli

The Qur'an, English	Paperbound	$7.95
The Qur'an, Arabic-Translation-	Hardbound	$30.00
Commentary	Paperbound	$25.00
The Holy Qur'an, Arabic-	Hardbound	$25.00
Translation-Transliteration	Paperbound	$20.00

Holy Qur'an by M.H. Shakir

The Qur'an, English	Paperbound	$7.95
The Qur'an, Arabic-Translation	Paperbound	$8.00
The Qur'an, Arabic-Translation		
(features 41 translations of the	Hardbound	$24.00
First Chapter – Sura Fateha)	Paperbound	$19.00
Wedding Edition	Hardbound	$24.00

Holy Qur'an by Muhammad Pickthall

The Glorious Qur'an, English	Paperbound	$7.95
The Glorious Qur'an, Arabic-Translation	Paperbound	$8.95
The Meaning of the Glorious Qur'an	Hardbound	$25.00
Arabic-Translation-Transliteration	Paperbound	$20.00
	Hardbound	$39.95

Holy Qur'an by S.V. Mir Ahmed Ali

The Qur'an, English	Paperbound	$7.95
Holy Qur'an, Arabic-Translation-	Hardbound	$59.95
& Commentary	Paperbound	$39.95

Interpretation of the Meaning of The Glorious		
Qur'an by Prof. (Dr.) Syed Vickar Ahmed	Paperbound	$7.95

Qur'an in Spanish, by Julio Cortes

El-Coran, Translation in Spanish	Paperbound	$12.00
El-Coran, Arabic Text and		
Translation in Spanish	Hardbound	$24.00

Arabic Only Qur'an

Large Size	Hardbound	$25.00
Medium Size	Hardbound	$15.00
30 Parts	Paperbound	$25.00

Tahrike Tarsile Qur'an, Inc.
Publishers and Distributors of Holy Qur'an
80-08 51st Avenue
Elmhurst, New York 11373